TO: Ele ' " "

MW00876643

Through Christina's Eyes

A Novel

By Julia Anderson

Julia Anderson

Introduction

Overall this book is a work of fiction. Many of the elements within it are factual – Christina Nilsson was my great-grandmother, Walter was my grandfather, Anna Christina is my daughter I have tried to accurately represent historical facts from Sweden and the United States' history. Dimensions of individuals' lives are fictional as there are no witnesses to all of the events described in this book.

I dedicate this book to those who inspire us. Some have passed into another world and some are still living here on Earth. This group of people, for me, includes my Great-Grandma Christina, my Grandfather Walter, and my three daughters, particularly Anna Christina.

I also thank those who have gone before us who smoothed out the path of life for subsequent travelers.

I hope you enjoy this book – Julia Anderson

I invite you to:

- Visit the website: www.throughchristinaseyes.com

- Like my Author Facebook page: Julia Anderson

Christina

Like most people, I have a story to tell. Mine was trapped in history, grasped in the hands of time for over one hundred years. To release it, to make it known, I searched for a path, several times unsuccessfully. At last, a pathway was opened. My story has surfaced through my great-granddaughter, who heard my voice and understood the markers along the path of our family's history. This was how these words came to be; this is my story, seen through my eyes.

My story, my life, winds its way through continents, generations, and experiences. Along the path of my life there were so many choices to be made that shaped the future. Some of the choices were mine to make, more often they were made by others and then my life was changed in some way. Their effects rippled through the generations to come after me, weaving a path through my family's lives. The course of my descendants' lives was changed in many ways by events and actions they couldn't have been aware of that had occurred many years prior.

Viktor Frankl, the prominent Austrian neurologist, notes in his book, Man's Search for Meaning, that "Everything can be taken from a man but one thing: to choose one's attitude in any given set of circumstances, to choose one's own way." As Viktor said, even in the confines of physical and mental prisons, "there are always choices to make". His perspective was mirrored in my life; how I chose to act and react to events in my life made a significant difference for me and for all of my descendants. Sometimes people aren't able to successfully navigate the circumstances of life by the choices made in their lives. They arrive at an emotional or physical end, crumbling under the weight of their experience. From my experience I can tell you that heartbreaking events are part of every life. No one is immune from situations that are detrimental. Some have more challenges than others - the quantity and impact of the challenges are not metered out in some grand plan. Things just happen that humans have to adapt to. During my life and now watching the lives of my descendants unfold, I've seen how a person chooses to react or adapt to a given situation affects their life, along with many others'.

I can't wait to tell you my story. Mine doesn't involve a physical prison or the horrific circumstances that Viktor Frankl experienced during World War II. My world was comprised of logistical, social, and emotional barriers and boundaries. Within the realm of my life, choices were made that were crucial points to my very survival. I would like to explain them to you.

By way of introduction, I am Christina Nilsson, born in the area called Hagnarp, Sweden, in December, 1866. The closest community which still exists today is called Verum. Hagnarp was a small, rural farming community as 85% of Sweden was at the time. Sverige is the Swedish version of our country's name; Sweden is how it is referred to in the English language. We were Svensk, referred to in English as "Swedish". Our family knew all of our neighbors, visited with them Sundays after church, and generally spent the other six days a week working on our small farm. I was the youngest of six children, which consisted of one boy, then the five of us girls.

As was typical in Sweden at the time, our last names were based on our father's first name. By the late 1800's most Swedish families had settled on a last name that they would hand down from generation to generation, as mine had done. A smaller percentage of families selected a surname relating to the name of the area where they lived or some aspect of nature. Most decided on their last name to be based on the father's first name, with 'son' as the ending. This is how my last name came to be Nilsson, or Nils' son. (Customarily in Sweden, the suffix added to the father's first name was patriarchal. In another Scandinavian country, Iceland, a person's last name also followed the gender of the child, for example: Nilsdotter, for Nils' daughter). Since Anders was a very popular first name in Sweden, one of the most typical surnames is Andersson in Sweden.

Just before I was born there was a great shift in the political system in Sweden. The King, Charles XV, wanted to continue his dynasty of power, which was proliferated through the House of Nobles. Representation of Sweden's people in this House consisted only of large estate land owners. In 1865 this system was converted into a parliament like group that was nominated or elected. Then further changes occurred in june, 1866 where the First and Second Chambers were established; these were similar to two legislative houses of representation. Members of the First Chamber were indirectly elected local level politicians. Members of the Second were elected by the people (those eligible to vote). This system stayed in place over one hundred years, until a single house of parliament was enacted.

When I was growing up in Sweden in the 1870's, the area of land under the Swedish King's control was much greater than it is now. It included what is now present day Norway (which has existed as a separate country from Sweden since 1906) and had previously controlled the land where present day Finland exists. My family lived in the area of land that has been a part of the country of Sweden since the days of the Kalmar Union, which was formed in 1397. Later in 1523 the unification of Sweden occurred under King Gustav Vasa. The land was divided up into provinces, called landskap, that describe a geographical area. Skane is one such landskap. It persists even today, when a landskap could now contain multiple lans (a lan resembling a county or smaller geographic region of a larger country.) The lans, of which there are presently twenty one, are governed in a pattern similar to individual states of in present day United States.

The countryside of the landskap of Skane, where I was born, is a farming community, even today. During my lifetime, the lan where we lived was Kristianstad. (It has since been combined into the lan now referred to as Skane). Skane generates much of the crops cultivated in Sweden, as it is in the southern area of the country, with less harsher winters than the far north. The soil is excellent for growing crops and has been farmed for well over a thousand years. Skane makes up much of the southern coastline of Sweden, where the Vikings, most famous for their ruthless crusades of much of Europe from 800 to 1050, lived.

Sweden is geographically roughly the size of the present day state of California in the United States. Like California, it varies in terrain and temperature from the north to the southern most regions. In the north is Lapland, with a peak elevation in the Kjolen Mountains of about seven thousand feet. Reindeer roam in these mountains, and in the winter castles carved from ice are made. Sloping towards the sea, in the south and east, are Sweden's central lowlands. The most southern region comprises fertile areas for farming and plains, where my family and I lived. Our climate was to have cold winter weather and warmer summers.

The land my family and I lived on in the Skane lan was distributed to my father's family during the Svaneholm Estate's redistribution of land reform. Between 1782 and 1785 Baron Rutger MacLean divided his estate land (called "fralsejord" – owned by the nobility) into pieces which were sometimes rectangular – others were square shaped. The novel part about what the Baron did was to move a farmer's home (wood, bricks and all) onto the piece of land that they rented from the nobility "fralsejord". Many countryside villages, including ours, were literally disassembled by this process. This process came to be known as "laga skifte" and expanded to other lan's starting in 1827, mostly completed by the mid 1800's.

This system is how my family's farmhouse came to be located on our small plot of land near Hagnarp. Farmers, who did not own the land (referred to as "torp" or "croft") they farmed, were called "torpare" or "crofter". This meant they paid rent to the landowner by working a number of days per year. There just wasn't the ability to amass the wealth required to be able to purchase land. By the end of the 1800's, the torpare system was replaced by tenants paying their rent for the properties monetarily. Larger pieces of land were leased out to others by their owners.

Another change that occurred in land ownership and tenancy was how it was passed down amongst families. Because of the large population growth in the 1800's, there were typically more children to divide the Swedish family's farm amongst. Work off of the farm was difficult to obtain – inheriting part of one's family farm allowed continuation of the family's way of life. Sweden's laws differed from other countries' in that as of 1845, both sons and daughters have had equal rights to inherit property. Children cannot be disinherited by their parents. While this put Sweden well ahead of other countries in granting property ownership rights to women, it also created a situation where each child must receive a portion of their parents' inheritance. Thus the piece of land would be divided up amongst all of the parents' children. Over the years it could be very difficult for the children's families to sustain themselves and their families from a small plot of land.

The population of Sweden grew exponentially in the 100 years between 1750 and 1850, doubling in size to 3.5 million Swedes. With such accelerated population growth, fears began to brew of overpopulation, influenced by the theories of Thomas Malthus. To alleviate this fear, the Swedish law that disallowed emigration was repealed in the 1830's. The door to leave, previously closed, had now swung wide open. The population continued to swell to 4.1 million people in Sweden by 1865, straining the support system in the agrarian based economy. Repealing the law permitted emigration for the large number of Swedes that chose to leave in the latter half of the 1800's.

Lars & Pernilla

My parents, Lars and Pernilla Nilsson, were part of the agrarian society. When they were born in Sweden, the average male and female, respectively, had a life expectancy of thirty nine and forty three (years of birth 1816 – 1840). It was somewhat of a miracle of their lives that they had met when they both were 31 years old, with only around ten years left to live, by the numbers. They married and then had their children late, compared to others of their generation. I don't really know much else about their background; there were no older relatives to ask as I got older. Neither of them spoke of their parents much, if at all. As in most Swedish homes, emotional feelings and history weren't verbalized. Infrequently, if ever, was there any raising of voices or shouting, indicating anger or someone being upset. Doing so would mean a person didn't have self-control to stop an outburst of emotion such as that.

In the 1830's my parents were in just starting out their lives as a married couple, working the plot of land my father had inherited in the Swedish countryside. As they were now their own household, they were responsible for paying the taxes the Swedish monarchy levied. For the largely agrarian workforce, the taxes were almost impossible to pay with the meager profits obtained from their farming activities. It was difficult for many farmers to clothe and provide for their families. Contrastingly, during this timeframe, extravagant, ornate castles housed the Swedish royal family, including Drottningholm. It was physical and cultural divide between the small percentage of wealthy landowners and the rest of the population.

My parents' marriage was not arranged by their families. Father made a 'suitable' choice in selecting my Mother. The criteria of selection included that she had not been previously married or involved in any scandals surrounding her (such as being romantically involved with another man). The drawback was she was 'old' at thirty one and didn't have any wealth or inheritance to bring to the marriage.

Our mother, Pernilla, gave birth to Lars, her first child, when she was thirty three years old. That was ancient back then to become a first time mother, with the average life expectancy in Sweden for a woman in her age group just over forty years old. Her life would be almost over according to that standard. She was a teacher prior to marrying our father; if a woman wasn't married after age eighteen she had to have some way to support herself – by either becoming a teacher, cook, cleaning person, or other non-legal means. I don't think mother thought she would ever marry, given that she was 31 when she did marry Father. But she did and they were married almost fifty years. She was also eight months older than Father, which was somewhat unusual in the small village where we lived. People thought that a wife should be younger than her husband, to provide a better chance to have more children and the health and stamina to survive childbirth. Mother was a sturdy, healthy woman, who would raise six children.

My Mother's life after she married my Father was that of a typical Swedish farm wife; she cooked at least twice a day, cleaned, laundered, fed the farm animals, and gardened to provide food for our family. The food we ate was referred to as humanskost, in English that translates to "plain food" which it was in terms of taste and variety. Our three meals consisted of frukost (breakfast), *Äta* (lunch) and Middag (dinner). Breakfast and dinner were typically hot meals – lunch was more of a cold meal, eaten faster so as to continue working. Breakfast would usually be fairly large, served after our morning chores on the farm. It would usually include by *bröd* (bread), *ost* (cheese), ägg (eggs), and *strömming* (herring). Lunch would be possibly meat on a piece of bread with *kaldolmar* (stuffed cabbage). Dinner was our largest meal, being served at the end of our chores and workday, with one hot entrée (usually ham or meatballs) and other side dishes, served cold. For a special treat, Mother would make risgrynsgröt, which is a rice porridge made with eggs.

The foods we ate in Sweden were fresh during the months they were available. We grew vegetables (those that could survive the short growing season in Sweden, such as potatoes, beets, carrots) and fruits on our farm. Our family fished in local lakes for varieties of fish. Father hunted wild animals such as deer, and some of our livestock was butchered for us to eat, including cows and chickens. Our diet would be called bland by modern day standards. We didn't have many spices or have fancy sauces with our meat and potatoes. The Swedes also learned, starting with the Vikings' preparations for long sea voyages, to preserve food by salting, dehydrating and curing. This was mainly done for fish and other meats. We preserved other vegetables in a root cellar, which was a small room dug into the ground to keep foods cool for months on end.

Since Mother had been a teacher, she read quite well and would read to us children in the long, dark winter nights in the Swedish countryside. Sweden, being located in the far north of the Earth, receives little more than five hours of daylight in the winter, making the winters seem long and sometimes intolerable. Our family often went to bed as early as 6pm in the winter, with daylight long gone and only so much lamp oil to light our home. The cold, snow and ice made it difficult to get into town but once a month in the winters. We had to socialize within our family – reading to each other, playing games we made up amongst us siblings, or simply occupying ourselves somehow for hours.

There was a natural phenomenon that brightened those dark days of winters, called the Northern Lights, the Aurora Borealis. We so looked forward to catching a glimpse of the streaks of green and pink seemingly painted across the dark night sky, giving a somewhat eerie glow during the nighttime. The Lights occur when a large numbers of electrons originating from the sun stream in towards the Earth along its magnetic field and collide with air particles. The air literally lights up, the colors based on the gases present in the atmosphere. We didn't see it very often, as the most visible time to see the Lights was between 11pm – 2am. We children were not supposed to be awake during these times, having gone to bed in the early evening hours. It was so exciting and special we would lay in our beds, hoping for a glimpse through one of our home's small windows of beautiful colors against the dark night sky.

When it finally did become warmer in the late springtime of the year, Sweden is then bathed in almost 19 hours a day of daylight, the opposite of the winter which has so many dark hours. In May the sun goes down around 11pm and then rises again around 4 am. Farther north from where I lived is the "Land of the Midnight Sun". The northernmost area of Sweden has this moniker due to the sun literally not going down in the sky all twenty four hours of the day during mid-summer. No wonder we Swedes celebrate many times over in May. The daylight is a welcome change from the long, dark winters. We also celebrated surviving the previous winter. We called these the Midsummer holidays, where pickled herring and new potatoes are part of the festivities.

With six children in our home, Mother didn't have time to focus on each one of us and what activities we wanted to pursue. She also had many tasks running our farmhouse that took up the majority of her time. She was generally a happy person, although typical Swedish stoicism kept her from displaying affection and verbalizing her emotions towards us children. We knew by her actions she loved us, although I don't actually recall ever hearing that aloud from her.

Both of my parents were reserved; they seldom if ever spoke of their feelings. Instructions to us children were given to teach us how to perform daily living chores. My parents did sometimes talk in the main room after we children were in bed. Most often they sat, each in their own chair, in wordless silence working on their own project of either mending something or possibly reading.

Reading books held a high place of importance in our house, although it was an activity engaged in only when all one's chores were completed. We didn't have access to a variety of books – the central book in our home was the Bible, which was read, re-read, and re-read again. Mother would read aloud in the evenings to all of us, where we heard the entire contents of the Bible over about two years' worth of evenings.

Father was what most Swedish men were like. He wasn't 'cold' emotionally – he just lived as he was taught to hold in his emotions and not talk all that much. He did love us children, I know, in his quiet, reserved way. His love was like loving someone from afar, not involved in their everyday lives, but love still there. Our physical proximity was quite close, as we all shared the space in our two room farmhouse.

Father worked hard on our farm to keep our family fed, clothed, and sheltered. He would rise every morning early in the day to tend to the animals – the cow, the horses, the chickens. I could hear his boots scrape the floor as he went out the door every day in the early morning. During most months of the year, due to Sweden's far north latitude, Father rose in the pitch blackness to tend to the animals. In winter the cold temperatures came, well below freezing, where icicles would remain on our barn for months it seemed. I liked looking at those icicles – so clear and translucent, each one unique. When the sun shone through them so many radiant colors of the rainbow were on display.

As I grew up, it was clear that Father made the decisions for our family and Mother's role was to perform chores that would support our family. Her efforts focused on the tasks that women were presumed to be responsible for in those days: those inside the home. I don't recall hearing them raise their voices at each other.

If there was a decision to be made my Father made it. Mother may have been able to subtly suggest her opinion or stance on a particular issue, but in the end it was Father who had the final say. In the event Mother disagreed with Father, she didn't verbalize or indicate her dissent. It was simply the way it was for her role as a farm wife at that time.

Father's work and daily life were at the whims of the weather. If it was raining hard when it was time for him to do his chores, his clothes would become soaked, sodden with the wet rain. Raincoats didn't exist back then, the only possibility being a leather coat which would keep some of the rain off. Farming, therefore our income and household livelihood, was very dependent on the weather. There were some years of either drought (little rain) or flood (too much rain) that ruined the crops. These situations greatly impacted our family's survival for the crops were both a primary source of our food and our ability to earn money to purchase other goods we did not grow. How frustrating that the very things needed to sustain us (sun, sufficient rain) were completely out of our control. We just had to accept that we would do the best we could, and then another force took over.

As I mentioned, what I knew of my parents' relationship was what I have observed – the situations and exchanges I saw and heard. I assume they loved each other – each spoke respectfully to the other. I never saw them actually touch each other. That public of a display, even within our family, simply wasn't done. They didn't argue or bicker with each other. Mother, as the female and the wife in the relationship, deferred to what father decided or said.

Mother did, however, influence Father in her quiet way prior to his decision or statement. She had an unassuming way about her. She just continued calmly and smoothly through her work day on the farm. I can only recall her being upset very few times, where she seemed distraught or unsettled. She must have been a very strong woman to be able to subvert her emotions and express them only in a reserved manner, never in front of us children.

The concept of love in our family was just that – a concept – not tangible or audible. I'd heard of it from the Bible – the Father's love for us humans. Our parents didn't expressly state they loved us children; we had to surmise their feelings from the signs they demonstrated. We were all taken care of : fed, clothed, kept warm, provided schooling and guidance. Those external factors, combined with a reserved demeanor of guidance to us children, were how we knew our parents loved us.

Siblings

My oldest sibling was my only brother, Lars. He was 13 years older than I; the hope of my family to carry on the family surname and prosper. Our family wanted him to get an education greater than high school – and, as the only male, funds and resources would go towards this end of bettering the whole family's welfare. Our father wanted him to have a trade or profession other than farming.

On a personal level, as older brothers go, he was a kind sort. Since our ages differed so much he was like an uncle to me. In this time period, the 1870's, boys and men were not involved in helping "around the house", doing household chores such as laundry, cleaning, or gathering kindling wood. When he was at home, he would be outside with Father, while I was inside with Mother. He was kind, when he spoke to me. There really wasn't much of an opportunity for us to interact – thirteen years and gender difference were a chasm difficult to leap over as we were growing up.

He left our farmhouse at age seventeen, to move to the university town of Lund, Sweden, about 40 miles away. In the mid to late eighteen hundreds in Sweden, the idea of a wider range of people attending a university was just coming into being. Prior to this, the number of students and space available for advanced studies was limited to only those who came from wealthy families. As the vast majority of Sweden's families' livelihoods were based on agriculture and farming, not many were in the group who had sufficient monies to pay for an able bodied young male to leave their household to study. The universities in the cities of Lund and Uppsala are among the oldest in the world and those that were among the first to offer higher level education to the broader public. (None of my family had ever visited Uppsala – it was much too far away from where we lived. It remains an important place of Swedish history, including Gamla Uppsala ("Old Uppsala").

Ruins and burials in the shape of mounds of the earth were there since as early as the third century AD. From that time on it was a significant religious, economic and political and learning center.)

Lars attended Lund University and graduated with a humanities degree. He then stayed on at the university to further study and become a teacher. He would never live in Hagnarp again. His life had moved to a new circumstance and place. Since he left our farmhouse when I was barely four years old, I don't remember him living at our family home, just when Lars visited during his school's breaks.

Next in succession in my family came my four sisters: Nilla, Anna, Johanna, and Elna. Nilla was born two years after my brother, then Anna within a year of Nilla. Our mother had three little ones under the age of three to care for. It must have been a very challenging time for her to keep up with all of her farm duties and care for her three children. Mother had a few years until Johanna was born, when Lars was six years old. Since he was deemed old enough, Mother tasked him to watch out for his three younger sisters while she might be outside performing a task of hers. Lars had a lot of responsibility for a six year old. On the farm that's what Mother needed, so that's what Lars did.

A few more years went by, then Elna arrived. By now Nilla was seven, so she replaced Lars as the child minder. Lars had moved on to tasks outside our house, helping Father with his farm duties of the crops and tending the livestock. Nilla made up games for her now three younger sisters to her, playing with them and even changing Elna's wet clothing. She was grown up in many ways by a very young age.

My siblings were separated from me ranging in age from five to thirteen years. The gap of our age differences also created gaps in our relationships. As the youngest of the children, I was the baby to be taken care of. Each of my siblings looked after me at various times during my life. Mother was very busy with household tasks and at times, such as when she was preserving food or helping Father gather in our crops, she didn't have time to watch me during the day. I don't recall spending much time with my Mother – one of my sisters was my typical companion. Father of course was out all day working the farm.

Nilla was my oldest sister. She seemed so much more knowledgeable than I, facing life's cross roads eleven years ahead of me. I looked up to her as role model. I watched how she conducted herself and how she interacted with people. I learned a lot from her by observing. She was a few inches over five feet tall with blond hair and blue eyes - what most people think of 'looking Swedish', except for her height. In the 1800's with the access we had to nutrition, she was of average height. As the oldest of the five girls in the house, she was like our second mother. She received the new clothes and shoes first; if she outgrew them they were handed down to one of us other four girls. She brushed her long blond hair every night to keep it shiny. I loved sitting off to the side of the room watching her brush carefully and methodically.

Nilla fulfilled one of the traditions of Swedish culture each year on the night of December 13th. As the oldest girl in our family, she assumed the central role of our celebration of St. Lucia Day. Before the Gregorian calendar was changed, this day was the shortest day of the year; the darkest day. Lucia was a Christian who died for her faith and was said to have brought food to Sweden during a famine, centuries after her death. Her representative visit once a year reminds us she lives on. St. Lucia comes in the morning to signal the family that light has triumphed over darkness. Per the tradition of this celebration, Nilla would put on a white robe or dress, a crown of branches on her head (sometimes with lit candles!) and waken each of us in the household, starting with our parents. She brought us special treats, including saffron buns. Since it is most often dark and cold during December in Sweden, being woken up from sleep by a young girl with light and aromatic scents is a welcome change from most winter mornings.

Some of my most memorable childhood moments are of Nilla, awakening on a cold, dark day in December, seeing her from where I slept. She really did look angelic holding the lit candles, the soft glow flooding her face. Sometimes they were inserted in the crown she wore on her head – other years she held the candles in her hand. The fragrant scents of the saffron buns and the candles were a sensory burst to awaken us.

Next in our family came my sister Anna. She was so close in age to Nilla it was almost like they were twins. In more current times this spacing of children is sometimes described as "Irish twins", since many Irish in the 1800's had children very close together in age. With two children still in diapers and needing parental attention for the basics of life, parents were challenged. Anna, being the younger 'twin' of Nilla, was most often trying to keep up with what Nilla was doing, although at a disadvantage due to being a year younger.

Anna was the feisty sister in our house; she often rebelled against what Nilla wanted or said. Of course she didn't verbalize it or make a scene in front of our parents; she would be reprimanded if she had. The undercurrent of competition and resistance was definitely present. I didn't get to know Anna very well – she was always 'out' somewhere, helping another neighbor with their chores or working on a church project. She wanted to be away from home, I think.

Anna would grow up to marry Lars Tulin when she was seventeen years old. This was the exit from our parents' house Anna was looking for. She was one of those children who didn't find fulfillment in the home she grew up in. Anna and her new husband formed their own household, ten miles from where my parents lived. They had one daughter, Alice. Then she successively had four boys. This was an achievement, to have four strapping sons to carry on the family name and participate in the farming duties. The boys were excellent assets for their parents in supporting the family's farm. Anna became somewhat distanced from the rest of our family, with her own five children to look after. She wasn't emotionally close with any of the rest of us sisters.

Johanna was next in the succession of children; she was quiet and reserved. Johanna was one of the most typical names for Swedish girls. She was what is known as a classic middle child in birth order analysis; she blended in with the patchwork quilt of our family. She stayed strong and steady; she connected those on the outer edges of the family. She was always helpful to Mother and did as she was asked. Johanna married when she was eighteen to Olaf Linde; I was nine years old when she left our childhood home. She was a kindly, quiet sister to me, although we weren't emotionally close.

Olaf was a man concerned with how things and people looked, and much less concerned about what condition they were in or how a person felt. I am fairly certain Johanna lived a fairly lonely existence after she married – Olaf was distant and always working at something away from their home. He was very ambitious, always striving for more than what he had at any given time. This drive pushed him to succeed at a stone quarrying business, which he later sold. They had two daughters, Anna and Ellen. I think Olaf never forgave Johanna for not having a male child.

Elna was my closest sibling in age, although she was sickly as a child, and thus wasn't able to be as active as typical children. She most often stayed indoors and helped mother where she could. As a teenager, Elna developed a cough that persisted for a very long time. She was very tired and had to rest most of the time. She was like a flower that didn't quite reach its potential; she died at age twenty from lungsot (a lung disease now known as tuberculosis or

TB). In 1875 tuberculosis was at its peak of deadliness in Sweden, Elna being only one of the hundreds of thousands to fall victim to it. *4 million people per year* across Europe died of tuberculosis in the mid-1800's. It was the most deadly disease in all of history – a death toll even greater than the plague. It was not yet known how a person contracted tuberculosis; it took until the 1880's to establish that it was a communicable disease. Around 1900 it was identified as a bacillus, a microorganism that attacked the lungs. She just wasn't able to fight off the infection in her lungs.

Growing Up Years

During the mid to late eighteen hundreds, the majority of monetary wealth in Sweden was held within less than 5% of families. Those families typically had some relation to Sweden's Royal family which was among the most powerful politically and economically in all of Europe. The grandiose castles of Slottsbacken (located in Stockholm, with 608 rooms, is the world's largest castle), Drottningholm, and Kalmar and were only for the Royal family. These palaces and homes were totally out of my horizon – both literally and figuratively. We lived on the south west side of Sweden – Stockholm, the capital, is on the far eastern shore, about 260 miles (over 400 kilometers) away. The thought of a palace, such as Drottningholm Palace near Stockholm, was not tangible to me at all. The luxuries available in the palace on Lake Malaren were in another world, far outside of my own. This palace, built in the 1600's, was the Swedish royal family's summer house (where they lived only part of the year). In current times it is their full time residence. Apparently it is so grand and ornate that it is called the Versailles of the North (Versailles being the elaborate French monarchy's palace).

As for my family, we were about average for Swedes in worldly possessions – we had a rough board wood home, made up of two rooms – one for sleeping the other for our daily living. There we sat by the fire, ate our meals, completed our studies, sang songs, told stories, cooked and mended. We did a lot of living in that small space. Our conversations centered on current events that were happening in our part of the world – how the crops were doing, what the weather happening that day meant. We didn't discuss our dreams and hopes for the future. During that time period our goal was survival. We didn't think of fancy dresses and having free time to compose a letter or play the piano. That was well beyond what was seemed possible for us Nilsson girls. Any finery we or our neighbors had was limited to possibly a small piece of jewelry or a lace handkerchief.

My parents gave us, their children, the gift of a comfortable life. I had a warm place to sleep, clothes, and enough food. They also gave us the gift of family. We would all sit near the fireplace in our home on the cold, dark winter nights. All of us would be working on something. For us girls that might be needlepoint or a mending task. I so enjoyed being with my family, being part of that community of seven or so people, depending on which time of my life my siblings were living at home. Most often we weren't even talking aloud; we were just *there* – together. We were, on a nonverbal level, sending messages back and forth via our attentiveness to what the others were doing: a nod of approval for a cross stich row finished, a small smile for a finished piece of wood carving.

Our parents brought us up to respect the church and the country of Sweden. Even though it was difficult for my parents to make a living in Sweden, with taxes making up such a large percentage of any income they had, they were patriotic. Church was a weekly commitment we always kept. We rarely missed attending on Sunday.

We went to church in the closest town, Verum. The Church of Sweden is the largest organization of the Lutheran faith. It was founded by King Gustav I Vasa in the fifteen hundreds, after his negotiations with the Catholic Pope did not end in an agreement. The church was where we saw a glimpse of art, writing, and life beyond our small village of Hagnarp. There were a few small, beautiful stained glass windows in the church, which one of the local craftspeople at the time donated their time and energy to create. Those windows were so lovely to look at, with their deep hues and shining color when the sun shone through them. It was a welcome sight during the long, dry sermons the minister delivered, and allowed me to sit staunchly on the hard wooden pews for over an hour 'listening' to the minister's words. I say 'listening' because I appeared to be listening, but really I was somewhere through those stained glass windows, floating through space in the beautiful streaming colored sunshine. A child was expected to sit still and listen throughout the time the minister was speaking, without either of my parents needing to intervene by a word or gesture for me to behave. If one of us dared to 'act up' in church, we would certainly receive a punishment, such as no supper later on. We knew the consequences of misbehavior; so we didn't do it.

The building itself was not large by today's standards, but had significant ornate details that made it stunningly beautiful to me. The gold encrusted chandelier, from which 50 candles were lit to illuminate the interior hung as a centerpiece over the area in front of the altar. As a child I used to count those candles as a way of passing the time. The minister, Olof Stille, made it difficult to sit through a long sermon telling us the evils of the world. Most of the time I tried to focus on something, like the ornate lectern where he stood above and separate from us in the congregation. All these years later, I'm glad that practice has changed to have the minister on the same level as the rest of the congregation. The minister is a part of the congregation just like everyone else.

It was there I was baptized on January 31, 1867, when the record of my birth was added to the church's records. That meant I was officially recognized as having been born in Sweden, under the care of my parents Lars & Pernilla. Inga Dopvittnen was the witness to my christening. Long before I was born, in 1686 church law was established that required each church to keep a registry of the residents of the congregation. The Church of Sweden was the official vital statistics record keeper for the entire country of Sweden until 1991. In the present day world this system established so long ago is recognized as one of the most complete of record keeping of families in the world. In 2000 the church and the government officially separated. There is no longer a link, financially or otherwise, between them.

Each lan (or county) was divided into parishes for church attendance and record keeping purposes. All through the eighteen hundreds the minister of the church was in charge of keeping the records of the households that lived within his parish. Most did so with great detail, by visiting each household to check on their wellbeing. This system was put into effect in the latter half of the seventeenth century; quite forward thinking to have a system of checks and balances for families' social wellbeing. This system is analogous to the concept in the United States today of a social worker, visiting families to see how things are going and noting any needs the family may have. The minister was responsible for connecting people and things. If someone wasn't able to feed their children, he could ask a family with more resources available (specifically the man of the house) to assist them.

The records kept by the minister gave an overview of the details of a household: who attended church services, all the inhabitants of a particular household (including boarders or older relatives), and which persons had completed communion in the church. They also detailed other aspects of life, such as a person's occupation and character, for example if they were a chronic alcoholic or mentally challenged.

Today the records containing the parish's household documentation are kept in regional archives, called landsarkiv. There are approximately 5 of these locations throughout Sweden, usually in the largest city within the lan. A few cities in Sweden, such as Stockholm, have their own landsarkiv, due to their size.

There were nine of us recorded into the church records that year: 4 boys and 5 girls. One of the girls, born in June of 1867, didn't receive a Christian name, as she passed away before a christening ceremony was held. This person's life was commemorated by being recorded, that she had been a part of this world and then departed within a few months. It was common practice not to receive a given name until the infant was christened in the church.

In the years between 1815 and 1865, Sweden's population had almost doubled, from 2.4 to 4.1 million residents. The population growth was primarily due to the increasing birth rate of children. The years of crop failures and the increase in the population in the mid-to late eighteen hundreds made being able to sufficiently nourish and economically support an entire family quite difficult. Thus I was part of a great population boom in Sweden, while agricultural production and the economy were anemic. Because of these strains on Sweden, of population growth and food shortages, starting around 1850 and continuing until 1930, over 1.2 million Swedes emigrated, comprising approximately 25% of the entire country's population. Economic related issues were the primary reason people chose to leave Sweden.

During my first year of life, in 1867, there was a severe crop failure due to a very wet summer with lots of rain, causing much of the crops to rot before they could mature to be harvested. This year's food shortages caused many people to not be able to feed their families or themselves, and many looked at other alternatives such as emigrating to another country, the most common being Canada, the United States, and Denmark. The provinces of Norrland, Dalarna, and Varmland experienced the worst crop failures; not enough food was produced to feed the burgeoning population.

Then in the following year, 1868, came an extremely hot summer with a devastating drought. There were simply few seeds to be sown. Between one third to one half of the cattle had to be slaughtered in some areas, due to the lack of crops and grass to feed them. The 1868 drought was particularly severe for the 'breadbasket' of Sweden, Skane. Most every household was affected by the failure of the potato crop, either by malnutrition or death by starvation. (Much like Ireland had endured). I was born in the peak years of the famine; with people literally starving at every door, I was one person to feed at our farmhouse. It was a tough choice for many parents – who to feed what and how to obtain enough food to sustain the family members. Since we did live on a farm, we grew most all of our own vegetables, had a few cows, pigs and an even greater number of chickens to provide nutrition to our family. I was very fortunate. All totaled about 15% of the population of northern Sweden died from this famine.

In 1869, when I was about two years old, there was an epidemic outbreak of smallpox. These were difficult years in Sweden for people to survive – if not from health concerns, from economic concerns. Infectious diseases such as smallpox, influenza, and diphtheria, as noted earlier, caused 20% of the yearly deaths among Swedes. As it was when I was born, the average age I would live to was forty six, given the possibility of disease, lack of food, and lack of medical knowledge of the basics of hygiene.

Our lives on the farm were run by routine. Time to milk the cows, time to feed the chickens. Our lives revolved around the needs of the farm. To survive we had to plan as accurately as possible – to not be out alone in a snowstorm or to preserve our food when it was ready for picking to last us through the winter. There was much planning, figuring, and factoring to optimize the results of our labors on the farm.

All of us children had to help with the chores, tasks that were necessary to sustain our lives. We children did what was asked of us without protest. We knew if we didn't our very survival would be at risk. Elna really couldn't help due to her illness, so she did what she could indoors – darning socks, helping Mother with the kitchen chores.

As a child my expectations, if I even had the concept of that word, were very basic. I was hoping to have enough food to eat, fuel to keep us warm, and not to get so sick that I would die. That was my world. Since we had no newspapers or written documentation of happenings outside of Verum, I knew very little of what was outside of my town. As to my future, I figured somewhere in the back of my mind when I was a teenager, about eighteen, I would get married to a man who was a farmer and then begin a new chapter in my life.

As a young girl, I recall going to church on Sunday was something we prepared for all week. We had to make sure our clothes were washed and clean. The Sunday dinner was prepared as much as possible the day before, on Saturday, to allow for a day of rest on Sunday. Living on a farm it is pretty much impossible to take a complete day of rest, as animals still need to be fed and tended to, crops watered, and daily living tasks such as fetching water from the well completed. Whatever tasks we could complete before Sunday we did. The process of the five of us girls out the door, into the wagon, and the one and a half miles to church was no small feat. My mother rose especially early on Sunday to ensure we all made it in the wagon on time. We knew we'd be in trouble if our Mother had to speak to us about hurrying up to get ready or we weren't meeting her exacting standards for our clothing and personal grooming.

Sunday was a special day; we would see our friends and neighbors at church. The grownups talked about the business activities of farming – the crop yield, the price of wheat or maybe the latest ideas about farming. I don't really know the details of what they talked about; I would have been outside after church to play in the yard with the other children. We children would play a game with a sock that had beans or rocks in it – kicking it around the yard. Other times we played tag – where you have to run away from the person who is "it". After about age ten, the boys and girls didn't play those sorts of games together – it wasn't really socially acceptable for a young man to touch a young girl, even on the arm or back. The boys would walk down by the river and toss rocks in or swing on a tree branch. We girls would talk while walking around the church yard.

Next to our church in Verum was the church cemetery. Many generations of residents of the Verum area were buried there, including my grandmother. In the 1800's when children didn't survive birth or their first few years of life, the gravestones were marked simply "child" - no name, no specific dates. These children didn't have a long stay on Earth or live to do 'great things' like publish a book, write a sonata, or start a business.

Looking back on this practice, it might seem odd in the present day to not commemorate the unique child who was here on Earth. The answer those of us who lived during that time period would give is of a practical nature. As many children died of a variety of diseases including the flu, typhoid, or polio, many parents didn't get too attached to children as babies. They didn't want to get their hopes up for one specific child, in the event they did wind up having to bury them. In the mid-1800's one in five children, 20%, died before reaching age one in Sweden. In Copenhagen, Denmark, during the mid-1800's parents made clothes for their babies that were used as either burial or christening clothes. What a sorrow laden task that must have been for a mother to sew clothes for her child knowing they could quite likely be buried in them instead of being christened in them, and live to outgrow them.

In the Verum cemetery the grave markers, for adults, usually noted a fact about their life, such as their profession. That gave the viewer a small insight into who the person was. Those who had less financial resources were buried with simple wood grave markings, which didn't survive very long into the next generation. The etchings of name, birth and death dates were erased by the gradual sanding of time – the wind and the snow and the sun. All erased into history.

Since we were farmers, even on Sundays there was never truly a day off. The animals and our crops needed tending every day – rain, sunshine, snow, or mud. The brief bursts of joyous holidays we celebrated dotted our year's calendar. Towards the end of winter/early spring would come Easter, a religious holiday celebrating new life. The next holiday occurred on the last day of April, where we Swedes celebrate the King's birthday by flying Swedish flags in respect for him. On that same day, the celebration of *Valborgsmassoafton* (Walpurgis Night) occurs in Sweden, which celebrates spring. The festivities are named after an English nun, Saint Walburga, who lived from approximately 710 to 777 and was canonized on May 1, 870. She was said to have brought food to Sweden during times of famine. Also she is often credited with being the first female author from both England and Germany.

The very next day, May 1, is the celebration of spring, May Day. (Much, much later, in 1938, it was also declared Sweden's Labour Day, celebrating workers and their efforts.) Along with our friends and neighbors, my family would light a huge bonfire of poplar tree limbs to celebrate the coming of the light and the end of winter. It was great fun to stay up as long as the light was in the sky, since at that time of year the sun doesn't go down until almost 11pm at night. It was a welcome relief from the dark winter days.

May Day is the traditional dance around the May pole to celebrate spring. This is the event we children, especially girls, looked forward to. It was an opportunity to add more 'sparkle' to our clothing and maybe receive some special ribbons for our dresses and hair from our parents. The Swedish colors of royal blue and yellow were very prominent in our clothing on May Day. In our town of Verum, there would be a parade down the small 'downtown' street, where everyone dressed up in their finest Swedish decorative clothing. After the long cold winter it was truly glorious to be outside and visiting with so many people. (And hopefully the sun was out, warming up our pale, wintery skin!)

During the season of Advent (meaning "coming"), we celebrated the coming of the birth of Christ, as had been done since the fifth century AD in Sweden. This season was hectic for our family, as farmers we needed to have all of our work completed for the coming coldest winter months. The ninth of December was called

"Anna Day". This was the day that we were to begin soaking the fish in lye, to make lutfisk, so that it would be ready to eat by Christmas Day. (The Swedish word lutfisk literally means "cod soaked in plutonium". This was a method to preserve the fish so that it could be eaten throughout the long, cold winter in Sweden.) And the baking would begin for the special Christmas holiday season. Following this was St. Lucia Day, December 13th, when candles were made and the meat for Christmas dinner to be prepared. And then Tomas Day on the 21st would be the end of milling and spinning, preparations for winter. After the 21st our town would have a Christmas fair, where all the farmers would convene and enjoy each other's company and fruits of their labor throughout the year – such as meat and breads.

Nilla

Nilla, the oldest girl in the family, was the first of us girls to leave home when she married Karl Bentzen, a man from a neighboring village. She was eleven years older than I, thus I was only eight when Nilla was married and moved away from our family's home with her new husband.

They'd met at a dance during mid-summer festival in May. Midsummer is such a joyous time in Sweden; we celebrated the arrival of summer, the long hours of daylight, and, quite frankly, surviving the winter. It is a time for renewal by many people to reengage with their neighbors and friends. Food, brightly colored clothing (especially the royal blue and yellow, our country's national colors), and gatherings highlight this time of year. Nilla married at a most opportune time; she was still young (only nineteen) and had completed her schooling.

Nilla and Karl married at the church in Verum, and within six months we learned Nilla was to bear a child. Because of the economy and to support his growing family, Karl had decided to become part of the wave of emigrants from Sweden and relocated to America. He left Sweden in 1875, before his child was born. During these years of 1865 through 1918, a total of 24.4 million immigrants to America came from European based countries. Sweden contributed close to 1.5 million of these new residents. The lure of the American economy and the want for a better life for his family had put its hook in Karl's mind.

Nilla's first son, Nels, was born when she was twenty years old. As her husband had sailed for America two months before the baby's birth, Nilla was alone to care for her newborn son. She named him Nels, after her husband's father. That was such a joy, their first child a son! Although it was difficult for Nilla, who was left with the tasks of caring for her infant son on her own. Karl sent money to Nilla to provide for her and Nels. She lived on her own with Nels for nearly seven years until 1882.

We had heard Nilla's husband Karl had settled in America in a place called Joliet, Illinois. Karl had chosen this location in America for several reasons, primarily because this area offered familiarity to him. There were many Swedes living in the greater Chicago area. By 1900 there would be 49,000 Swedish-born residents, who had 96,000 American born children. That meant he could easily translate his knowledge of working with Swedes from home to his work activities in America. His work was with natural resources in rock quarrying and mining. He went to work as a stone cutter in a Joliet quarry, and in the winters, he worked inside in a steel mill. The climate and surroundings of the Midwest / Chicago area were similar to Sweden – cold winters with warmer summers, although Illinois could be much warmer in humidity than Sweden. The area outside of Chicago had an expansive base of farm land with rich dark soil, quite like where we lived in Sweden.

Karl, having come to the United States through the port of New York City, had to pass through the United States Immigration office. Clearly he was able bodied and planned to work once he reached his destination. His name, Karl, was a very popular name for males amongst Swedes. The immigration agent didn't know, understand, or probably even care about Swedish naming customs, so he had 'renamed' Karl to Charles. His last name, Bentzen, was also spelled differently than the agent was used to. His last name became Benson. As of the time he passed through the American immigration office, he was known as Charles Benson.

The goal for many immigrants to America, including Karl/Charles, was to earn as much money as possible to establish a home in America and then send money for his family's passage. Charles achieved his goal in 1881, after saving and prospering for six years, when he sent money for Nilla and Nels' passage to join him in America. They had lived on different continents for seven years.

He had successfully established himself in the industry around Joliet and literally had left the farming life of Sweden behind.

There were sad moments as Nilla prepared to leave Sweden. I was becoming a young woman – fifteen years old. Most of us that saw her off believed this would be the last time we'd see her on Earth. The cost of a trip to America was just too great for only a visit. The passage on the ship was taxing for a person's health – one must be in good health to make the journey and survive it. Our parents realized it was part of Nilla's obligation to her husband to follow him wherever he was in the world, knowing it might be the last time they would ever see her again. That is what came to pass. Our parents, Lars, Anna and Johanna would not see Nilla again.

Looking back on this I wonder how our mother truly felt. She kept her feelings to herself. She didn't share with us what her emotions were. She did shed tears when Nilla left Hagnarp, which surprised me, since I don't recall her crying in front of us children – ever. Clearly it was difficult to see her oldest daughter and first grandson leave, most likely to never return. Her tears indicated the importance of what was happening to our family. Part of the future of the family had left for another place and life.

Nilla sailed away from Sweden with her 7 year old son, Nels, and arrived in Joliet on February 9th, 1882. Nilla's husband, Charles, was employed in Joliet and had found a small house for the three of them to live in. Upon her and Nels' arrival in Joliet, Nilla immediately began setting up her household. She was adjusting to life without any extended family. Only her immediate family of her husband and son persisted in her new life. She corresponded with our mother via letters every three months or so.

By the time Nilla and Nels arrived in 1882, Chicago contained the densest population of Swedes in the United States. Chicago was known as "little Sweden" and had the second largest city of Swedes in the world (Stockholm being the first). The transition to America, culturally, was easier with so many of our fellow Swedes living in the same area. Around this time was when American Swedes began to integrate further into American life and culture, having previously clung to the familiar and 'old' Swedish ways.

Chicago was beginning the process of making its presence known on a global level. One of its distinctive features would be as the first city to have an elevated electric railway, called the "L" (for elevated). Thomas Edison and a partner, Stephen Field, impressed the attendees at the Chicago Railway Exposition in June of 1883 with a locomotive running on a one third of a mile track. They carried almost 27,000 passengers proving the viability of an electric train. This demonstration was important for the city of Chicago's future.

Soon after Nilla had begun her new life in Joliet, she was expecting another child. Then another child arrived the following year. She bore a total of ten children, nine of which were born in Joliet. Her family grew to consist of 5 boys and 5 girls. She fulfilled her role as a provider of children, particularly multiple sons. This was seen as 'success' as a mother and a wife in America.

Choices

Part of my sister Nilla's letters to my parents told them of the opportunities for a young Swedish woman. As the only unmarried daughter remaining in their home, they considered the options available to me in Sweden – to marry or remain living with them with a small chance of finding work to add to the household income. The job opportunities for me weren't great in our rural area of southern Sweden. For young women it was limited to possibly a teaching position or working in a nearby town (it would not be typical for a young woman to move alone to a city). I had no prospects for marriage - no strings to attach me to Sweden, other than my parents.

By this time my older sisters Anna and Johanna were married, and my next closest sister in age, Elna, had passed away years earlier. As noted in the parish register, Elna unfortunately had always been sickly.

My parents made the decision for my welfare that the opportunities in America presented the most promise for me. They scraped together the money for my passage and booked me a ticket. By this time the cost of passage was half of what it was twenty years earlier in 1865. More Swedes could find the money to pay for a ticket to America, thus it encouraged more emigrants to leave Sweden.

The lure of the United States offered the promise of work with decent pay and conditions for many aspiring immigrants. At this time Sweden was in the midst of yet another famine; families couldn't feed all their children. Thus families would even risk sending unmarried women to America, in the hopes of the women finding work and a better life.

The primary jobs for young Swedish women in the late 1800's in America were for household helpers (known as domestics) : cooks, childcare workers and maids. In Sweden 'domestics' often were also farm workers. There was no prestige with this work and little in the form of compensation. Barely enough food to survive was provided by a domestic's employer. In America domestics enjoyed higher wages and a greater social appreciation. Thus emigration from Sweden was appealing from both a living and social standing.

Preparations were made for my travel to relocate near my sister in America. I was one of the millions of Swedes between 1850 and 1930 who emigrated from our country. Emigration out of Sweden peaked in 1869 and then again in 1887 (the year before I came to America), the main impetuses in those years being crop failures (thus lack of available food) and disease. After about 1890 the rate of Swedes emigrating began declining, since there were increased opportunities at home and the economic driving force was tamped. This is when the lure for (male) immigrants who could homestead land in the Western portions of the United States ended. The homesteads had reached the Pacific Ocean, concluding the opportunity for 'free' land.

During the peak years of the Swedish emigrations, the two primary economic motivations were to:

- Homestead a farm – these were primarily families who came to American in the years between 1865 – 1890. This option ended in the 1890 timeframe, when settlement had reached the Western edge of America – all the way out to San Francisco, California and Seattle, Washington.
- Obtain work in the cities – this group of Swedes was most often young, single people, particularly focused on the area around Chicago. Chicago had become known as the "Swedish capital of America". The Illinois Central Railroad sent agents to Sweden to recruit young men to help develop the railroad, many of whom settled in the Illinois area.

At the end of the American Civil War in 1865, there were approximately 25,000 Swedes that had settled in America. By 1890, following the peak years of Swedish immigration, our numbers had become 800,000.   1% of the Swedish population emigrated *each year* during the 1880's.   Sweden's economy had not yet achieved improvements in industrialization, which, when accomplished, would lead to more jobs and greater efficiencies.   That would conclude in 1914.   The economy in Sweden remained poor until the early 1900's, accelerating young Swedes' desire to emigrate to seek increased employment and earning opportunities.

Records of the Swedish emigrants were kept starting in 1869 by the police in Malmo and Goteborg, the primary ports of egress from Sweden.   All who passed through these ports had to register with the police. The registration included name, age, gender, parish of origin, and destination (most often either Canada or the United States). The Landsarkivit in Goteborg stores all of this information, which was collected from large archives left by the Larsson brothers, who had been emigrant agents in Goteborg.   This information is a treasure for descendants who wish to research their ancestors migration, a gift from this company who kept impeccable documentation.

America had recently finished the Reconstruction period in 1877 from its Civil War. Conditions and work were improving, and the positives for immigrants lured many to try their luck in America. The nation was recovering and healing from the assassination of their President, Mr. Lincoln, in April 1865 in Washington DC, at Ford's theatre.   In 1875 the country had passed the civil rights act, to give rights to people regardless of race or previous servitude. Slavery had just been abolished.   America offered the promise of being the land of opportunity.

My Father had made the journey with me to Goteborg to see me off from Sweden.   I'd said my goodbyes to Mother at home.   This was the one occasion in my life she told me that she loved me.   I treasure that moment that she verbalized her feelings. Father was more stoic at the ship's dock – he, somewhat stiffly, hugged me. That gesture was difficult for Father to make; he was not at all demonstrative of affection, and especially in public around others. Then we said goodbye, for what would be the last time.

In 1888, I was twenty one years old and sailed alone on a Wilson Line ship from Gothenburg. My destination was New York City, New York, in the United States of America. As we left the harbor of Gothenburg, I looked back at my homeland, Sweden. I didn't know if I would ever return; I thought it not likely due to monetary constraints. I said my final goodbyes, whispering into the air. I knew I had to make the best of the new life I would have in America and that I had literally sailed away from my life in Sweden. I chose to think about it as a positive change and to do my best work possible. There weren't many other options. In the future I could write to my family, where letters took 6 weeks or more to reach their recipients. That was the only means of contact available with my parents, brother, and sisters.

The route to New York took me to the port of Hull, England. We passengers then boarded a train across England to Liverpool. There the steamship waited that would take me to New York. The journey was long and full of seemingly endless waiting. I tried to think of things in my head to keep my mind occupied. I endured three weeks of existing on a bunk in a windowless lower cabin of the ship. Because there were no areas to gather (and little to do anyway) most of us third class passengers stayed in our bunks for most of the twenty four hours a day. Twice a day I forced myself to go up on the deck to get some fresh air. Our toilet was a bucket that was thrown overboard periodically. If a person was ill in the bunk room, the stench was overwhelming for days.

We did the best we could. The trip was hard for even those of us considered healthy enough to be allowed on board the ship. The days were seemingly endless – little light, food that was heavily salted for preservation, and little fresh water made it almost like what I thought being in a jail would be like. Although we were technically allowed to move around the ship (within guidelines – which meant not in the first class cabin), it was a very confining trip.

Much later I learned of the experience the Irish had in their crossings; the ships were called "coffin ships" as many died during the crossing due to disease and truly dismal conditions on the ships. The Irish onboard were often fooled out of their money by inflated fares and charges for basic necessities, such as water and food, while onboard the ships.

Once they arrived in America, their lives often didn't get much better. Fellow Irishmen known as "runners" greeted the ocean passengers, transporting ("running") them to businesses who most often exploited their new clients. They quickly promised to help, but in reality took even more of the precious monetary resources the new Irish immigrants had remaining. The Irish boarding houses were quite likely to be filthy, vermin infested places. Often the owners would steal their boarders' luggage, and when the boarders had no other resources left, tossed them out on the streets of New York with no clothes, food, or shelter.

Being in America without resources, many of the Irish stayed in the ports they'd arrived in : New York, Boston, Los Angeles. They tended to settle in the same areas as their fellow (former) countrymen, seeking cultural and social support. In 1860 there were over 200,000 Irish in the New York City area, over 25% of the population! In the next forty years, 2 million more people from Ireland would arrive in America. By 1910 there were more people in New York City of Irish heritage than in Dublin, Ireland. History has noted the impact of the Irish immigration to America and the places they settled and established – such as Boston College, Notre Dame University, the major work force behind the construction of the Erie Canal, and celebrations of St. Patrick's Day in March.

It is less well known that we Swedes, during the late 1880's, made up the third largest group of immigrants to America. There were many similarities in the conditions of Ireland and Sweden in the 1800's, namely the agrarian economies that couldn't support the population growth and religious persecution. We all came looking for a better life. Swedish immigrants would found Augustana College, Nordstrom department stores, Walgreens drug stores, and produce the well-known writer Carl Sandburg.

On American Soil

One of the most important days of my life occurred on June 3, 1888. The steam ship I had been aboard for the previous three weeks pulled into New York Harbor. I had arrived to America. Land was such a welcome sight after the constant rocking motion of the boat in rough seas. The magnificent Statue Of Liberty greeted us as our ship entered the harbor; it had been dedicated not even two years prior to my arrival. She stood watch over all who entered the harbor, like a patron saint guiding our paths into this, for many of us, new world. My fellow passengers and I were hopeful that we might, in the future, become American citizens. Ellis Island, the primary immigration processing center for the United States, had not opened yet. (It did in 1892 and until 1954 over twelve million immigrants passed through this small island). We came ashore on the docks at the harbor. Having been a third class passenger, we were the last to disembark the ship. Those hours of waiting to get off the boat were some of the longest in my life; the anticipation and excitement of the "New" world in America was exhilarating, yet for those hours still out of reach.

Finally it was my turn to disembark the boat, and as I walked down the gangplank, and set foot on American soil, I relished the moment. This was truly a new beginning for me. My life would be forever different from this point forward. I was then ushered to stand in a line of about 150 people long for another few hours. This was somewhat anti-climactic, being thrown back into the waiting game. At least I was in America, and I passed the time making small talk with my neighbors and thinking about seeing Nilla soon.

When it was my turn to approach the table with the immigration agent behind it, my stomach fluttered with a mixture of excitement, fear, and uneasiness. The agent outstretched his hand and said something to me in English. I had seen others before me hand him their passports and travel papers, so I did the same. He took them and began examining them, so I assumed I did the correct action in response to what he'd said. I was terrified he would find something out of place with either me or my travel documents. I waited in suspense for what would happen next.

The agent waved me on to the next line, that one for health examination. I breathed a small sigh of relief, thinking I had passed at least the first part of the admittance process. If a person had become ill on the journey or deemed not able to hold a job (work), they would be sent back to the ship to return to their origination point. I did have the benefit of having a specific destination, as my sister was my sponsor who was already a United States citizen at this point.

The anticipation and concern was palpable as I awaited the medical review. I wondered if there was anything about my body that would make me not able to enter the United States. I didn't have a cough, I had never been sickly as a child. The medical exam even included a doctor looking in our mouths at our teeth. Thankfully mine were in good shape.

The last desk was the decision point for either being turned back or let in to America. The agent spoke to me in English, which I knew a total of about 15 words from having talked with some with fellow passengers on the journey. I mostly nodded what the agent was saying – I couldn't understand the meaning of his words. They flew by like birds – gone away in the air. He wrote on his papers….Christina Nelson. After what again seemed like an eternity, he selected a stamp and pounded it down on my documents and motioned to me to move along. Much later, after I could read English, I saw that the stamp said "Accepted". And my name was now Christina Nelson (not Nilsson as it was spelled in Sweden). Even with this adjustment to my name, I was in!! I was on American soil, headed for a new life in Illinois.

What is now the city of New York did not form until 1898. When I arrived, the area was a spread out collection of businesses and residences, teeming with activity. The area included Manhattan, Brooklyn, parts of the Bronx, Queens, and the county of Richmond.

Grover Cleveland was the President of the United States at that time. This was the answer to one of the questions I knew I would likely be asked by those who were checking to see what I knew about the United States. (Granted in my earliest days in America, I didn't know much of its history.) He was the first Democrat elected after the American Civil War had concluded, almost 20 years earlier.

When he took office in 1885, he was a bachelor. During these times socially and politically it was more advantageous for a man to be married; even more so representing the United States to the rest of the world. In 1886 he married Frances Folsom, becoming the first President to be married at the White House. Frances was almost thirty years younger than her husband; they would have five children. As a model for the American public, she kept their personal lives separate from the public life of her husband.

Another passenger from the boat, who was also a young Swedish woman, and I went in search of a boarding house to stay in prior to our departing on the train for our respective destinations. We wandered through the streets, heading to Water Street to find one that had a visible sign in Swedish. At least we could then communicate in our known language. The boarding house owners also preferred to provide lodging for their fellow countrymen. I didn't even think of the option to search for a boarding house owned by a non-Swedish speaking person. At home in Sweden there were no varieties of people and languages. I had no knowledge of different countries, their customs and their people. Like many others, I clung to what I knew.

Carrying my suitcase through the streets, walking in shoes with narrow two inch heels, my co-traveler and I stepped into a boardinghouse with a sign written in Swedish, stating it was for women only. We paid for our spot to sleep in the house (a bunk in a large room) and put our things down underneath the bed. I slept rather fitfully that night. Other than the boat I'd never slept overnight anywhere other than parents' house. Since it was June, it was fairly warm. The windows were open during the night; it was a welcome feeling for even a slight breeze to blow in keeping the air fresh in the sleeping area. Sleeping amongst many people unknown to me was like the experience of staying on the ship. During the night others talked, groaned, or made other unfamiliar noises. Other noises of the city laced my thoughts and dreams: horses clattering through the streets at all hours and deliverymen tossing their cargo onto sidewalks for the next day's trade.

I awoke in the morning with the sun streaming in the windows. Although I hadn't been a deep, fortifying sleep, I reveled in the glory of the place I was in. All of the activity, the challenges, the newness…it was intoxicating. It did seem like the land of opportunity with so many people rushing here and there, business being conducted most of the hours of the day and night. I felt small and insignificant compared to all of this activity, and was infinitely glad to have my sister's home to look forward to.

The two nights I stayed in New York City were disquieting, educational, and sometimes thrilling. I saw things and types of people I'd never seen before. The smells and sounds were totally foreign to me; spice scents drifting in the air on the streets, peoples' varied clothing styles and customs. It was by far the largest city I'd ever been in; back in Sweden I had not visited the largest cities there, Stockholm and Goteborg. My eyes must have been truly 'wide open' as I walked around the city streets. I had to watch out for the carts and buggies that splashed water up on the sidewalk as they went by. All kinds of refuse was thrown out into the streets, which necessitated my being aware of where I was stepping. It seemed to me to be a bustling, often dirty place. I wondered how people lived there their entire lives. They never seemed to slow down. The pace and structure of my life in the countryside of Sweden seemed to have very few things in common with lives in New York City.

In the city I even saw something called a 'saloon'. One had a bright red lettered sign outside with a picture of a woman with red circles on her cheeks. I later came to find out that's called rouge – we didn't have makeup where I lived in Sweden, and we certainly wouldn't have put it on our faces. Some of the men walking into the saloon looked at me with leering eyes – it made me uncomfortable so I crossed the street. I had no idea what a saloon was, and why there was a woman's picture on the sign, since only men seemed to be entering the door.

During my negotiation of the street made of compacted dirt, I was splashed at close range with dirty water launched up by a wagon wheel. I made sure to be back to the boarding house by dinner time; as a young single woman it wouldn't be proper to be out on the street near or after dinnertime.

Just down the street from where we were staying, was the Svenska Kyrkan, the Swedish Seamen's Church. It ministered to seafaring Swedes and also Swedes resident in New York. Since it was a weekday, the church was open without services being conducted. I walked in and sat on one of the long, hard pews. It was comforting to have the feeling of being in a Swedish place, although it was on American soil. It calmed me to think of all the Swedes that had passed through here, and those that were thriving in the big city of New York.

While in New York I had to seek out for myself, for the first times in my life, the necessities of life including food. As I stepped over the threshold doorway of the boarding house, I was terrified of the new sights and sounds around me, but exhilarated at the same time.

I found businesses, called restaurants that offered food prepared in exchange for what seemed to me like a lot of money. It would have been a mouthwatering treat to me to have a warm meal, after the three weeks on the ship with cold, stale food. I just couldn't spend the money at the restaurant, though, because the money my parents had given me had to last all the way to Illinois. I was also uncomfortable sitting alone in a public place; it wasn't proper for me as a young, unmarried lady. The compromise was that I went to a General store and purchased bread, a few carrots, a tin of some sort of fish, and an apple. That food carried me through to when it was time to leave New York City.

Only having been on American soil for two days, I still didn't know much of the English language. I walked around in wonderment of the signs posted and conversations others had – I had no idea what they said or what they meant. It was joyous to find a business run by Swedes, where I could read the postings and say a word or two to a fellow customer in Swedish. I tried to find patterns in what I was looking at and hearing in English, but thus far I couldn't make out what the words said. In one Swedish shop I asked the proprietress how to get to the train station. After my purchase was completed, she very kindly instructed me how to get there and what I should expect.

The night before I left New York City, I had cleaned myself up for the journey I would take on the train the next day. At the boarding house I took a bath and washed my clothes, which cost me more of the small sum of money I had for my entire trip. It was astounding to have to pay for every task of living – washing, eating, drinking, sleeping. Back home I rarely even came in contact with money, since my parents traded what we had for things others had that we needed.

I set off for the station to find the train that would take me to Illinois. It was early in the morning as I began the approximately three mile walk. Unfortunately the proprietress' instructions were off by a few streets as to the location of the train station, so I had to inquire about the correct location by some other means. I approached a woman who was neatly attired in a somewhat worn calico dress to ask for assistance, figuring she would take a moment to help a stranger. I didn't ask the women in fancy dresses, who looked straight past me, seeming to hurry to their next destination. The woman in the calico dress must have understood what I meant, as I motioned with my suitcase. She pointed her finger in a direction and held up three fingers. I set off in the revised direction she'd pointed to and after about three blocks I'd arrived at the biggest building I'd ever seen.

New York City's Grand Central Station was amazingly complex and busy – people hurriedly going every which way, racing past each other on their separate journeys. Everyone seemed to have a place they needed to be right *then*. I wondered if this pattern of behavior was typical of how people behaved in America. Standing at the Station, it sure seemed like it.

Inside the station I was searching for the Pennsylvania Limited, which had established train service between New York and Chicago on June 15, 1887, about one year prior to my arrival. This train was the first to have a vestibule, an enclosed platform at each end of a passenger car. That was nice for those of us ladies who didn't really want the outside smoke and air billowing directly into the passenger cabin.

The smoke billowing out of the trains was fascinating and suffocating all at once. It was amazing to see these immense, potbellied steam engines taking multiple cars and passengers off to unknown destinations. Finally I located a sign that read "Chicago" which was where I had written down as my destination. I walked over to the train line and put my foot up on the step to board the train. I struggled with my suitcase, hoisting it onto the train car's vestibule. It almost seemed like getting on a horse, having to swing one's luggage and self up to board the train. Walking into the cabin, there were hard wooden benches on either side of the cabin. I sat down on a free space and put my suitcase underneath my feet.

The seat was hard at the beginning of the trip. It developed into a rock-like feeling on my behind over the next 18 hours of travel. A man in a uniform entered the cabin. His uniform looked to me like a military uniform, but I wasn't sure. It was blue, darker than the Swedish military uniforms. He had a shiny object in his hand that looked like a pair of scissors, but didn't cut paper like scissors do. He approached a couple closest to the door and said something to them in English. The man of the couple reached inside his pocket and handed him his ticket, made of paper, which stated their destination. The conductor took the ticket, made a clicking noise with the scissors type device, and then handed the ticket back to the man. Good thing I'd observed this process; when the conductor stood in front of me, I handed him my ticket. I felt a mere shred of confidence as I looked up at him. He did the same clicking noise to my ticket and handed it back to me. He didn't smile; he didn't say anything; he just moved to the next person. I felt that I'd passed that test and breathed a small sigh of relief.

Inside the train car during the journey we all jostled around, sometimes crashing into each other with a jolt of the train. When I closed my eyes to rest I was awakened by the train's lurching movement on the tracks. The train cut through the air, snaking through the hills of eastern Pennsylvania. During the daylight hours, in the car it would have been nice to have fresh air coming in from the windows. Because of our car's proximity to the engine, with the window open, remnants of black smoke came rolling in. A person couldn't breathe very well with that situation, so the windows were pulled up, closed. It wasn't that easy to breathe in that environment either – a warm day with many passengers in the car. I had a purpose in mind as to why I was making this journey, which made the trip easier to bear for me. I thought about seeing my sister Nilla again, this time in Joliet. It had been six years since we'd last seen each other.

My New Life

The majority of young women immigrants came to America, as I did, between 1885 and 1895; I was only one of the hundreds of thousand people in the migration wave. This was the only time in America's history where the majority of immigrant waves were women. Most of these young women, including me, arrived in America to work. My profession would be a domestic. In the Chicago area by 1900 25 percent of domestics were Swedish. We Swedes had a reputation for being honest, diligent, hardworking, willing to learn, and unlikely to complain. As these were all traits I was taught as young girl in Sweden, they came naturally to me. American families preferred American born domestics; Scandinavians were next in the order of preference, followed by the Irish and Germans.

After the long train ride from New York, I arrived at Chicago's Union Station, on Wells street. This railroad station was built by the Pennsylvania Railroad in 1881, having completed seven years of operation prior to my arrival. It was also massive, confusing, and an extremely busy place of passage for so many travelers and trains. The head house, which looked out to Canal Street, took up several city blocks. I felt disheveled from the twenty hour ride, jostling back and forth. I had tried to straighten my clothing and hair before stepping out of the train onto the platform. My next big task was to find my way to the train to Joliet, where I would meet my sister Nilla. Since I hadn't seen her in over six years, I had some trepidation as to what she might look like and if I could still recognize her. I couldn't read any of the signs that seemed to be posted all over, with numbers next to them. I saw odd looking words like "Kankakee" and "Paducah". I really wasn't sure what to make of this place that seemed to have these odd words plastered all over.

After about an hour's train ride, this commuter train pulled into Joliet's train station on East Jefferson Street. I had arrived in Joliet.

This was my first look at the city that was to be my home. As I stepped off the train, I saw Nilla standing on the platform. Accompanying her were three of her children, all boys. After the six years we had been separated, Nilla looked much the same as she had back home in Sweden. It was wonderful to see her familiar face, having weathered the challenges of living in Joliet with her expanding family, at the train station. She quickly introduced me to my nephews Art and John, who were under five years old. Nels, my oldest nephew, was shy upon being re-introduced to me. He was now almost a young man at thirteen years old. Nilla was visibly pregnant with her fifth child - good news. They escorted me to their home where I would live in the downstairs extra room until I found work. Nilla had talked to others at church and let people know I was going to be arriving and looking for a household position. All of the tasks I learned from my Mother at home were excellent training for my first real job outside my parents' home.

In the years since I'd seen Nilla, Charles and Nilla had become ingrained in Joliet's Swedish community and adopted the customs of America. They taught their children the laws and customs of the United States, provided religious guidance by taking them to the Swedish Lutheran church, and emphasized speaking English as a means to show their Americanization.

They prospered in Joliet; owning 2 cows and a horse and buggy. Charles worked hard in support of his family; his efforts had garnered the desired results of economic stability and prosperity. One of his business endeavors was owning a sand and gravel pit, which did quite well financially. This success enabled him to provide a house big enough for each of their ten children to have their own room. As they grew up, their second and third sons, Art and John, took care of keeping the horse groomed, harness cleaned, and the buggy shined. When they were in high school they could use it to take their girlfriends out on dates, the modern equivalent of having a very nice car to pick up a date in high school.

Nilla was quite busy during the day with (for over 20 years!) having children, making clothes, and tending to the household. She became part of the higher echelons of Joliet's Swedish society, resulting from her husband's status as a successful businessman. In Joliet there were distinct communities of ethnicities; the Swedes knew the Swedes, the Irish knew the Irish.

Her family practiced the Lutheran religion devoutly. They never missed a Sunday at church that I can recall. Their celebrations of Christian holidays were to the greatest extent possible. A large meal with a variety of food selections was served at both Christmas and Easter. One diversion in their home from typical Swedish male dominance was that during the holidays, the boys in Nilla's family did all the cleaning up and dishwashing in the house after the big events. I suppose it gave the girls a break, since on typical days they performed these tasks. As a special treat, after the Christmas party, the whole family went ice skating on a nearby frozen pond. Nilla and Charles adapted their family lifestyle to a more American based approach, to provide more individualized opportunities for their children.

The city of Joliet was large compared to my hometown in Sweden; already by 1870 there were over 7,000 people living in just this one city! The city had a library, court house, schools, and businesses. Downtown Joliet bustled along on a typical weekday, with horse drawn carriages and delivery carts winding their way through the streets. Very busy, very congested compared to the countryside of Sweden.

Joliet is situated on the Des Plaines River, making it a waterway stop and transportation hub. Where a person is from in Joliet is referred to as either the "East side" (of the river) or the "West side". The city was originally established by several developers –

Mr. Campbell, Mr. Demmond, and Dr. Bowen. It started out as a town, called Juliet. You may be wondering why it seems the city's name "Joliet" is misspelled. The answer is the city was renamed from "Juliet" to Joliet in 1845 by the Illinois state legislature. Two of the possible explanations that I learned of for the town to be called by the name Juliet were:

- The area was originally named Juliet in conjunction with the naming of Romeo eight miles away. Juliet and Romeo (as in the lovers of William Shakespeare's book) were in the middle of Lockport, which at one point was intended to be the largest city on the canal.
- Juliet may have been a misspelling of Louis Joliet's name, who was a companion to Father Marquette on their first exploration of the area. The mound of earth discovered nearby was named the "Joliet mound" in 1821.

Joliet developed as a city in the mid eighteen hundreds. There were no graded streets or sidewalks until 1857; Eastern Avenue (developed by Mr. Campbell) was the first. The material left over from that effort was hauled into Jefferson Street to fill that area in, which enabled people and wagons to more effectively navigate it. Until then it was mostly impassable, due to the slough consisting of mud and the ground not being solid enough. The first development of homes and businesses in Joliet were on the West side of the river. In successive years development occurred on the East side with the construction of the Courthouse in 1848 and the Public Library – what is now considered 'downtown'. This was all established prior to my arrival.

Nilla escorted me to her home on Francis street, on the West side of the river. The city streets were bustling with activity, nicely paved with asphalt and brick. Horses clattered along taking their passengers and cargo where they needed to go. Electric trolleys were not yet available in Joliet; this type of trolley had begun service in the city of Chicago in 1877.

Once we arrived, she showed me to a small bedroom towards the back of the house that wasn't being utilized. I had use of a small bed and a table to store my things underneath. My small suitcase contained all that I owned. This was my temporary home while my employment prospects would be finalized. I was nervous about employment. I knew I had to perform my work satisfactorily and not be asked to leave – I had nowhere else to go.

While I stayed with Nilla and her family, I helped Nilla with her household tasks. She had four small children then, so there was of course always something to do. We cooked, cleaned, washed, bathed, and dusted it seemed like morning until night.

A few times during the week there were church activities to go to – Wednesday nights the ladies met for a Bible study. Nilla took me with her twice; it was a large social gathering of women who were established in society (almost always through their husbands). It was a new experience for me being introduced as a young single woman, and not as my parents' daughter. I looked around the room and wondered if I would ever fit in with these women. They were all polite to me, since my sister was in their group. It was unspoken that I wasn't part of their group, and wouldn't be, until I was a regular attendee of their church and had a husband who was financially successful.

On a few occasions either after our mid-day meal or dinner, for a diversion I would take Nilla's children on walks around the city. We saw many buildings made of limestone, the stone that earned Joliet the nickname "City of Stone". It looks a bit bluish-white tinged. The stone was shipped by the Illinois & Michigan Canal to other cities along the river- some made its way into the buildings in Chicago. Much earlier in 1858 a state penitentiary was opened in Joliet, the walls and cells built out of the local abundance of stone. That building still stands. The demand for Joliet limestone continued, and spiked after the great Chicago Fire in 1871. Everyone was interested in building with stone or brick instead of the wood that had literally gone up in smoke in the Fire. In 1890 the Joliet Quarries shipped greater than three thousand railroad carloads of stone per month! The limestone and the demand for it created many jobs for quarry workers and stone masons. Many of the Swedish men had come to the area, hearing of the stone industry, to continue in America their work experience they'd gained in Sweden.

One of the beautiful stone buildings we saw on our walks rose multiple stories over the street. It truly was a massive building; the façade of red Illinois sandstone and red brick imposed itself on the view of the street. It was comprised of over forty rooms with more than five huge fireplaces to heat the building. Later I learned it was built in 1876 by a railroad tycoon, Jacob A. Henry. He also had a quarry of his own that he brought in to lay the foundation and the entire basement floor. Each porch, of which there were many, was made of a single slab of limestone – twenty feet or more in size! The interior was said to be made of intricately hand carved black walnut and oak. Huge parties were held, attended by Joliet's society, which we once or twice spied through the beautiful windows.

Joliet was lucky to have multiple industries fueling its growth: steel was another industry that took off starting 1869. Bessemer converters manufactured in Joliet were of the highest technology at the time in the entire United States. This earned Joliet the additional nickname of "City of Steel", and many jobs were filled by thousands of primarily southeastern Europeans. The Joliet Steel Company built their beautiful main office building in 1891. From the front entrance of the building, with the arched doorway and gabled roofline, it looked like a grand residence, not a business office.

The third in the trifecta of Joliet's industry prominence was as a shipping transportation city. Being located as a major port on the Illinois & Michigan (I&M) canal, this provided the means to enable boat traffic to transport goods to ports up and down the Mississippi river. Work on the I&M began in 1836 and completed in 1848, on which many Irish immigrants labored. The canal was a route of commerce between Chicago, Joliet, and many other cities.

Joliet also had the second largest railroad facilities in the state (Chicago being the first). The railroads that were centered or passed through the city were the Chicago & Rock Island, Chicago & Alton, the Atchison, Topeka & Santa Fe, the Illinois, Iowa & Minnesota, the Michigan Central, and the Elgin, Joliet & Eastern. The Elgin, Joliet & Eastern's extensive presence in Joliet covered over twenty acres of buildings, shops and tracks north of East Jackson Street. These railroads provided transportation to every direction from Joliet.

Social standing in Joliet, as in many other locales, came from typical hierarchical measures such as family ties and wealth. Another factor of social ranking in Joliet came from what year you or your family had arrived to the area. The pioneers of the county had formed the Will County Pioneer Association, which, when it was formed on July 3, 1880, allowed only those persons as members who had come to the county before 1850. Later in 1895 they amended their constitution to allow members who had come to Will county before 1870. Since none of our family had arrived prior to either of these dates, we were not part of the society. Dr. B.F. Allen was president in 1887, the year I arrived in Joliet. He was a medical doctor and very well known in Joliet in a completely different social circle than I was.

Domesticity

It only took a few weeks before a Swedish family had hired me as their household maid. A title of domestic sounds a bit nicer, although in everyday life the tasks I performed were those of a maid, tending to their household cleanliness. The man of the house, Mr. Petersson, was a manager with the Elgin, Joliet & Eastern Railway, which served the Joliet Steel mill. I would live at the Petersson's home; it was socially preferable for a young single woman, working as a domestic, to live with the family they worked for. I wouldn't want to draw attention to myself as a "woman adrift" as a woman boarder was called then. The label "adrift" applied to all life circumstances a woman living alone could be in, including divorcees, widows, and unwed mothers. If you lived alone, people would suspect you engaged in sexual misbehavior or that you were immoral.

On my first day of employment with the Peterssons, I walked the fifteen blocks from Nilla's home to theirs with my suitcase in one hand. As I approached the house that was to be where I would live, I looked up in awe at the two story, multi–room home with limestone facade. It was one of the biggest houses I'd ever seen – certainly bigger than any I'd seen in Sweden. It even had four chimneys – incredible! There were also multiple entrances to the home; one in the front – two others in the back. I went to the back door on the right side of the house as I was instructed to do by my sister; as a member of the household staff I was not to enter through the front door of the home.

After I had walked in my new workplace and residence through the kitchen entrance, I was introduced to the other household staff – the children's nurse, the cook. Fortunately we all were Swedish, and thus spoke Swedish, as I still couldn't conduct a conversation in English. I was replacing the previous maid who had left to get married. They handed me a broom, mop, and rags and explained what rooms I would clean at which times during the day. After the overview of my work had been imparted to me, I was led to the small room at the back of the house where I would stay. There was enough room for the twin size bed, a small nightstand, and a low table. I put my suitcase on the table, opened it up, and unpacked my small quantity of worldly possessions. I refolded my clothes and put them in neat piles on the table. My comb and brush I put on the nightstand, along with my copy of the Bible. It took me all of about 5 minutes to unpack – I didn't have much.

The seven Petersson children (ages 12, 10, 8, 6, 4, 3 and 1) had assembled inside their home for lunchtime. The baby, age 1, was sitting in his high chair. The back door by the kitchen was opened and the screen door slammed as the other six children entered the house, breathless from their escapades in their yard - even the girls! I was briefly introduced to them while they were readying for their lunch. It wasn't expected that I would converse with them – I was told their names and that was all.

I was aware that these children, whose father was a railroad executive, had a high standard of living. I was simply their maid, and they were also my superiors, providing me direction and tasks, in addition to the lady and man of the house. The children had been guided by their parents of their standing in society; they knew they outranked me. For example, they made no attempts to clean up their discarded clothing, dishes, or bathing items. It was my job to silently come along behind them and put the dirty laundry in the bin, tidy up their rooms, and remove their dishes to the kitchen where I would then wash, dry, and put them away. The hierarchy of social position was like it was at home in Sweden – there were upper classes that I did not have a pass to enter into as a result of the class of my birth family.

In my first few months in America, learning English was a tool in the effort to becoming independent and more sought after as a domestic. I didn't speak much those months, as I was listening to the children and my fellow domestics to hear spoken words. I was trying to assimilate them to words I knew in Swedish. My coworkers, the children's caregiver and the cook, also helped me associate words from Swedish to English, although we had little time to talk and discuss. Most often our work was conducted silently and methodically.

The Peterssons primarily spoke English in their home. They seldom spoke to each other in Swedish. The sooner I learned English the sooner others couldn't tell how long I'd been in the United States. It was socially more acceptable to appear as if you had lived in America for several years, as opposed to just arriving a few months ago. Speaking English was one way to give that appearance. It also indicated a person's dedication to becoming American. None of us wanted to appear as if we were clinging to the old country; learning the language spoken in America was one of the means a person was accepted into society, and certainly Joliet.

During the time I was employed at the Petersson's, the lady of the house, Mrs. Petersson, was most often pregnant or recovering from pregnancy. I attribute her cranky demeanor to what changes her body was undergoing during particular months. She wasn't available to advise me on what she wanted or direct my work; I was supposed to just "know". So I did what I thought best and had been shown by my mother.

I had some challenging moments where my work didn't meet Mrs. Petersson's expectations. One episode occurred early on in my employment regarding the way I had folded the family's bed sheets. I had folded the bed sheets in half, then in half again, then again. They had been stored until the next time to put them on the beds. Apparently this was not acceptable to Mrs. Petersson; she felt it showed lines in the sheets at incorrect places. She ordered me to rewash, dry, and iron the already clean sheets to eliminate any fold lines that would be visible once they were on the beds. After spending additional hours relaundering the sheets, you can be sure I followed her instructions exactly all subsequent times.

I worked hard as a domestic for the Petersson's. My days were filled with work – tasks, chores, then more tasks. Each morning before the sun rose, I began my work methodically and diligently; that's what I knew from growing up on a farm. On my one day off per week, it wasn't easy for me to revel in the short window of free time I had. I almost didn't know what to do on my day off, as during my growing up years working every day on our farm had trained me that there were no days off, there was always something that I needed to do. To me it was a great luxury to remain in my bed after the sun had risen and spend some time on my own personal tasks of washing my clothes, reading, or walking downtown to the general store.

Sunday mornings the schedule was not as the other mornings' – that was the day we all went to church. My responsibilities included preparing the clothes for the Petersson's to wear, which must be precisely the way Mrs. Petersson wanted them. By early Saturday evening I was to have laid out the freshly laundered and pressed clothing. This allowed for a smoother preparation time on Sunday morning, as they dressed and departed for their church services.

Recall that back in Sweden there was only one church, the Swedish Lutheran Church, which was run by the government. (The minister being a Swedish state employee.) A smaller portion of the emigration from Sweden was due to persecution some Swedes felt from the state church. As a result here in America many Swedes went to churches with different names and beliefs than I had heard of : Swedish Baptist, Swedish Methodist, Swedish Congregational.

After the Peterssons had departed for church, I met my sister's family at the Swedish Lutheran church they attended. After the services I would occasionally have the opportunity to accompany her home to help with Sunday dinner and watching her children. Most often the Peterssons wanted their household help to assist with Sunday dinner at their home, thus I would return to my work place to continue my duties.

In the fall of 1888 the Presidential election process was all new to me and was somewhat confusing, as in Sweden we didn't have elected officials. As both a non-citizen and a woman I was not an eligible voter in the American election process. The system didn't make sense to me, as the election results showed the current President, Cleveland, of the Democratic party, had actually received more of the popular vote in the United States (meaning in total numbers of votes he received the most votes). However, because of the electoral college system of voting, Mr. Harrison, the Republican candidate, received more electoral college votes. Thus Harrison was elected the next President, his candidacy having benefitted from the monetary contributions received from large manufacturing companies and Cleveland's request a year earlier to reduce high protective tariffs, which the Republicans used as a campaign issue.

A year had gone by, almost before I knew it. Days filled with work, routine, then more work.

To advance as a domestic, the role of cook for a family was the most sought after position within a household. The cook in home had less menial tasks to complete and primarily spent their time in the kitchen, away from interactions with the family. The physical demands of the work were easier than being a maid, and the wages were better. However, to earn that spot one had to demonstrate cooking skill and the ability to serve food at appropriate temperatures. It really was a challenge to time the various food dishes arriving simultaneously to the family's table at the right temperature, especially given that the wood stove could be quite temperamental in either achieving or sustaining a specific temperature.

My opportunity to move into the cook position came when the previous cook, Ursala, became ill. She somehow had contracted polio, and couldn't stand for long enough periods during the day to complete her cook's duties. One day Mrs. Petersson asked me if I would like to try the cook position to see if I would be a fit for it.

I was so nervous on the Thursday my chance came. I had thought ahead for many nights as I lay trying to fall asleep about what I would cook. Breakfast was fairly simple, as it was a weekday, and that involved making Mr. Petersson his soft boiled egg, bacon, and toast, to be ready at 6:30am. Mrs. Petersson and the children ate similarly, but at 7:30am. Then the children were off to school, walking with their lunch pails. Lunch for the children was fairly simple – maybe a meatloaf sandwich with some cold boiled vegetables. Mr. Petersson would eat at a restaurant somewhere near his downtown Joliet office. Mrs. Petersson was home during the day with her younger children, where a hot lunch was to be prepared.

Dinner was more complicated – a main dish, vegetables, bread, and a dessert. I selected a beef roast with boiled potatoes, cooked green beans, and apple pie for dessert. It all had to arrive to the table at the correct temperature and appropriate time. They had a bell which announced dinner was served; the children knew to report to the dining room quickly when the bell rang so as not to anger their father. I was so glad I had the experience of cooking with my Mother – at least I knew basics which would allow me enough variations to cover a week or more of meals.

After consultation with her husband, Mrs. Petersson approved of the day's meals I'd prepared, promoting me to the position of cook at their household. I was excited but nervous to perform well in my new job. Thus began my days of planning menus, shopping for the family's groceries, and negotiating with the butcher for the choicest cuts of meat. The menu choices were quite like those in my native Sweden, with the exception of some fruits and vegetables. Fish varieties that were available came from the local lakes – including trout, bass. The Illinois climate and seasons were similar to those in Sweden, however here in Illinois we had abundant fresh vegetables and fruits in the summer and early fall from the large gardens cultivated on the Petersson's property. In the fall we would can whatever we could to preserve foods for the winter and early spring.

The food in America was overwhelming. The smells; the quantity! Back home we had very little or no excess – here in America they actually threw food away in the refuse pile – potato peels, carrot tops, sinewy scraps of meat. At home we used absolutely everything to provide for our nutritional intake. In America there was butter, eggs, bread, and meat almost every day. This was in great excess compared to the porridge, potatoes, milk and rye bread that were our diet staples in Sweden. Even the American general stores, which stocked food staples, had so much more to choose from than in Sweden. If I had more time to look around, I would have loved to examine the variety of boxes and packages contained inside the general store. The packaging of various items - soaps, crackers, preserved fish – were colorful and had many words written on them. With being responsible for both the shopping and the meal preparation, I didn't have much time in between breakfast and lunch to get to the store and back. I had to be expedient in my trips to the store.

I learned American cooking as quickly as I could, perfecting my craft, to hold my place in the hierarchy of domestic positions in the house. The man of the house was the first piece of the puzzle I had to satisfy with my cooking. Since he was paying my salary, foods were to be prepared how he liked them – the doneness of a soft boiled egg or the color of his toast in the morning. Toast was specifically hard to get just perfect – with the temperature variation of the wood stove, the toast could easily burn or not get hot enough. There was precious little time to perfect my cooking skills – my job was at stake.

To keep my position as the primary cook in the household, I had to provide a high standard of food, in both taste and presentation. The criteria were defined by the man of the house. If a roast was underdone according to Mr. Petersson, he would rap his fork on the table in anger. Hulda, the maid, would slink into the dining room to determine the source of the issue. Then she would pick up the offending item and return it to the kitchen. Once back in the kitchen, with the door safely closed behind her, she would fume and sputter at me the identified problem. If Hulda became unhappy with me, that didn't help my day, either. Thus I learned to time the start of cooking to the household schedule for the day, so that food was delivered when wanted at the appropriate temperature.

As time went on, my specialty in my cooking became breads; the rising of the yeast is so tricky with the exact temperature and timing to get the bread to come out fluffy and light. Especially when I was first cooking I made a few errors in judgment regarding the water temperature to get the yeast to rise the bread. Those times I had to toss the whole mixture and start anew, requiring extra time. Scrapping the ingredients wasn't something that could happen very often if I wanted to obtain and retain the Petersson's favor. On special occasions I made limpa, the Swedish rye bread, sweetened with molasses, which has dried fruits and nuts in it. The weekly baking of bread and desserts took up most of my day on Thursdays.

In the years when I was working as a cook, the prices of things I purchased went up quite a bit. I didn't understand why wool clothing and cloth would get so much more expensive so quickly. It turns out it was due to a new tax the United States Congress, led by Ohio Representative William McKinley, had levied. It was called the McKinley Tariff, which had added cost to the prices on imported goods from other countries. The effect of this tax that affected me was that prices of all goods went up – the American companies raised their prices also. The tax was very unpopular –

none of us wanted to pay more for goods because of laws our government had enacted. Representative McKinley's political career was affected, also, as the voters in Ohio opted to not reelect him in the fall of 1890 because of "his" tariff.

Social Life

There wasn't much time for socializing on my own. Tuesday, my day off, there weren't a great number of fellow domestics that I knew who I could visit with. I could either go to Nilla's house to help her or run some errands for myself, looking in the shop windows along my path. A few times I was able to attend dances or gatherings at the church. Some of the other girls would spend much of their income on clothes, hats and shoes – sometimes up to $150! Since I needed to support myself and didn't have any other means of income, I didn't feel comfortable spending my money I'd earned on extra dresses and pairs of shoes. I saved most of what I made by hiding my money in a coffee can, which I kept in my second drawer in the dresser in my room. That coffee can held the next steps to my future; it was all the money I had in the world in 1890.

One thing I never quite understood was why women in Chicago at that time were so fussy about their hats. It seemed to be a status symbol; a subversive competition to show the tastefulness and prestige of the wearer. It became a symbol of upward mobility, the fancier the better, even amongst all of us domestics. I felt a twinge of envy seeing the beautiful hats passing by on a city street in Joliet or on Sunday at church. But I knew that was not for me; I was to be sensible and save my money. It wasn't possible for me to keep up with the spending and race to get the 'latest' in fashion. The race was over before it even had started for me.

Some of the other girls who did have fancier hats and clothes attracted more attention from men. It may have led to them getting married faster, thereafter having the potential of financial security through a husband. The prize of marriage we all were looking for was a financially successful, older man. If the man was older, it was believed he would die sooner, thus, less time required as his wife. And, after he'd passed away there would be sufficient funds to keep the household running.

During the times we had to converse amongst ourselves, none of us Swedish girls spoke of our collective goal of finding a stable, non-alcoholic man, wealthy, older man. One of the primary fears we all had in marrying was if a husband turned out to be an alcoholic or abusive. This was a very real fear; alcohol was a significant issue for many men. Men during the eighteen hundreds drank approximately *six times* as much alcohol as the typical American man does in the 2010 timeframe. If a husband became belligerent or abusive during a drinking binge, there was little that could be changed for the woman's life. Mostly a wife had to endure and hope for the best in their husband's behavior. Most commonly the women in abusive situations couldn't bring themselves to say anything to anyone; they suffered in silence. Culturally it's not what we Swedes did; we don't expose our emotion and the negative aspects of our lives to others, even close family or friends. Swedish women endured the difficult times. We would rarely share our troubles with our friends; it just wasn't the Swedish thing to do.

One of the girls I knew, Ursala, did confide in me about what was happening at the house she worked in. She was upset and didn't know what to do. The man of the house, who was a railroad line manager, would call her into his study after dinner and close the big wooden door. He would force himself on her and told her to not call out or tell anyone what happened. What could she do? Her life depended on having work and a place to live, which he controlled. As domestics we didn't have a way to protest or complain – there was likely no one who would listen or even believe what we said. I listened to her, nodding my head in sympathy over a coffee hour at church, knowing there was nothing I could do to help her. This went on for almost a year; then Ursala suddenly was gone. She had begun to "show" (what is now called a "baby bump") and had to leave immediately. For where, we never found out. She probably moved to another town, telling people her husband had returned to Sweden, had the baby, and then continued working.

As part of our working life, if one of us 'girls' had become ill while we were working for a family, our contract could be terminated at will during one week's time. Back in Sweden household help enjoyed a stadja (one year contract). In America, a prolonged illness or personality conflict with the homeowner could result in dismissal within a week, leaving the domestic with no place to live or income source. As a result, we didn't complain or object to work we were asked to perform; we did as we were asked to keep our jobs.

Most of my own social life occurred in the hour or so after the church service on Sunday. We would gather as part of the congregation to have some coffee and possibly a roll. My fellow Swedish domestics and I always spoke English – even if we were only among Swedes. We were trying to ensure we were becoming Americanized. We would compare experiences amongst the families we worked for or talk of the local news. Rarely if ever was the word 'homeland' mentioned; we all had left it behind, both physically and mentally.

Once for a special treat I went to Chicago with one of my fellow domestics to visit for the day. We went to the train station in Joliet for the hour plus ride up to Chicago. Upon arrival at Union Station, we would walk towards Lake Michigan, window shopping and looking at all the sights and sounds of the big city. We discreetly looked at the wealthy ladies all dressed up in their fancy dresses, with purses, hats and gloves to match. The world of finery they lived in was outside of anything I could even dream of. For a few brief moments I liked having a glimpse of the fashions they wore and what their lives might be like.

In the spring of 1891, the Mayor of Joliet, Patrick C. Haley, moved into his three and a half story high residence, located on South

Center street. It was like a castle (made of Joliet limestone) – so many rooms, huge front porch. Inside it was said to have woodwork in oak, cherry and mahogany, with stained glass windows, detailed friezes and fancy adornments. I walked by it during one of my days off; it was so amazing to see the enormous house, like a palace in our city of Joliet.

At a spring picnic put on by my church, one of my domestic acquaintances introduced me to a tall, blond, strong, Swedish man. That day my long, dark hair was pulled back in a tidy bun, the humidity not getting the best of it. He asked me my name, to which I replied with my eyes cast down somewhat, not directly meeting his. In turn I asked his name, which he said "Charles Anderson". His name was really originally Karl back in Sweden, but was changed to Charles as he entered America. After that we stood for a few minutes without saying anything; then he asked if I'd like to watch him throw horseshoes. We walked over to the horseshoe pit, where he threw the shoes quite accurately.

When that was completed he asked if I'd like to go to the lunch table to eat some food. I followed him there – we selected some food off of the long white picnic tables laid out by the women of our church. We then went to a picnic table where we sat across from each other, both of us pondering what to say. Charles wasn't shy; he was a man of few words. One topic would last about two sentences, then we'd return to the awkward silence where nothing is spoken aloud. That was alright with me; I didn't really know topics to ask him about. We kind of smiled at each other (very slightly, as to not expose any sort of feeling in public) without saying much. It was a comfort, though, to converse with someone who was also from Sweden. He told me he had come to America in 1886, roughly one calendar year prior to my arrival, to earn a better living than he could make in Sweden. In the past his family had impacted by the young men being drafted into Sweden's wars and religious battles, causing some ill will towards Sweden's government.

He asked if he could come to call for me at the house where I worked. I told him yes – he was the first man who had ever asked for me. I wasn't head over heels in love with him, not that I had experience with romantic love, but he seemed decent enough. He wasn't a great conversationalist or interesting personality. He seemed like a stable, steady, reserved Swedish man. I realized my options in America for marriage were limited – dictated to pretty much a Swedish man, given my upbringing and familiarity with the culture. When a man came asking about me I didn't say "No".

Charles had an intense personality – very terse, to the point, no nonsense. He was a skilled craftsman; a stone mason who worked hard, laboring all day, Monday through Saturday. He was a man of habit, consistency, routine. He didn't drink alcohol, so as not to ever change his mental capacity and his actions. This was fortunate for me, as when something deviated from his baseline/norm/typical, he could become very angry. His anger could have gone more out of control if alcohol was involved.

During our 'courtship' in the spring and early summer of 1891, Charles asked me on a few outings – once to the movies, once to a soda fountain. The soda fountain was new to me, since I had never visited one. I couldn't spend my earned money on an expensive treat. I did enjoy the fizzy soda, with chocolate sauce mixed in it, and the creamy vanilla ice-cream scoop floating in it.

Life with Charles

After about two months, Charles asked me to marry him while we walking in Bush Park, which is located on the southern side of Joliet, near Rockdale. We were out for a walk on a nice summer evening in June. I had already weighed my options if he were to ask. I had reasoned to myself that, unless I wanted to be a cook in someone else's house the rest of my life, I would make the choice to accept Charles' marriage proposal. My options were limited for prospective husbands. I was a domestic with no family support and over twenty five years old. That age was 'old' for a woman to be married. My prospects of marriage were getting slimmer with each passing day.

I knew our marriage would begin as a union that made economic sense. I wanted the security of a home and a husband's income, Charles wanted a wife to run a household and have a morally approved sexual relationship (within a marriage), including children. Our marriage would not be, given the status of the development of our relationship, a marriage of passionate love. That may grow in time; at the beginning it would be something that worked out for both of us. We both knew our roles and what the other expected. And, as common in this time period, as a wife my performance of my duties were more required than a husband's intended commitments. Husbands had much more leverage in their duties – they didn't have to provide their income all to their household – they could choose to spend their earnings how they wished. They could also go out and drink, be physically abusive to their families, and not help out with chores around the household. The wives and families were left to deal with the impacts of the head of the household, the husband and father.

Charles was a support to his family back in Sweden. He had three sisters and two brothers. Charles had saved money and sent it back to Sweden for his brother, Klaus, and sister, Sigrid, to join him in

Joliet. They arrived just three years after he had to America. This demonstrated his hard work to provide for his siblings and family.

As I'd mentioned during my days as a household domestic, there were some avenues available to help a wife and the children if the husband wasn't performing his societally imposed duties to his family. But they were limited – more of an advisory nature. Even a minister of our church wouldn't really get involved if a husband was physically abusing his wife – he might say a word to the husband, but wouldn't press the point if the husband rebuked him. The policemen of our city weren't interested in getting involved in domestic disputes, either, unless someone was severely injured (where a doctor had to be called to save the person's life).

In 1890 there were 1.1 million people in Chicago. Swedes made up the third largest immigrant group, given that these were the peak years our immigration. At this time the Swedes had settled into the area surrounding Clark and Foster Avenues (3200 North), which became known as Andersonville. The name had two possible sources. It may have been named after the central figure in the Swedish community, the Norwegian minister, Paul Anderson. (Norway was ruled by the Swedish monarchy at this time). The other was John Andersson, whose farm was on this site prior to homes and businesses being built there. There were also Swedish enclaves on the south side, in an area known as Englewood; in Irving Park and Logan Square, in Humboldt Park, and the far south side (including Pullman). Just to the north of Chicago in Evanston also held a great number of Swedes.

The Germans and the Irish held the rankings of the largest groups of immigrants to Chicago during this time period. Chicago's population was literally doubling every ten years; in 1880, 503,000 people lived in Chicago.

Swedes in Joliet formed their own types of support systems, funded via private channels such as our churches. One such venture was the Swedish Orphans Home, located one mile southeast of the city, near Manhattan road. The Home is a large stone structure which opened on February 11, 1896. The home grew quickly to almost one hundred children as residents - "inmates" as they were called at the time. We heard about this fundraising effort at church, which we supported to the extent we could. Oftentimes if a mother wasn't available to assist with raising her children, by either death or sickness, the children would be sent here if no other relatives were available to take them in.

We were married on July 25, 1891, at the courthouse on West Jefferson Street in Joliet. We were married there because there weren't many others who would attend, and it was less expensive and quicker than a church wedding. It was a hot summer day in Illinois and very humid. The only attendees were our witnesses, Charles' brother Klaus and my friend, Mathilde whom I worked with at the Peterssons. My sister Nilla wasn't able to be there; she was in the process of delivering her sixth child. After the brief ceremony, Charles and I went to have our wedding photo taken (see Photo 1 in the Appendix) then out to lunch downtown.

Following our lunch, we walked back to the rented flat which would be our first home to begin our lives together. The flat was half of the first floor of a large home, with a small grassy area outside and a back porch. It seemed so quiet and lonely as we walked through the doorway, as husband and wife. I had prepared myself mentally for what would likely happen next. I was anxious about it but knew the decisions for my life were now up to my husband.

Our first night of marriage Charles exercised his husbandly right of intercourse. I was not at all prepared for how this would feel – no one had ever spoken to me of sexual relationships and their dimensions. (Other than, at church, I had heard that sexual thoughts or interest was not something proper Swedish women had). That first night, like many to follow for me, was difficult.

On our marriage bed I lay down and was trembling out of fear of the unknown, waiting. Charles came over to the bed, removed parts of his clothing and mine, and proceeded to have intercourse with me. It wasn't really a shared experience; more like I waited until he was through with what he wanted and then I allowed myself to relax a bit. The tension flowed through my body and lingered until into the night. Intercourse was something all of us women knew as a duty in marriage, something to be endured for production of children.

The day following our wedding was the start of what would become ritual for my life; cooking, cleaning, shopping, tending the garden. Our first few months of marriage was a steep learning curve for me of Charles' habits and requirements for my position as his wife in the household. My work for the Petersson's had concluded one day before we were married, as Charles insisted that I not work outside our home, as that was the practice in America. He felt it made us more American to pattern our lives after what other Americans were doing. Back home in Sweden most women would work in addition to being mothers; typically the work they would perform was in the fields and with the family's livestock.

I learned to stay out of Charles' way and prepare his food and house the way he liked it. Laundry day was on Thursday, which for just the two of us didn't take but half a day. I had to warm up water on the stove , lug the heavy basin full of water to the clothes washing tub, then pour it in the washing tub. The clothes were washed in the yard up until late September, when the weather in Illinois generally became too cold to wash outdoors. Thereafter through the winter the clothes were washed on the back porch, and hung to dry in our pantry or kitchen, near to the stove, which generated heat for the room.

Charles came home each weekday after 5:00pm, working a full day at the stone quarry on the outskirts of Joliet. He left in the morning at 7:00am sharp, when I needed to have his lunch packed in his metal lunch pail. Most often his lunch included a bread sandwich, butter spread on both sides, with possibly a piece of beef or cheese inside. Maybe some salted fish, a boiled potato or some pickled vegetables accompanied the sandwich. In the summers we had fresh fruits and vegetables from the trees and garden in our yard. In the winter we made do with what was left over from canning I did in the summers. We didn't often have beef, as it was expensive to afford on Charles' salary.

He approached his work and daily habits with the strictness and rigor you might expect from a Swede. He was not tolerant at all of any deviations to his schedule and routine. I did my best to keep to the rigid schedule and pattern, quietly, steadily working throughout the day.

As the weather began to chill that fall, I began to feel somewhat different throughout the day – my stomach seemed to be constantly upset, I had a bad aftertaste of food from the last meal I'd eaten. I knew I was most likely expecting a baby as my monthly cycle had disappeared. It took me a few months to realize this was indeed the case.

In my day we didn't see a doctor until it was time for the baby to be born. I just went on with my life – washing, cooking, cleaning, going to church on Sundays. My belly grew larger and firmer with the baby's growth. It was a whole new experience for me to see my physical form change over the months of my pregnancy. I loved feeling the baby kick – knowing it was moving around inside of me and that was a good sign for its health.

The baby's presence in my belly wasn't a deterrent for Charles insistence on continuing our sexual relationship. Only towards the very end of the pregnancy, when it was too cumbersome to have intercourse did that abate. It wasn't my choice – I had to go along with what he wanted. I didn't have leverage in our relationship to disagree with him.

Since both Charles and I had tried very hard to assimilate into American society, we left most of our Swedish customs, practices, and language behind when we moved to America. We chose not to teach any children we would have the Swedish language, so that they might become more fully American. The only items that were of Swedish language in our home were a few books, purchased when Charles was not yet able to read in English. They stood next to Charles' family bible, written in Swedish. The bible remained with him, as he was the eldest son in his family. In the first few pages of it were recorded his ancestry, dating back to the 1600's.

Children

Our first child was born one day short of nine months after our wedding day. Charles was very proud that we had a child quickly after we were married. I was somewhat frightened to have a child, to be honest, because I had no experience whatsoever with what exactly occurred when a woman was giving birth. I didn't know what to expect or what was needed (sheets, water?). Charles called a midwife to come when I went into labor, and she helped me through my child's birth. I didn't think I should cry out or scream with the pain; that wouldn't have been within the range of acceptable for me, even given that I was in my own home, in my own bedroom. There was a code of conduct, unwritten, that I was to maintain composure at all times. Some may think that odd that even in my own home I could not express my emotions, which were hidden beneath my surface.

During the birth process, I did the best I could. I clenched my teeth on a rolled up sheet during the childbirth pains. I was aching and tired and sweaty. Thankfully the birth went fairly quickly, only ten hours of labor. My body was ready to birth our child; I was twenty five years old, which was considered 'older' for my first born child. We – I say we, although my opinion wasn't really input to the 'we'- were hoping for a boy. Charles really wanted a first born son.

I was tired from being up all night in labor, the pains coming every fifteen minutes or so. Charles had gone to sleep for the night, rising when the midwife called him when the baby's birth seemed imminent.

Herbert - April, 1892

At last our baby was delivered at 7 am in the morning. He had a shock of dark hair – just like mine. He had clear blue eyes like Charles. We named him Herbert, after a man Charles had worked with for several years. It was an American name. We wanted to demonstrate that we were truly American.

I was thankful our first child was a boy, as this took some pressure off of me, proving to Charles that we could have sons. Having a boy relieved both the spoken and unspoken quest to produce a male child; someone who would carry on Charles' family name. In the late 1800's a child's mother was held responsible for the sex of the child. (It is now known that genetically it is the father that determines the sex of the baby.) Girls were looked on as additional household help, not as able laborers to assist with the family's vocation, in our case working in the stone industry. Charles was satisfied with my effort in producing our son. The next day he expected me to be up again, tending to my household chores and the baby. No time for bed rest or having another woman come to help me with my household duties.

Herbert embodied many mysteries of how to care for an infant, as I had never been around babies before at all. I marveled at his little hands and feet, how perfectly formed they looked. Even while he slept I watched him, his eyes covered by his eyelids with their beautiful black lashes. Experience was my teacher as to how to care for infants: bathing, diapering, feeding. At times my learning came through trial and error – I had to use my own intuition to mother Herbert. We didn't have any pacifiers or bottles, so all feeding of Herbert was completed by me. Sharing of childcare duties was not even a glimmer of a possibility with Charles – he expected me to be able to keep the baby quiet whenever he was around. If the baby cried during the night, I would instantly have to jump up and quiet him, before he would wake or disturb Charles' sleep.

During the daytimes when Charles was at work, Herbert and I had quiet time together. We were able to nap at the same times. I fed him (breastfed, as that was the only option) and talked to him; it was just the two of us for several blissful hours during the daytime. He was my companion throughout the day. In addition to my household chores, I sewed clothes for Herbert.

When Charles returned home from his workday, he expected his dinner ready when he came to the table after washing up. He didn't converse much with me – or I with him. We didn't talk of his work. That was for men and not a topic he believed I would understand. I didn't have much news to report from the home front, either. We spent many dinnertime meals eating in silence, with Herbert's occasional vocalizations. After dinner Charles would go to the living room where he would drink a cup of coffee and read either the newspaper (the Joliet Daily Republican) or a book. Most nights he would sit in his chair in the living room until about eight in the evening. Towards the end of the daylight hours, he would light the kerosene lamp to continue his reading. He would then take the lamp to our bedroom where he would ready himself for bed.

That action was my cue to have completed putting Herbert in his bed for the night. This was time that belonged to Charles, whether or not there were other tasks and actions going on in the house. I reported (for lack of a better word) to our bedside, to lie down beside Charles. Probably five nights out of seven he wanted to have intercourse with me. I was to be available – there wasn't a choice from my perspective. Since I'd stopped breastfeeding Herbert, my monthly cycle had continued. Charles did not require me to have intercourse when I was bleeding – too messy.

During the summer of 1892, Herbert was just three months old. In June there was a big meeting in Chicago of the Democratic National Convention, where they had nominated Grover Cleveland as their candidate for President and Adlai E. Stevenson of Illinois for Vice President. Our city of Chicago was in the national news. Charles was not a Democrat – far from it. He was a staunch Republican, believing that each man should represent himself in the world of work.

That summer there was turmoil in Illinois. In June the steel workers went out on strike against the Carnegie Steel Company. It was called the Homestead Strike and there was literally a battle – physically – between the steel workers and the Carnegie Steel company's security agents. The state militia had to be called in to quiet the violence that was occurring.

The strike slowed manufacturing, as parts and supplies to businesses were not being produced by the workers who we out on strike. This in turn affected business in the entire city of Joliet, as a manufacturing and steel center. The strikers' families had no income, and families were starting to crumble with having no food or money to support themselves.

The iron and steelworkers' attempts to unionize dissolved with the softening of the strikers' will. The picket lines were crossed, weakening the impact of the general strike. By October the strike had collapsed to the point the state militia did not need to be present, which ended the 95-day occupation. The strike would not officially end until later in November.

During the last few weeks of this manufacturing and industry slowdown, Charles and I became a United States citizens on Oct 26, 1892. This was a proud day for our family. The three of us went to the brick court house in Joliet on West Jefferson Street where Charles and I took the oath of citizenship.

Herbert was about six months old, and he had begun eating 'solid' foods such as mashed up vegetables, cow's milk, and ground meat. Since he was eating 'table' foods, I stopped breastfeeding him. Mothers started their babies eating solid foods as early as possible, given the extra demands of breastfeeding on the mother's body. It was a new phase of life for me to adjust to – Herbert's nourishment now came primarily from sources besides me, a first step in his independence.

In November of 1892, Cleveland was again elected as President – the only US President to be elected to office, leave office, and be re-elected into office. In the four years of President Harrison's Republican leadership, he had alienated many in his own party, clearing the way for Cleveland's reelection.

Entering into 1893 the American economy was spinning into the most severe depression in its history thus far. Times were getting tough – fewer jobs, banks and businesses closing. Estimates of the millions of unemployed workers rose three to four fold; almost 12 million people were out of work. The national unemployment crisis was caused by the collapsing of many of the major railroads, including the Philadelphia and Reading, Northern Pacific, the Union Pacific and the Atchison, Topeka & Santa Fe Railroads. In total over 15,000 businesses and 500 banks would fail.

This depression would hit Joliet with the vengence felt across the United States. Some of Joliet's primary industries of steel and railroads were squarely in the path of this destruction of jobs and finances. In the spring the coal miners struck, which also led to violence in our state. Coal was an important industry to our area also, as evidenced by places such as Coal City and nearby Carbon Hill.

Just ten days before President Cleveland assumed his office, the Philadelphia and Reading Railroad had failed. The start of his Presidency found him focused on the Treasury crisis (where the dilemma was to decide the basis of the US currency system – should it be gold or silver?) instead of dealing with the general public's most visible issues of business failures, farm mortgage foreclosures, and unemployment. He was able to secure the repeal of the mildly inflationary Sherman Silver Purchase Act and, with the aid of Wall Street, maintained the Treasury's gold reserve. The issues the President put at the top of his action list were in conflict with those being experienced by much of the general public. It made the President seem as if he was out of touch with the American worker and primarily focused on big business

By now Herbert was about a year old. My monthly periods had stopped again, after just restarting following his being weaned to table food. It reminded me of the swells in the ocean on my passage over to America – up and down. I was wondering if I was pregnant again – I didn't have morning sickness and queasiness like I had experienced when Herbert was to be born. I just wasn't sure what was happening inside my body. There was no point in a visit to the doctor. There was nothing to report that they could do anything about, and we didn't have money to pay for a non-essential visit.

One day in March, I went out back to go to the outhouse. As I was hiking up my skirts to relieve myself – I felt an usually strong urge to urinate – I looked down and saw blood had run down my skirts and undergarments. My stomach suddenly felt all knotted up and painful – like something was moving through my insides and trying to move out. In a whoosh of release, fluid, mostly blood, was pouring out of me. Something from inside had released and was now outside my body. All of that fluid slipped into the cesspool underneath the outhouse. I was slightly dizzy, even though it wasn't hot outside – in fact it was a crisp, rather cold day that day.

I really didn't totally understand what had just happened. I knew I needed to get myself cleaned up and my clothes washed before Charles came home for the day. I was trying to sort through my thoughts – should I say anything to Charles about this? I was quite sure Charles wouldn't relate to my experience on any level. I decided that it was information that only women would understand and would ask one of the women I knew at church about it.

That next Sunday at church, with Herbert balanced on my left hip, I asked a friend, about what might have happened to me that past week. She told me I probably had a baby that didn't make it into this world, and that the baby needed to leave my womb before it was ever born into this world. I stood there listening to her, speechless, because I had not considered that as a probable cause for what had happened. Her explanation did seem probable. I remembered from growing up on the farm sometimes baby animals were stillborn, yet had developed enough to see their shape. I had never considered those circumstances occurring in humans, specifically to me.

I grieved some for this child that wasn't to be. Was he a boy? Was she a girl? Was this my imagination of a child or my body playing a trick on me? I had a variety of thoughts where no answer came. I prayed to God to not let this happen again to me – the whole experience of losing all that blood, the cramping in my stomach, the confusion of having no one to talk with about what had happened was exhausting in and of itself. And I had to move on with our daily lives as if nothing had ever happened.

The next month my monthly cycle returned and our lives continued as they had been before – daily chores, caring for Herbert, celebrating the American Holidays of Decoration Day (this holiday became known as Memorial Day in the early 1900's) and the Fourth of July.

Even though my sister Nilla lived not too far away in Joliet, I rarely had the time or opportunity to keep in contact with her. She and her family had moved literally 'across the tracks' from my home to a much bigger house on Polson Place. As her husband owned his own business, a rock quarry, they were therefore of higher rank in society. My husband Charles was a laborer who worked for others. Part of the social distance between our families was because of this difference in economic, and subsequently social, stature. This aspect of separation rippled through subsequent generations; in years to come Nilla's children did not accept mine as equals.

Our relationship as sisters wasn't close – the first point being that she was eleven years older than I. She had married and moved away from our home when I was eight. Thus we didn't grow up together to form childhood memories together. Later in life, once we were both living in Joliet and married, there just wasn't time for us to socialize. Nilla and I stayed cordial, but distant. I know she was very busy with her 10 children; I was busy with mine. We weren't able to connect emotionally. The thought that sisters are best friends, that they are emotional support for each other, is not true in all cases.

A Memorable Day

One of the few times Charles and I did travel into Chicago together was for the World's Fair, in the summer of 1893. This was a bright spot in our lives given the difficulties our city, state and nation were going through. The Fair's official name was the World's Fair: Columbian Exposition. The name referred to the celebration of the 400th anniversary of Christopher Columbus' arrival to the New World in 1492. (The dedication ceremonies for the Fair occurred on October 21, 1892, thus the 400 year calculation.) The fairgrounds were actually opened to the public on May 1, 1893. The Chicago World's Fair was held on the grounds of what is now called Jackson Park on the waterfront of Lake Michigan.

The Chicago World's Fair was also a celebration of how the city had been rebuilt since the Great Chicago Fire, which had destroyed much of the city in 1871. The refuse from the buildings burned in the fire was dumped into Lake Michigan, which formed the land that Grant Park now sits on. The fair was a triumph for Chicago to the American spirit of rebuilding after loss and being host to a worldwide event.

Chicagoans were proud of their efforts in hosting the World's Fair. One newspaper editor, Charles Dana of the New York Sun, became exceedingly tired of hearing Chicagoans boast of "their World's Fair". In exasperation he called Chicago the "Windy City," referring to how ebullient its residents were about their city. This nickname is still used, although most thought it was referring to the wind that comes off of Lake Michigan, blowing fiercely on the downtown streets and buildings.

One of the new innovations Chicago could showcase to the world at the Fair was the elevated, electric railway that had recently been put into service by the Illinois Central Railroad. This railway was called the "El" (short for Elevated). In 1895 the electric railway service was expanded to originate on Chicago's Franklin Street and connected to Chicago's famous Loop (the railway the forms a loop around Chicago's downtown) by 1897. The "El" and the "Loop" are still used to describe the railway system in Chicago.

There were very few events that would be considered worldwide in the late 1800's – the Fair being a foremost event. Harlow N. Higinbotham from Joliet was the president of the organization which oversaw the event's planning and progress. We, the people of Joliet, were pleased that one of our residents was in such an important role.

Our son Herbert was one year old, and I'd left him in the care of our neighbor for the day. Charles and I took the train downtown to Union Station, then walked over to the fairgrounds towards the Lake. We walked and walked and walked. The fairgrounds were over 600 acres full of exhibits, rides, and sales booths. I had never seen so many people in one place in my life. Over its five month run, 27 million people visited the fair.

The day we were there was a very hot day in July. Walking as much as we did in the shoes I had (black leather, two inch heels, with buttons up the sides) was not easy. I struggled to keep up with Charles, staying in the shade as much as possible. Charles was a very fast walker, as he was very physically fit from his labor work, and six feet tall, making his stride much longer than mine.

There were over 200 buildings built for the Fair, the Palace of Fine Arts (now the Museum of Science and Industry) and the World's Congress Building, located in Grant Park, much closer to downtown. This building is now the Art Institute of Chicago, where its two bronze lions (donated by Mrs. Henry Field, of Marshall Field's department store) on either side of the stairway guard the doorway to some of the world's greatest artistic treasures. The Art Institute of Chicago was founded in 1879 as both a museum and school, and first stood on the southwest corner of

State and Monroe Streets. It opened on its present site at Michigan Avenue and Adams Street after the Fair had concluded in December of 1893. The building had been constructed overtop of rubble from the 1871 Chicago fire.

We saw as much as we could in one day. This included a demonstration of a rounded glass bulb that shone light, a phosphorescent lamp. That was really amazing to see, for all of the light in our home came from either oil lamps, candles or the sun.

One of the most exciting exhibits for Charles and I was the replica of the Gokstad Viking ship that had sailed all the way from Bergen, Norway to the waterfront of Chicago. Captain Magnus Andersen and his crew crossed the Atlantic in the ship in 28 days, then made the 1,500 miles voyage to reach Lake Michigan. This journey removed any doubts regarding the possibility the Vikings could have made a transatlantic voyage, since the same type of ship was used during the Viking days, back in the years between 800 – 1000. People cheered the ship's arrival; all of us Swedes (which included those from the Norwegian region, part of Sweden at that time) were very proud to see the ship at the Fair on Lake Michigan.

Another exciting experience at the Fair was an enormous ride that had cars where two or three people sat that twirled them around in a circle. The 'ride' that people went on for fun was taller than almost any building I'd ever seen. Some people screamed in terror, others laughed with joy. I had never seen such a thing. The only 'rides' I knew were gliding over the snow back home in Sweden in a sled. I learned this turning machine was called a Ferris wheel.

How glorious the Fair was – all the buildings, people, and new things to see. It truly was a meeting of all of the world, although some cultural representations weren't precisely accurate. For instance the American Indian had a booth that showed them sitting in a circular position, as a kind of curiosity. As an average American living in a populous city, I didn't know much at all about their culture or traditions. We were separated by geography and cultural norms.

There were also dancers from a place called Hawaii performing a dance called the hula. Their pictures were on the outside of the exhibit where they were performing. I looked away from the pictures as we passed the booth. It was quite shocking to me that women would not have their bodies covered with clothing and also that they would sway their hips. Not at all what my Swedish Baptist church would consider acceptable. Charles steered us across the walkway from the exhibit, so that I wouldn't be in close proximity to it. (A few years later, in 1898, Hawaii was annexed as part of the United States.)

There were many food vendors and booth exhibitions of new foods. It reminded me of my few days I'd spent in New York City, with varieties of cultures presenting their traditional foods. The smells were so different than I was used to – curry, paprika, sauerkraut, rice. Many new foods were introduced to the world at this fair that are still sold all these years later, including Juicy Fruit gum, Quaker Oats, Cream of Wheat cereal, Shredded Wheat cereal, and the 'hamburger', which was ground beef in a patty served between two slices of bread. The hamburger was the most novel item to me – how incredulous that meat and bread were in the same food item.

Charles bought me a lemonade drink – it was tart, cool and refreshing. The rest of our meal we brought with us from home, as we didn't have extra money to pay for food available for purchase. We ate mostly in silence on a picnic table in Grant Park. Nearby to the Fair, Scott Joplin performed his music called 'ragtime' on his piano and trumpet.

We walked back to Union Station at the end of a very long day. It was one of the most experience filled days of my life. The other such days so far in my life were:

- when the ship I was aboard docked in New York harbor and I'd set foot on American soil for the first time
- the day Charles and I were married
- the day my son, Herbert, was born

The train whisked us back to our home in Joliet; the skies were turning to black of night. We went back to the realities of our daily lives.

I didn't have that long to wait for more effort to be added into my reality; I discovered in September that I was pregnant for the third time. This launched a cycle of having a child every eighteen to twenty four months. While breastfeeding, a woman's body does not produce a hormone, prolactin, which is necessary to ovulate, thus providing a natural form of birth control. Not long after my children had been weaned on to cow's milk and food, I would become pregnant once again. This process would go on for almost twenty years.

The Economic Panic of 1893 continued for the remainder of the year. The city of Joliet and the overall United States economy was in tough shape. Almost 20 percent of America's workers were unemployed, which included one-third of the wage earners in manufacturing and 25 percent of urban workers. Confidence in the economy was low, as one out of ten banks had shut their doors to depositors. The resulting loss of workers' savings and jobs pushed many to the Western cities of the United States, hoping for a fresh start. Cities such as Portland, San Francisco and Seattle saw a marked increase in their populations. Railroad construction had fallen by 50 percent, and the market for steel rails fell by one-third, forcing dozens of steel companies into bankruptcy. This particularly affected the economy in the Joliet area, "the city of Steel" home to many large steel and manufacturing companies.

Elmer - March, 1894

Bad economy or not, my second child, Elmer, was born the following year in 1894, just about two years after our first child, Herbert. Maybe he was a "World's Fair" baby from the summer before? Throughout history often there is a boom of babies being born following major events, such as the World's Fair was for Chicago or the end of a war.

Charles was happy to have a second son. The challenge of keeping up with the household work continued, with the added work of caring for two children under age two – diapering, feeding, burping, bathing. Rarely now did I have an opportunity to go out shopping, even for groceries. Either I took both boys with me, or a neighbor girl came to watch the boys while I was gone. I would pay her with a home cooked meal or sometimes I had some change to give her. Occasionally Charles would do home maintenance work on weekends for our babysitter's family, paying them back for their assistance to us.

In the early summer after Elmer's birth, the railroad, which we all relied upon to transport goods from their origin to stores in our local city, began to have interruptions in service due to strikes of their workers. The initial strike began in May with the Pullman Car Company workers over several issues they had raised to the Pullman company. Most Pullman workers lived in Pullman, Illinois – just north of us in Joliet. The town, founded in 1880, was the invention of and owned by George Pullman. He owned everything in the town, including the homes, the stores, the schools. The town's design won awards and had many amenities that the majority of us didn't have, including indoor plumbing, gas service and sewers. The crisis started when Pullman, during the depression which followed the economic Panic of 1893, _had cut the company's workers' pay per hour, laid off hundreds of workers, and would not lighten up the workers' sixteen hour workdays or drop the rent he charged for their residences.

The strike of the Pullman company's railroad workers mushroomed into a system wide strike. By June 26th the American Railway Union (the first United States wide union) members refused to run trains containing Pullman cars, resulting in the cross country railroad system grinding to a halt. I didn't know of the details of the strike, but did notice the effects when I went to shop in Joliet. The store shelves, which relied on railroad deliveries from various parts of the United States, had quickly thinned out due to the lack of completed deliveries. We didn't have much variety in what was available for purchase; some household items weren't available at all. These strikes effectively shut down commerce, the moving of goods between sellers and buyers.

The strike escalated in both violence and destruction; 13 strikers were killed and 57 were wounded. An estimated 6,000 rail workers did $340,000 worth of property damage (about $8.8 million in 2010 dollars). In Illinois these impacts primarily occurred in Chicago, although there were several confrontations across Illinois. Even though the governor of Illinois, John Altgeld, did not want President Cleveland to use federal troops to break the strike, the President did so anyway. "If it takes the entire army and navy of the United States to deliver a post card in Chicago," President Cleveland asserted, "that card will be delivered."

It was confusing to the public as to who was making the decisions – government or business? Many people wondered whether the nation was on the brink of either anarchy or presidential tyranny. Cleveland's handling of the strike alienated many Northern workers from the Democratic Party. This was especially impactful to all workers in the Chicago area.

Labor Day (an American holiday celebrated the first week of September) became a United States federal holiday in 1894 after the strike when President Grover Cleveland and Congress made appeasement of organized labor a top priority. Legislation for the holiday was pushed through Congress six days after the strike ended. Samuel Gompers, head of American Federation of Labor, which had sided with the government in its effort to end the strike by the American Railway Union, spoke out in favor of the holiday. Charles appreciated the recognition of labor at a national level, although he stayed far away from the violence and politics of the labor unions.

Throughout these turbulent times in our country, I was feeling tired all the time, day and night, caring for our two small boys. The winter of 1894 came; the two boys and I were indoors much of the time. I welcomed the spring of 1895. I would open the windows of our home to let the fresh breezes blow in. It gave me a better mental outlook, after what seemed to me to be a long, cold, dark winter.

By later in the springtime, almost early summer, I realized I was again pregnant. Less than a year had passed after Elmer was born. To layer over my general tiredness, another pregnancy made the tiredness seem as if it had soaked into my bones in my body. I couldn't shake the feeling. Herbert and Elmer slept through the night, but of course sometimes they did wake up and require my attention. There was no thought of Charles helping with the children; their care was solely my responsibility. He would be angry if the children woke him up; I had to get to them quickly to quiet them.

Even though I was married and had children, my life in Joliet was mostly solitary. Neither Charles nor I had close family members who could help out when the children were sick or after I had birthed another child. Charles wasn't interested in hearing or discussing my daily trials and struggles. I had to keep going every day, alone in my parenting and quest to make our home comfortable. My feelings and thoughts were tucked up inside of me with no chance to escape.

Sometimes another woman from our church would come by after I had a baby to help out around the house. That was out of the goodness of their hearts – no one had asked them to do so. Charles wouldn't consider paying them, so to thank them I would give them something of what we did have - food or later, when I was back to my typical schedule, caring for their children. Out of sheer necessity, even though eventually there would be eleven other people living in our home, I went quietly about my work and routines of what was expected of me. My hopes and dreams were limited by the day to day activities of living; I had little to no time to dream of anything other than the world immediately around me. Dreams I dared to hope for were focused on my children to thrive and survive. Concern for me and my physical wellbeing were not prominent factors in our household's priorities.

Living with Charles was a lot like when I worked for the Petersson's. If I were to become ill for any extended period of time, I felt like I would practically be 'let go' from the house. After each baby, I had about one day to recover, then I had to get up and resume my household duties. It was not easy, to say the least. Conveniences such as indoor plumbing slowly arrived to our home, requiring much of my work to be manual – carrying in water, preparing baths, and pumping water from our well.

Thankfully Charles didn't drink alcohol or ever become physically abusive to me. If he had been, I would have had little recourse to change matters. I had no family to go back to for support – my parents were in Sweden, my older sister absorbed with her family. Who would I have been able to tell that would or could change the behavior? I knew I had to work within the boundaries of what was set for me – including Charles' personality and behavior and what society expected of me. That is what I did; I ensured I ran our household the way my husband wanted and isolated any inconveniences of household life from his attention. I learned to stay out of his way when he became angered over something, waiting out the time for his anger to subside.

Charles and I both had roles to play. We both knew what was expected of us and we did it. For him it was to provide for our family and father children. He was a hard worker – very physically strong and persistent. He consistently found work as a stone mason and was usually the last man to leave the job for the day

If you are wondering what 'stone mason' implies, let me explain. In Joliet and the surrounding areas there were (some still exist today, although the demand is miniscule compared to earlier decades) limestone stone quarries. This limestone was used to build many of the Chicago area's buildings following the Great Chicago Fire of 1871, when most buildings were made out of wood and were therefore consumed by the Fire. People didn't want their homes and businesses to be wiped out by another fire and sought more permanent materials from which to construct buildings. This drove the demand for both the material, stone, and people to construct with it. Being a stone mason – meaning you worked with this more expensive material – was and is a craftsman's job. It requires visualization of how the pieces will fit together, the shape and contour of all sides of the particular piece of stone, and the sheer ability for a man to be able enough to lift and complete the repetitive motions of laying stone.

Charles had all that; he was very strong. Being a stone mason meant he was on the most skilled side of the construction worker spectrum. He had control over his portion of the building process, to make the decisions about which stone would be placed where. His role in the construction of a building was looked up to and revered; he had a skill that not everyone had. Nonetheless, he was a worker, and not an owner or foreman. His wages were slightly above the $830 per year, which was the average worker's salary. Our rent for an apartment was approximately $25 per month, where we lived in the early years of our marriage.

I endured, and did what I needed to do. Monday was the day I did our household's laundry. This involved multiple steps of adding wood to the stove, heating up the water, carrying it out back to wash the clothes, grating the clothes on the washboard, turning the hand crank to squeeze out the excess water, hanging the clothes on the clothesline in the summer (and in the pantry in the winter). Completing these tasks would take me most of the daytime hours. Charles demanded clean, folded laundry and would be angry if it wasn't prepared to his liking. He required order and consistency in his home, clear down to his laundry.

I did enjoy the days I was able to extract myself from our home and go downtown Joliet to shop. It was just over a mile walk there. It was such a bustling place, the courthouse, the stores. Wagons and buggies crowded the streets. Inside the mercantile stores (Joliet had four of them – quite a metropolis from my point of view) were hundreds of items, ranging from food to horse shoes to thimbles. I didn't have enough time to look at all the items – I had to get back home within a few hours. I pretty much had to find what was on my list, make my purchases, and be on my way. I knew we didn't have money for luxuries like scented soaps or premade clothing.

In the cold winter months our food consisted of what was left of vegetables and fruits I'd canned from the previous summer. We also had a barrel of lutfisk (salted fish) that was our protein source for much of the winter. This is commonly eaten by Swedes, as back in Sweden we preserved fish and other foods by salting them for consuming in the winter months. The cod soaked in salt and lye became known in America as lutefisk, which is the Norwegian spelling of the word. To keep up with how Americans referred to it, we changed how we referred to this salted fish to the Norwegian spelling. No matter what it was called, it didn't taste very good at all; we ate it because that's what we had and it was affordable on Charles' income. Since Charles didn't work during the cold days of winter, we had less money in the winter to buy groceries. That barrel of fish was a primary source of food for us, seeing us through the winter.

Richard - November, 1895

Eighteen months separated Elmer and our third son, Richard, born on the last Thursday of November, 1895. This day was not yet designated as a national holiday of Thanksgiving. That would not occur until 1941. Our family, along with many other families, held a small celebration of Thanksgiving on the last weekend of November. Our meal included stuffing (bread crumbs baked in the oven), mashed potatoes and gravy, and vegetables. Birthing a baby was still not an experience I relished, in fact it was quite painful. But that was not something I could complain or really do anything about – it was part of my life to bear children.

It was winter time, and the outdoors were cold and dry, particularly so that winter. Since I now had three children small children to care for and Richard was an infant, we stayed in our home most of that winter. We ventured out very seldom until the late spring of the following year, as I had no way to transport my three young boys and winter was a bad time, anyway, for their health.

In 1896 the volume of Swedish immigrants to the United States had reached its pinnacle. In America Swedes formed the Vasa Order of America, whose purpose was to assist Swedish Americans with social services and networking. There are still some recreational facilities and organizations that bear the name of this group. Since the United States was still going through a depression, where over 14 million people were unemployed, the Vasa Order helped Swedes try to find work and provide stability for families.

My family was fortunate that only infrequently did Charles not have work. Most of these times were due to the cyclical construction timetable and funding available from banks. At one point there were no construction jobs to be had in all of Joliet for Charles. It was a very difficult time, as we had no income. Most stressful on us was Charles' demeanor when he didn't work. He was struggling with his belief that he must provide and be a strong man for our family. For me it meant we had to stretch our food staples farther than ever, especially with more children to feed. I especially had to stay out of Charles' path, so as not to anger him with how I was completing my work. For most of our married life he was not at home when I performed my household duties and chores. On the unusual times he was there to observe me, he had an opinion as to how I should be performing my tasks. His direction to me mirrored how a stone mason works: carefully, planned, and exacting.

The summer of 1896, following the cold winter, seemed extraordinarily warm. The three boys and I did what we could to stay cool during the hot summer days. I let my older two boys play on the back porch shirtless, not something we would ever ordinarily do. Charles would insist on always being neatly and properly attired, even if the weather was extremely warm.

We had a cellar which stayed cool during the summers, where we could store a block of ice. This was only a very occasional purchase for our household. It was such a treat to have a piece of cold ice on our tongues and feel it reverberate through our body. For a brief moment of time the oppressive heat of the summer in Joliet was evaporated. Once the ice chip was melted in our mouths, the heat would wash back over our bodies.

Again the Democratic National convention held their candidate nominating meetings in Chicago. Illinois' Governor Altgeld was still incensed at President Cleveland for calling out federal troops to help settle the railroad strike of 1894. He used his influence to block President Cleveland's reelection bid. Instead the Democrats nominated Illinois native William Jennings Bryan. The workers of Chicago were ecstatic that the national presidential candidate was from Illinois.

Meanwhile the Republicans nominated William McKinley, led by the urging of a wealthy Cleveland businessman Marcus Hanna.

McKinley ran his campaign with "front porch" talks from his home in Canton, Ohio. A New Yorker named Theodore Roosevelt campaigned vigorously for McKinley, aiming for a choice appointment after the election victory. McKinley would go on to win the election by the largest majority of popular votes in over twenty years, taking office in January of 1897.

Times were changing for our country, having now been settled from coast to coast. The days of the great Wild West were over. Most of the Native Americans had been swept off the land where settlers established ranches and cities.   Railroads, telegraph, and telephone lines connected cities to each other. The depression of 1893 had almost – finally - run its course. The economy was improving.

America was just exiting the depression that had hovered over us for over four years. Most of us working class Americans were numbed by the lack of prosperity that had continued on for many years. We saved everything and reused everything where we could. Brand new items were not a part of our lives, unless we made it ourselves.

These times were great times for businesses – industry developed at a previously unprecedented pace. Large businesses held much power and influence in America. President McKinley called them "dangerous conspiracies against the public good," but they still held a grip on the economics and working conditions in America. At least there was work, for those able. Finally the land of opportunity had returned.

Following McKinley's assumption of the Presidency, he called Congress into special session to enact the highest tariff in history ("the McKinley tariff"). America turned its attention to places other than our continent, now that our own lands were somewhat 'in order'. President McKinley thought Roosevelt was a brash young man, but, owing to the assistance in getting him elected, nevertheless nominated him to be the assistant secretary of the Navy. Roosevelt championed action against Spain, who he believed had interfered with Cuba's efforts for independence.

After the national presidential election, my third son, Richard, was a year old. I discovered I was pregnant once again with our fourth child. My delivery date would somewhere in the summer months, which caused me a good helping of dread. For my first three children, I delivered them in either early spring or the winter months, so that the last trimester of the pregnancy was not in the hot, uncomfortable months of the year. My fourth pregnancy was harder on my body than the first three had been. I was increasingly tired with the heat and the later stages of pregnancy, struggling to keep up with the household demands.

Esther - July, 1897

Happily for me, after having three boys, I delivered a daughter in July of 1897. I so wanted a daughter, and felt blessed by God to have her. Charles was what I would describe as "sour" about our daughter – he thought that since we'd had three boys, the next child would also be a boy. Charles named her Esther, since he had just reread that chapter in the Bible. Esther looked different than the boys – her coloring was more like Charles' – blond, blue eyed. As she developed from infant to the toddler stage, Charles became more taken with Esther, since she primarily resembled him. He became more of a doting father to her than he had with the three boys – she was an engaging, 'good' baby. I think she knew even as an infant what her role in our household had to be: seen but not heard, no crying or outbursts, smile and look happy.

Charles and I did not practice many, if any, of our Swedish traditions. We continued in our belief that since we were citizens of the United States of America, we should no longer follow the Swedish traditions. We did not speak Swedish to our children. In our view they were Americans and should speak the language of their country, English. Esther, our oldest daughter, wouldn't be instructed in the role of St. Lucia to our family when she became old enough. That was one of the traditions that we left behind in Sweden.

Automation, as far as mechanical items, was just coming into being – Henry Ford had yet to introduce the automobile that we 'average' Americans could buy. In 1898 only very early versions were available, being sold by Thomas Edison's company, which were very expensive and not very reliable. Some of the more well to do businessmen around Joliet owned these. It was a symbol of prosperity for a Joliet resident to drive an automobile in our city. It was amazing to those of us walking on the sidewalks to see a 'horseless carriage' go through town. They were almost frightening to see on the Joliet streets trying to weave amongst the horse and buggies. The horses had a hard time getting out of the automobiles' paths and were spooked by the odd noises emanating from their engines. Between the horse traffic and the automobiles, downtown was a very busy place.

My life had become almost an automation of functions and tasks – preparing meals, laundering, cleaning. Even the cycle of having my children was appearing to be on a schedule. The time demands of my days were mapped out long before I actually lived through the specific day. Some of ordering and automation of my life was necessary to complete all of my tasks in the amount of time allotted and to the set standard. My household tasks had to be completed by the time Charles arrived home for dinner time.

Our home on William Street was finished in 1898, when we moved in with our four children. Photo 2 in the Appendix was taken when our home was under construction. Fifteen men worked on the foundation of the house. Charles employed many of the workers he knew from his work on construction sites.

Charles laid some of the brick and most of the stone that formed the basis, the real foundation, of our home. The carpentry was completed by other craftsmen Charles knew. In the timeframe our home was built, we had no option to take out a loan from a bank to help us build it. We funded the construction as it was completed. Charles had saved and saved from his years of working in America to be able to purchase the materials for building of our new home. Many of the work hours to construct our home were donated by Charles' co-workers and some of the men from our church.

During the timeframe it was built, electricity had not made it to our corner of the world outside Chicago. Running water and sewer was not yet an option, either. We had an outhouse for our sanitary needs, and fresh water was carried in to the house from the well pump in the backyard. To me our new house was expansive, with two floors and three bedrooms upstairs. The first floor had a living room, a dining room, kitchen, parlor, and entryway. It was large enough to require daily cleaning, and our growing family added to the chores to keep our home tidy.

For Charles and me, owning our own home was a realization of our American dream. Back in Sweden it was quite unlikely that as farmers we would be able to afford to purchase our own home or land. We were very happy and proud of our home, although we never outwardly showed that to others. It was something we were happy about within ourselves. I think Charles took pride in the work he did on the foundation of our home and the coordination he undertook to make all the construction tasks happen. He may have boasted once or twice to some of the men he worked with; other than that, we quietly went on with our day to day lives. The building of our home was one of the great accomplishments of our lives.

Our home's interior had dark wood trim finishings on all of the doorways and flooring. The kitchen, like the rest of the first floor, had hardwood floors, which, over the years, became marked from constant use. And some spills of water caused them to buckle around the edges. That floor was used most of the day, all day, every day. Much activity went on in our kitchen, which included the work of preparing meals, preparing the laundry, washing dishes, and also eating when it was just a few of our family present. Many, many conversations, some spoken and others unspoken, occurred there between myself and the children, primarily my daughters, about their lives. My sons and Charles were doing other things – getting fire for the fireplace and stove, carting water in, sweeping off the front porch, or tending to the livestock we kept out back in our barn.

The main staircase, visible from the front door and entryway, led up to the second floor. The stairs were made of solid wood blocks, stained a shiny dark mahogany tone. As they were narrow steps, a person needed to be careful walking up and down them to avoid slipping. The women in the family generally had smaller feet which allowed for being able to put one's entire foot down on an individual stair. The boys' feet were larger and didn't fit all the way on each stair. It was trickier for them to go up and down the stairs, which they accomplished mostly by using the toes of their feet. There was also a banister, which sometimes the children would fling one of their legs over and slide down. It was a daring act of rebellion for them to attempt this. Charles especially would not tolerate what he called 'foolishness' and a punishment would ensue to the offending child.

Our dining room was used at least twice a day for breakfast and supper, and for lunch on weekends. We had a bay window which enveloped our large dining room table. It extended out from the flat side wall of the house. This was a luxury – it added a change to the linear shape of the house. I loved those three windows, one large glass window flanked by two smaller windows. Those windows represented one of the few differentiators of my life from typical. They were different from the ordinary, an extra expense that we allowed ourselves to make.

My world was contained within the walls of our home on William Street. I did hear some of the news that was occurring from Charles, who read the Joliet Daily Republican. This newspaper was sufficiently conservative in its political views, and thus Charles allowed it in our home. We were constant subscribers until September of 1906 when it ceased being published. My view of the news was filtered further by Charles, to whatever topics he decided to mention. Occasionally I took an opportunity to read the newspaper in between my household tasks. I tried to relate to what the article was discussing, but my world on William Street was quite different than what I read about. Most of the time I was preoccupied with other things and the day would slip by without having the time to read the newspaper.

In the early spring we had completed our move into our home; Esther was about eight months old. We had heard the news in late February that a United States warship had exploded in Cuba, bombed by Spain. We had no idea what that meant to America or why the ship was there.

Despite President McKinley's message of neutral intervention in April 1898, Congress voted upon resolutions that were the precursor what would be called the Spanish American War, the purpose of which was to liberate Cuba from Spain as an independent county. How long this war would last or what it would mean to our lives was unknown. This was the first war that America had entered into since I had lived here. The thought, and reality, of War rattled me somewhat – there had been no wars in Sweden while I lived there and none in the United States until now. How would our daily lives change? Illinois sent more than 12,000 men to push forward America's effort.

During the war, all of which occurred in the space of 100 days, America destroyed the Spanish fleet outside Santiago harbor in Cuba, seized Manila in the Philippines, occupied Puerto Rico, and gained control of Guam. There were a group of volunteer American cavalry men, called the Rough Riders, the now former assistant secretary of the Navy, Theodore Roosevelt, joined to show his support for this effort. The war was over by August, and the peace treaty was signed in Paris in December.

Because of the elapsed time of the War, it became known as the 100 Day War. America was ceded by Spain the properties of the Philippines, Guam and Puerto Rico. Cuba was made an independent country of its own, then United States annexed the Philippines, Guam, and Puerto Rico. During this time the islands of Hawaii were deemed a United States Territory. Much had happened on the world campus in 1898. In Joliet the 100 Day War didn't impact my life to much an extent. I did know some women from church whose sons had volunteered to go. Other than that the war was over quickly, and my family continued our lives in our new home.

Esther was nearing two years of age in 1899 when I determined I was pregnant for the fifth time. This cycle of conception was becoming apparent to me; towards the end of my breastfeeding a child or not too long afterwards pregnancy occurred. I accepted – that might be too strong of a word – I lived the role that was expected of me, which was to submit to my husband and do as he asked. I made the choice to remain in the pattern my life was following.

Time moved on into 1899, the year before a new century was to begin. The summer saw more automobiles appearing on the Joliet streets, with their odd noises they made and disruption to the horse traffic. To be honest they scared me – no horse was in front of them to move them down the road. The noises were unfamiliar and often steam seemed to ooze out of various parts, causing them to need attention. It was common to see a driver parked on the side of the road trying to figure out what was not working on his automobile. Many of them were made by the Detroit Automobile Company, which Henry Ford had founded. They were still too expensive to either purchase or run for those of us in the working class.

I preferred to run my errands of obtaining our groceries or supplies from the store by either walking or waiting until Saturday when Charles would take us all downtown with the horse and wagon. Our four small children had to wait patiently with Charles in the wagon while I shopped. Any acting up in front of Charles would be met with a rap on the knuckles for the child. He would not tolerate any crying, whining, or foolishness. The children were to sit, quietly, and wait. For children this can be difficult to do, especially since our four were all under the age of seven. Even at these young ages they learned to behave as their father expected them to while in his presence.

Edith - December, 1899

Fall yielded into the winter of 1899 – our child was due within a month or two. It was hard for me to move around the house, being in the last month of my pregnancy and trying to keep up with the household tasks with small children. Christmas was approaching and the extra preparations for meals and guests were looming. Charles' brother, his sister and her family came over for the celebration on Christmas Day. I served our big meal at two o'clock, prior to that I had been on my feet much of the day preparing the food, setting the table, cleaning. Then my pains of labor had started before I was finished with the cleanup tasks from the dinner. The guests had departed for their own homes.

I finished up the cleanup as best I could, then went into Charles who was sitting in the front living room. I told him my time to deliver our new baby had started and that I was going to go upstairs and lay down. He listened to me, said he would be upstairs in a while to check on me, and then resumed reading the newspaper. Our four children were playing in the parlor – it was up to Herbert, at seven years old, to watch his younger three siblings. I don't think they had a clear picture of what exactly was going on – they did know that I would be having another baby soon. They would see a different person, the midwife, come into our house and sit with me while the new baby was being born. The children knew nothing of what happened behind the bedroom door. I would go in with my belly large and emerge a day or so later looking tired and a new baby would live with us.

My second daughter, and fifth child, was born the day after Christmas, December 26th. She had the same birthday as my father did. He had died 23 days before Edith was born. He lived a long life of eighty years; his generation's life expectancy was thirty nine.

Charles named our newest daughter Edith, again drawing on a name from the Bible. Her middle name was Anna, owing to

Charles and I both had a sister named Anna. The day of Edith's birth saw a fierce storm blowing through Joliet. Snow was drifting up against the buildings. The horses were having a difficult time breathing in the cold air to complete their tasks of moving people and deliveries around. The midwife barely made it to my home to attend to me. The toll of the holiday preparations and giving birth exhausted me. All of these factors made this a challenging time in my life; I had to somehow meet the expectations Charles had of me and continue on with my day to day household tasks.

Because Edith's birthday was the day after Christmas, in the years following it was lost in the shuffle of the Christmas holidays. We didn't have any energy or resources for another celebration so close to the biggest holiday of our year. Most often her birthday was just a typical day. She learned to not expect anything special for her birthday and grew to not want anyone to remember it at all. Especially in her later years, she would not attend a gathering intended specifically for her birthday. She just wanted it to go away – to be absorbed in the rest of the days of the year.

By this time in Chicago's history it had become a bustling commerce center. It contained the world's largest railroad hub and one of the busiest ports in the world, shipping traffic coming and going via the Great Lakes. The Chicago Stock Yards dominated the meat packing industry. By 1900 Chicago had swelled to nearly 1.7 million residents – astoundingly large, resulting from the rapid expansion of the late 1800's. Comparatively, there were just 300,000 residents in 1870.

In 1900 Joliet had 29,353 people listed as residents of our city. 29% were foreign born, which included Charles and myself. An additional 32% were children (of which included my children) born to the 29% in the United States. A total of 175 people of the population were stated to be Negro, and 15 Chinese; we were not a very diverse city. The population had expanded from 7,263 in 1870, just thirty years earlier.

Meanwhile at a national level, in 1900 President McKinley was running for reelection to his office, with a new Vice Presidential candidate, Theodore Roosevelt. The Vice Presidential candidate, Roosevelt, actively campaigned for the Republican ticket, and stopped in Chicago more than once. Since Roosevelt was the person on the ticket that came closer to where the voters were, he was the one most talked about in our newspaper, the Joliet Daily Republican. Our household was staunchly Republican, believing that each person should make their own opportunity through their work. Of course only Charles was able to vote; we American women did not receive the right to vote until 1920, via the 19th Amendment to the United States Constitution.

The big topics of the election focused on what America's worldwide future and presence would be. President McKinley had sent William Taft to the Philippines (which America had received as part of the 100 Day war) as chief civil administrator. There Mr. Taft helped improve the economy and infrastructure. He also set up a means of participation by the people in their government.

The economy was doing much better; everyone was happier and more prosperous. Important for Joliet and the surrounding area was the main channel of the Chicago Sanitary & Ship Canal to Lockport was opened. The flow of the Chicago River was reversed. This provided a faster, more efficient means to transport goods between Chicago and Joliet, furthering Joliet's presence in the transportation industry.

Another year passed, and now I had five children to keep track of. Our oldest son, Herbert, was barely nine years old and attended school along with Elmer and Richard. I ensured they were ready for school in the mornings with their lunch pails, where they would walk the two blocks to Farragut school on Raynor Avenue and back. The neighborhood children would walk to school, the older ones watching out for the younger ones, during all types of weather

– snow, rain, stifling heat. If for some reason they became ill at school, they would have to walk themselves home.

Towards the late spring of 1901 I realized I was pregnant with my sixth child, due in the fall. There was no element of surprise in this discovery – I was now familiar with the signs and implications. I accepted this pregnancy as part of living my life being married to Charles. I felt I had only two choices in how to live my life: the first being to stay steady in my life as a wife and mother in our home in Joliet, the second would be to renounce my family. The second option wasn't really a viable option for me – I could not leave my children or my home. On a daily basis I needed to adapt to the circumstance I was in, to get through another day.

Several very large construction projects were underway in Joliet in 1901 which used a great number of stone masons to lay the limestone. This boom was good news for our family; Charles was busily employed on some of these projects. One project was a brand new High School for our community, Joliet Township ("JT"). It was built and opened in 1901. All of my children and some of my grandchildren would attend this high school. The arches, castellated walls and towers illustrate the popular "Collegiate Gothic" architecture of the time. In the years to come the building would be expanded several times to meet the needs of the growing population, making it a very large building – over a city block in size. It would also become the first location of the United States' first Junior College, Joliet Junior College (aka "JuCo").

Another project Charles was involved in was in downtown Joliet; work had begun on a new Post Office, a central point for commerce for most every Joliet resident. It was a fine thing to us to mail a letter, because it meant the sender was able to afford the two cent postage to send it. After finishing his work on the High School, Charles began working on the Post Office, laying some of the limestone façade. Those stones he laid are still there, as you read this. His work endures, despite over one hundred years that have passed. The granite entrance steps also remain.

Unfortunately for America, on September 6, 1901, President McKinley was assassinated in New York as he was standing in a receiving line at the Buffalo Pan-American Exposition. The President died eight days later, on September 14th.

Theodore Roosevelt, as the Vice President at that time, became our twenty sixth President. Many prominent Republicans of the time were not thrilled with this occurrence. Mark Hanna, who had been so instrumental in McKinley's election, lamented that "that damned cowboy is president now." I do remember being abhorred that the President was assassinated. The access of people in America to their political leaders amazed me; in Sweden the people were kept separated from our political leaders.

Ruth – September, 1901

One week following our country's loss of a President and the assumption of a new one, our third daughter was born. Charles named her Ruth, following the precedent of Biblical names he'd established in naming Esther and Edith. (The books of Edith and Ruth are close together in the Bible.) He wasn't very happy to learn we now had three girls in a row, following our first three children who were boys. Ruth's birth was a one day aberration in our household schedule – the next day it was back to the usual chores and household routine. My feelings of tiredness had continually ground me into functioning on an even slower pace. I had just completed having six children in nine years, stressful on any woman's body.

Our city of Joliet was adding to its infrastructure with more advancements on a continual basis. One of these was a sprawling network of street cars, run by electricity, which went to all sorts of destinations including Plainfield, Aurora, Bush Park, Ingalls Park, and the Swedish Orphans' Home. One could ride the electric railroad all the way to Chicago, on the Chicago & Joliet Electric (CJ&E) Railroad starting this same month of September 1901. That was a thrill for people in those days to go away from Joliet and return the same day in a much shorter time than if a horse and buggy was the transportation mechanism. Charles rode on one only once to try it out. The fare was extra money that we really didn't have.

Our new President Roosevelt, beginning with his first annual message to Congress in 1901, called for increased preservation of America's parks and forest land. He set aside 146 million acres for this purpose, which included 50 wildlife refuges, 5 new national parks, and began designating National Monuments (such as Devil's Tower National Monument in Wyoming). He had been influenced by his experience after both his first wife and mother had died in

1884, when he had moved to North Dakota to become a rancher to sort through his grief.

Many years later my children, their children, and their children would enjoy these parks and monuments. I am glad that President Roosevelt thought into the future to preserve these parks for future generations. His efforts were rewarded with his face being carved into the rock on the famous Mount Rushmore, near Rapid City, South Dakota, alongside George Washington, Abraham Lincoln, and Thomas Jefferson.

The new President's daughter, Alice, quickly became an instant celebrity and fashion icon for young women in our country. She set many fashion trends, smoked, placed bets, and partied with socialites. None of these activities, or anything remotely close to it, would be a part of what Charles would allow for our girls in their future. Alice Roosevelt was a symbol to many American women to go outside of the societal rules set for us at the time.

Our family was pleased that Sweden was brought into the world spotlight when the first Nobel Prizes (in <u>Swedish</u>: *"Nobelpriset"*) were established, having been provided for via the will of Alfred Nobel, who died on December 10, 1896. The awards ceremony takes place annually (since 1901) on the date of his death, where the King of Sweden presents the prizes in Stockholm. This event brings worldwide focus to Scandinavia every December.

The first to be awarded these prizes in 1901 were:

- Physics: Wilhelm Conrad Röntgen for his discovery of X-rays.
- Literature: Sully Prudhomme, a French poet, whose most famous poem is *Le vase brisé*. There was some protest of the award, as Leo Tolstoy (the Russian author who wrote the novels War & Peace and Anna Karenina) had been expected to win.

- Physiology (Medicine): Emil von Behring for his antitoxin he'd developed to treat diphtheria.

There is one Nobel Prize which is awarded in Oslo, Norway, to commemorate the country of Mr. Nobel's birth. This is the Nobel Peace prize. The first recipients in 1901 were very active in the peace movement, who were:

- Frédéric Passy, co-founder of the Inter-Parliamentary Union, and
- Henry Dunant, founder of the International Committee of the Red Cross.

During the last quarter of the year, Henry Ford was busy working on developing his automobiles in the Midwestern states of America. He had designed, built, and successfully raced a 26-horsepower automobile in October 1901. With this demonstration of capability, many stockholders in the Detroit Automobile Company formed the Henry Ford Company on November 30, 1901, with Ford as chief engineer. This was a big step forward into the introduction of an automobile that would be sold to many, many more people, putting them into frequent use by the general public.

Our home fell into routine patterns. Sunday was our day of rest, which, taking a step back, is actually a misnomer. It wasn't really restful getting our family ready and out the door to arrive at church by 9am. I had to ensure all my children had clean clothes, looked tidy, shoes cleaned. Sundays would begin at 6 am, which was sleeping in compared to the other days of the week. I would rise before most of the household was awake, sliding out of bed, my feet softly touching the floor so as not to wake Charles. If I did inadvertently wake him up he might want to have intercourse and thus provide another opportunity for another pregnancy. I tried to be quiet as I left our bed and quickly dress so as to not get chilled - our home was not heated during the night. I would softly make my way down the wooden staircase, trying not to step on certain spots which would creak in protest. In months other than the summers the floor and rooms were very cold in the mornings.

I made my way towards the kitchen, where I would put a few logs in the stove to begin warming the kitchen up and ready for breakfast. My next task would be to put a large metal pot on the stove to boil water for coffee for Charles and myself. For freshness of the coffee I would put raw egg on top of the coffee grounds; when I poured the hot water over the grounds the egg would absorb some of the coffee's bitterness. Thereafter I would begin cooking the eggs that one of my children had gathered the day before from our chickens.

Our barn in the back of the house sheltered our wagon, horses, and a cow. We also had a chicken coop, where the chickens provided us both eggs and meat for our dinner. The barn was also home to a few barn cats that took care of the mice or other types of rodents that might have been about.

For our personal needs – aka a bathroom – we had a one seater out house. This was a small building over a pit that was dug fifteen feet deep, by five feet wide, in the yard. I mention "one seater" because that meant only one person could be doing their business in the outhouse at a time. When we had all of our children living at home, this sometimes became complicated. The children learned to be quick and not take too much time in the outhouse. In the winter in Chicago, it was most often so cold a person was incented to be speedy as it was literally freezing outside. In the summer a person didn't want to spend any extra time there because of the heat causing quite a smell emanating from the pit. It was a necessity of life, although at times an inconvenient one. We did have bedpans in the house for overnight needs - those had to be emptied in the mornings. It was one of the chores of our household to complete.

Regarding bathing, each person took a bath once a week. We would set the steel tub on the kitchen floor, when the room was transformed into where we would all bathe in – our bath room. We heated up the water on the kitchen stove, which would be running pretty much all afternoon to heat the required hot water. The children had to share the tub, two at a time, for their baths on late Saturday afternoons. The girls would bathe, then the boys who were just finishing their chores for the day. When the children were all completed, Charles would take his bath towards the early evening. Then I would take mine; this was the one time in my entire week I was alone in a room of our house. The kitchen was fairly quiet, no children running through it, and I had a few precious, peaceful moments to myself.

Mornings in our home the children knew not to delay in getting ready for the day. The consequences of protestations from the children would be harsh from Charles. I would wake up my oldest daughter, Esther, who would then go around to the other children to wake them up. Charles would usually hear noise at this time and wake up on his own. I really didn't want to go back into our bedroom to wake him up, for fear he'd keep me there longer. The children would quickly dress themselves before breakfast, the older children helping the younger ones adjust their clothing and complete dressing. Since each child had three outfits of clothing to wear, it wasn't difficult for them to figure out which of them they were going to wear for that day. The first order of the day was quite often a trip to the outhouse out back. It was an exercise in coordination to get everyone's trip to the bathroom completed in the mornings. I always worried about the younger children going on their own because of their size; quite often an older sibling accompanied them to ensure their safety.

After the breakfast, cleaning the dishes and table, dressing, and readying to leave, on Sundays we all would head out to the barn where Charles would have readied our wagon to take to church. We had two horses, Nellie and Charcoal. They lived in our barn and backyard and provided us transportation around Joliet. We would all load into the wagon rain, snow, or sun shine, and make our way to church. The Swedish Bethel Baptist church was about 2 miles from our house, making it just far enough away that walking wasn't really an option. Charles and I would sit in the front seat. It felt grand to me to sit up so high and have a whole new view of the world. My neighborhood just seemed to look different from that high seat in the wagon. Once at church Charles would park the wagon, where we would all get out by stepping on the thin wood step and walk into church together as a family.

The Baptist Church in America was somewhat more relaxed than the Swedish state church I had attended as a child. It did teach us the same sorts of messages of obedience, compliance, and duties to our families. We never drank alcohol – that was considered a sin – something that made a person do things they shouldn't do.

The roles of women in America were not as defined as they were in Sweden. We had church socials where both women and men socialized in the same room, although a wife wouldn't dare to think to address a man, other than her husband, directly. If a woman did such a thing, she would be met with disapproval and possibly the other women not talking to her. The church provided familiarity for us of our original home in Sweden: the customs of the church, the songs (sung in English), the gathering together with other Swedes. The traditions were comforting.

Then in the late fall and winter of 1902, the coal workers of the United Mine Workers of America had decided to strike. This action jostled the routine of our lives, as to us it meant much higher coal prices for whatever amount we could find for purchase. The higher cost was especially hard on us during the winter, as Charles wasn't able to work every day due to the temperatures outside being too cold for laying stone. At the very point of the year our income was the lowest, the price of fuel to warm our house had increased dramatically. It was freezing, for sure, in

Illinois during this time; we really needed to heat our home. It wasn't that there wasn't enough coal, it was that the supply was suspended by the railroads who wouldn't transport it.

The early months of 1903 were, as typical for the Chicago area, cold and blustery. The winter felt extra cold that year because of the lack of available fuel and its subsequent cost. I worried for my children that they were not warm enough, that they might get sick from being too cold. Finally in March of 1903 President Roosevelt helped the strike end by nationalizing the coal mines and railroads until the crisis was over. This was the first labor episode in which the federal government intervened as a neutral arbitrator, in this case between the miners and the coal companies. The action did help those of us that needed the coal to heat our homes, and also set a precedent for the future of the role of government in labor disputes.

In many cities across America, child labor was a significant issue and risk to America's children. They worked long days as the adults did, but at much lower pay. Illinois was the first state in the country to pass a law, in May of 1903, to regulate hours for child laborers. An eight-hour work day and a 48-hour work week was the new maximum for child workers. Many families where the parents weren't able to make enough to provide for their households' needs had to send their children to work to sustain their lives. Thankfully my children were all able to attend school and earned money by completing odd jobs for our neighbors – delivering papers, helping out the corner grocer unpack the new arrivals or watching another family's children. Because of Charles' skill as a stonemason, he was able to keep all of our family fed, clothed, and sheltered, for which I am grateful.

In the early summer I realized that I was expecting another child; this would be my seventh. Charles was busily working throughout the summer. As the new school year began, our three girls were still at home with me. These were busy times; I was trying to keep the children's clothes mended and clean. As they were growing very fast, this was a feat in and of itself. My children seemed to inherit their father's height – they were tall for their ages in their school classrooms.

Walter – December, 1903

Walter was my seventh child. He was born in December 1903, during the cold winter months, arriving just eighteen months after my daughter Ruth. His birthday fell on St. Lucia day, marking a special significance to me from my Swedish upbringing.

Walter was born during a great year of innovation in America, which included:

- President Roosevelt working on opening new trade routes via the Panama Canal. This was something I couldn't relate to, the focus being so far away from where I was in my neighborhood in Joliet.

- Henry Ford's demonstration that his automobile invention could reach over 90 miles per hour. He continued work on a version that would be affordable to the average American worker, which he planned to launch via the Ford Motor Company, having been reincorporated during the year. We weren't at a point where we could afford an automobile, but this was an exciting possibility.

- The first box of Crayola crayons was made and sold for 5 cents. It contained 8 colors; brown, red, orange, yellow, green, blue, violet and black. My children loved these crayons – their colors vastly different from the white chalk used at school or the lead pencils on paper.

- The soda company Coca-Cola removed a substance, cocaine, as a key ingredient from their formula. At the time, Coca-Cola contained approximately nine milligrams of cocaine per glass. We had this soda only at summer picnics to celebrate American holidays – we couldn't afford to purchase it at other times.

- William Harley and the Davidson brothers started their bicycle company in Milwaukee, Wisconsin. We did not know of this at the time – it was something our family would learn of later.

- On December 17 in Kitty Hawk, North Carolina, Orville Wright successfully completed the first documented, controlled, powered, heavier-than-air flight. We did not hear of this event until January of 1904. It was amazing news to think of people being able to fly in the air – preposterous, really, was the word I thought. We did not even have access to an automobile which ran on land – it was beyond our thought that people could fly through the air like birds do.

A few more weeks later in December, on the 30th, there was a terrible fire where over 600 people of the estimated 2,000 inside died at the Iroquois Theater on Chicago's Near North side. The theater had just opened in November. Chicago was devastated, because we didn't want to be known for fires that had plagued our city and killed so many. The mayor ordered all theatres to be closed for six weeks. This tragedy led to increased building safety measures and devices to handle fire conditions.

Walter had joined our household of six other children, where our oldest child, Herbert, was eleven years old. Truthfully we almost barely noticed his presence. Other than being responsible for feeding him (by breastfeeding) I had little time to devote to focus on him. He simply became part of the household and the daily activities we engaged in to keep our lives running. He was a good baby - slept well and thrived. His older sisters enjoyed playing with him, much like a doll, since we didn't typically spend money on toys for the children. Esther especially enjoyed helping me take care of my younger children. I was so grateful for her help - there literally was no one else to help me around the house. Given my Swedish background and the lack of verbal communication between Charles and I, I didn't express this to Esther. I kept my distance and reserve; I generally didn't show emotion of either happiness or sadness to my children.

In the summer of 1904 *finally* Chicago was host to the REPUBLICAN National Convention, where they nominated Theodore Roosevelt to run for a second term as President. Charles was very pleased that the Republicans had met in Chicago – giving press to Chicago with a Republican party twist. That is why I capitalized the word Republican – Charles was a staunch Republican.

In 1904, President Roosevelt campaigned for election on the merits of his "square deal", which was aimed at helping middle class citizens via three primary ideas: conservation of natural resources, control of corporations, and consumer protection. Since Charles was more conservative politically than he believed Roosevelt to be, he would have preferred the Illinois Republican Robert R. Hill. Roosevelt did go on to easily win the Presidential election in November, defeating the Democratic candidate, Alton B. Parker, who was also from New York State.

During his Presidency Roosevelt furthered America into the world leadership. He worked to minimize the European powers' actions and influence away in the Western Hemisphere. He utilized his "Roosevelt Corollary" to the Monroe Doctrine to justify American intervention throughout the Western Hemisphere. He was convinced that stronger nations must bestow the benefits of their civilization upon the weaker nations.

For our part, we continued life as usual. Our world was on a local level, not the national or world political scene. For Joliet, this was a prosperous time. There were over one hundred businesses flourishing, providing one of the highest levels of pay to manufacturing workers in the whole state. The average annual wage for each employee was $631. Banks, railroads, steel mills, coal refineries and product manufacturers were the primary employers. Our schools were increasing their enrollment at a dramatic pace.

In early 1905 I discovered I would be expecting an eighth child later that year. Walter was just about one year old; just recently he had begun to toddle across the floor. I was resigned to the process that was underway – this would be my eighth child in less than fifteen years. All I could do was to go on – there was no turning back, no way to stop the process that was occurring in my life.

Alice – June, 1905

Eighteen months separated Alice's birth from Walter's. She was our eighth child, bringing our family's total to four boys and four girls. Charles named her Alice, after our President's daughter. This was a symbol of national pride to name your child after a prominent political figure.

I now had even less time for specialized attention to my newest daughter. I had five children to get off to school in the mornings; the youngest three were home with me. I had to move my attention away from the previous child to the newest born child for feedings, changing, and moving them around with me where I was doing my household work. My attention to my children was limited to their basic needs of food, cleanliness, and warmth; anything past that there really wasn't time for.

In 1905, Alice Roosevelt, along with her father's Secretary of War, William Howard Taft, led the "Imperial Cruise" to Japan, Hawaii, China, the Philippines, and Korea. This trip was the largest diplomatic mission in U.S. history at that time, composed of 23 U.S. Congressmen (including her future husband Nicholas Longworth), seven senators, and other diplomats and officials. It truly was a stunning accomplishment for a woman in American at that time. Women just weren't involved in the political process and didn't even have the right to vote until fifteen years later.

Later in her life Alice Roosevelt reflected on what held her family together, saying "There is always someone in every family who keeps it together." I couldn't agree with her more. In our family my son Walter would fulfill that role.

Our family pursued all things American. One of those was the sport of baseball, it being the "American" pastime. Charles approached this activity with gusto, in an incessant quest for information and progress. Charles always read the statistics of the games, noting the top players and their averages. Our hometown of Chicago hosted two professional league teams, the Chicago White Sox and the Chicago Cubs. The people of Chicago know you must pick one of these teams to root for – you don't root for both. The Cubs are based on the North side of Chicago, while on the opposite side of town are the White Sox, based out of the South side of Chicago. Where one lived in proximity to the teams was a factor in preference of which team a Chicagoan would root for. Since we lived on the South side of Chicago, our home, like most of our neighbors, consisted of White Sox fans.

Chicago has been the home of these two professional baseball teams since the early 1900's, although some of their characteristics, such as name and home field location, changed in the years following. The North Side team originated in 1876 and was known as the Chicago White Stockings. They would then change to the Chicago Colts in 1894, then play as the Chicago Orphans starting in 1898. In 1902 they became known as the Chicago Cubs, which remains their ball club name. The "Cubs" name resulted from the Chicago Daily News (paper) story which referred to the great number of young players on the team that year, including Joe Tinker, Johnny Evers, and Frank Chance.

The South side team, which first played as the Chicago White Stockings in 1900, had their original home field at 39th and Princeton Streets, which was referred to as the 39th Street Grounds. The field originally was the playfield for Chicago's Wanderers, a cricket team, during the 1893 World's Fair. A wooden grandstand, which seated 7,500 fans, was built by Charles Comiskey on the site in 1900 for the baseball team. The team changed its name to the Chicago White Sox in 1904. They played at the 39th Street Grounds until July of 1910, when Comiskey had built a new "Baseball Palace of the World" at the corner of 35th Street and Shields Avenue. The park's name quickly became known as Comiskey Park, where that name has persisted for over a hundred years.

In the early fall of 1906 there was a classic cross town rivalry underway, as both teams in baseball's World Series were from Chicago, the White Sox and the Cubs. Neither of the teams won a game of the series on their home field. The White Sox team, despite making it into the World Series, had been dubbed "the hitless wonders" by the Chicago newspapers. It was a joyous day in the early fall of 1906 when the White Sox won the World Series of American Baseball from the Chicago Cubs. That was one day Charles showed outward excitement and very nearly joy.

1906 passed without the delivery of a baby for me; I had turned forty years old that year. I pondered if Alice was to be my last child, thinking it was possible that my body wouldn't support another pregnancy. From watching and hearing of other women at church I knew that as a woman became older in years, pregnancy became more dangerous for one's health and increasingly difficult to sustain.

I believe that in the late fall of 1906 I experienced another miscarriage. My cycles had stopped for a few months, but I wasn't sure that I was indeed pregnant. Then a few weeks before Christmas I had an episode of excessive bleeding and cramping in my stomach. It was painful, more so than during the births of my children. The pain was confusing, since I wasn't positive of the source but thought it might be a baby that wasn't surviving to full term.

I went through this experience on my own – there was no one to tell, ask, or assist. Charles was impatient with me that I wasn't able to complete my chores that day. It happened to be a Saturday when he was home from work, and thus he was impacted by my not being up and around to monitor the household that day. Our children were left to get their own meals and supervise themselves

126

– he would not involve himself in those activities. The next day I resumed my household work, as I couldn't stay in bed and rest with eight children to care for.

With each year and additional child, my body seemed to tire, a tiredness that set into my bones. I couldn't shake the lack of energy I felt – it was present with me all the time. I would have some bursts of energy, where I accomplished many tasks. Most often I would have to slow my pace and get as much done as I could. Luckily my children were able to assist with many of the household chores, so that I didn't bear the entire burden of them. Esther, who was now ten, moved into a role of being my 'mother's helper' with the other children and cooking. She was a quick study and approached her tasks with an adult like calmness. I was so thankful for her and her help – I don't know how I could have made it through that time without her. What a blessing it was to have her – both her personality and her presence. My older boys helped where they could. Charles' influence encouraged them to not participate in 'women's work'. But they were my sons, too, and they wanted to help me. I appreciated that about them.

America was expanding its presence and influence on the world scene. Towards the end of the year, on November 9, our President Roosevelt left for a trip to Panama to inspect the construction progress of the Panama Canal. This was the first official trip by a sitting US president outside of the geographic United States. Very soon after that, in December, President Roosevelt won the Nobel Peace Prize for his work in settling the Russo-Japanese war – the first American to win any Nobel award.

The spring and summer of 1907 was made up of baseball for Chicagoans, although "our" team, the White Sox did not make it to the World Series this year. This year was the Chicago Cubs' year, and this time they were the champions. They swept four games in a row, holding the Detroit Tigers (led by Ty Cobb) to a combined three runs, to win the World Series. These were glorious years for baseball in Chicago.

We decided to have a photographer come to our home to take some photographs of our children. Photo 3 in the Appendix shows Ruth, Walter, and Alice on our front porch. The fur rug in the picture was a symbol of prestige and wealth – fur rugs were expensive to us. Ruth is holding a doll, a rare item of luxury for my daughter. There were other photos taken, but those did not survive the test of time, and are now gone.

By this time of the year, it was quite clear I indeed was pregnant for the ninth time, to deliver sometime in the fall. The summer seemed longer and hotter than others. The heat exacerbated the swelling of my feet and my tiredness. I was amazed how my latest pregnancy was impacting my body. I felt as if I could barely continue my daily tasks and had no idea how I was going to weather this storm of a ninth child.

Charles expected me to continue to perform all of my tasks of our household, pregnant or not. I spent all day on Sunday cooking our meal, along with my three older girls helping where they could. Alice played in the corner, watching us work. With eight children and about to deliver my ninth child I was teetering on the edge of exhaustion.

As the winter of 1907 approached, the Presidential race was being formed. Roosevelt had decided the man he'd appointed Secretary of War, Taft, should be his successor.

Burt - November, 1907

After eight other births, the delivery of my ninth child, went quickly. This birth was different for me, though, as it seemed to take some energy out of my body that never returned. The baby was a boy who we named Burt. He was born on the same day in November as my son Richard. This was even more unusual given that we had no technology to determine a specific birth date. When I had my children the babies came when they decided it was time. There was little, if any, intervention to induce labor.

I was forty one years old, older in years for a mother. After his birth, it took me almost a week to get back up and doing all the tasks I needed to do for the household. My body just couldn't rebound very well this time, just couldn't bounce back to my typical activity level. Hiring someone to help me was out of the question. I wouldn't dare suggest that idea to Charles. He wouldn't have permitted an outside helper to come into our home or want to pay the woman's wages. He simply expected me to meet all the demands of our household. Once again my daughter Esther was able to step in and be a 'mother's helper' to me. She assisted with my duties when I didn't have the energy and strength to complete them all.

Herbert, our oldest, was now attending Joliet Township (JT) High School. It was a large school; 1,000 students taught by 38 teachers. It was thought to be a superior school of the time, where Universities would promote graduates from JT into their second year of college. Our community strongly supported the public school system. One of the reasons given for its strength was the 'recruitment and retainment of male teachers'. Women teachers were seen as flighty and disruptive to the learning process. Six of my children were represented in the over 6,400 students enrolled in the Joliet school system, which had almost doubled in quantity in ten years.

By now our son Walter was four years old, running around the neighborhood and exhibiting his curiosity of life and quest for knowledge. Since he was pretty much left to his own to find something to occupy his time, he invented games, things to try and learn more about. For example he decided to investigate a bee nest that had lodged itself on the back corner of our barn. He was fascinated watching the bees fly in the nest, then others flying out to go investigate the world outside the nest. The impact came when Walter reached his hand towards the nest, and he was stung several times on the hand and arm. He came running back to the house, burst through the door, and asked Esther to help him. He wouldn't have thought to come crying to me as his mother. He held back any tears of pain and knew that Esther would have more time to attend to his bee stings than I did. He was a tough, determined child.

Walter's curious and challenging nature grated on Charles. Charles didn't want to talk or expend any energy on managing our children when he came home from work. Walter posed an impediment to the peace and quiet that Charles wanted (demanded, really), and therefore was not well liked or appreciated by Charles.

Early in Walter's life he was brushed off by my husband Charles. Charles paid minimal attention to Walter. He saw him as a nuisance, and often told him he wasn't going to do well in life, since it appeared to him that Walter was not going to be serious enough to be a hard worker when he reached adulthood.

Charles "played favorites" with our children, and very few were on his favorites list. Herbert as the oldest, and a boy, was the most favored child. Our next two children, Elmer and Richard, were most often put in the position of trying to be held up to the spotlight of Herbert, which Charles exacerbated by his comments and where he focused his time – on Herbert. Charles talked to Herbert more on a man to man level ; the younger boys were never part of that inner circle. The girls were mostly seen by

Charles as household helpers. He did appreciate Esther, our oldest daughter, for her organization and contribution to keeping the household running, on a nonverbal basis, of course. Our youngest three girls did not receive much attention from Charles, although he did like Alice's cherubic nature.

He particularly didn't appreciate Richard and Walter – Richard being the third son, he thought him lacksidasical and not as work driven and intelligent as Herbert and Elmer. Walter's personality spurred Charles' dislike for him. Charles wanted to be obeyed and didn't appreciate Walter's playful, curious nature. Walter was often reprimanded for not lining up his shoes in his designated spot on the back porch or for being outside when the dinner bell was rung.

One evening Walter was late to dinner. As Walter walked into the dining room where the rest of the family was seated, Charles extended his arm and struck Walter directly on his left ear. The rest of the children heard a popping noise; Walter winced in pain. He dared not yell out which would anger Charles even further. Walter sat in his seat at the table, choked down his food, then went to his bed to lay down on his side. His ear hurt beyond comprehension – the pain was throbbing. He could hear a rushing sound in his ear. Charles had punctured Walter's eardrum, and caused Walter to lose hearing in that ear the rest of his life. Oh how I wanted to intervene – to stop this from happening or at least go to Walter to comfort him. Because of Charles' will and what he wanted, I made no motion or action, other than to observe and pray for Walter's healing and Charles' patience. In retrospect I am not proud of those moments, to let myself be subjugated to my husband's will, which in this case had crossed a line of acceptability and had caused physical harm to one of our children.

Life on William Street

We now had nine children to tend to; only our oldest boy, Herbert, and our oldest girl, Esther, received any individualized attention. I infrequently (if ever) had time to focus on only one of my children. Most often I was absorbed my tasks and interacted with the children primarily to ensure they were finishing the chores assigned to them. With the sheer number of people living in our home it was unlikely that only one or two were in any given place at a time. There were three sleeping rooms upstairs in our home – Charles and I slept in the bedroom in the back of the house. The girls slept in the bedroom which looked out onto William Street. The boys slept in the other bedroom that faced our back yard. We had double beds, which had space for two of our children to share one bed, each sleeping on half of the bed, one head to the other's feet.

My greatest happiness came from seeing my children grow, although it was almost as if I watched from afar when I was present on Earth. I had so many chores to complete, so much to do. I really didn't have time, which sounds odd even as I write this, to be fully present. I was mostly worried about getting the children off to school, making sure we had bread baked and clothes folded. My tasks seem trivial now that I look back on it; the moments of showing my children how to tie their shoes or dress themselves long since stolen by the need for efficiency and time. As I look back on these times, I wish I had taken the time to enjoy the everyday moments with my children.

I say that because most people can detail out a particular event or moment from their childhood where they can remember even the smallest parameters. It's surprising how detailed the human memory is, especially when it's something either very positive or very negative. Although it doesn't have to be an extreme – children can remember the specific smell of their mother's oatmeal cookies or what she wore to attend their graduation ceremony. I let many of those moments go by without recognizing a pivotal point in one of my children's lives.

After Burt was born, I started having more frequent episodes of tiredness and breathlessness. I couldn't keep the pace I had years earlier. I had to take short breaks and ask my older children to assist with some of the chores. My legs and feet would be swollen by the end of the day after standing and moving around much of the day. I tried to get the time to literally 'put my feet up' to reduce the swelling. I did this in the kitchen after dinner. Charles wouldn't have liked to see me changing routine or seemingly 'doing nothing'. He wouldn't have understood how I was feeling, so I didn't mention it to him. I just soldiered on with my tasks and work in our home. The swelling didn't cause me sharp pain; it was more of a throbbing pain, making it uncomfortable.

Having nine children in fifteen and a half years took its toll on my body – I was successively more tired on a continual basis after each birth. I did feel fortunate that none of my children died in childhood as this was still a very strong possibility through the early 1900's. That truly was the Grace of God that kept them all healthy through adulthood. The effect on a woman's body of carrying a child and giving birth is draining – like running many miles. I had to slow down my pace of work – in the garden, I had to stop and rest while weeding, in my kitchen I had to sit down in a chair for a few minutes before rising on my feet again. It seemed just part of keeping up with the children and the house.

I imagine any woman that has nine children is tired – there is so much to do and little time for rest for the mother. In our house I was the primary cook, cleaner, washer, and child minder. I was continuing my career as a domestic, working for my husband and children in my own home. Each day was a long day to prepare food, ensure clothes were clean, make sure the children were dressed, get everyone on their way to their destination (i.e. work for Charles, school for the children), prepare mid-day meals, clean house, organize the house, prepare dinner, wash all dishes. The list of things to do never seemed to end. At the close of the day there were always tasks I just hadn't completed that day. Only when my body couldn't do it anymore is when I rested.

Charles' skill at stone masonry provided well for our family. We always had food, clothing, and shelter. Sometimes, especially in the winter months, we didn't have much food and lacked variety, but we did have enough food to not go hungry. It was difficult to stretch the groceries we did have across over all of our family; especially with 9 children to feed. I often took smaller portions of food so that my children might have more.

In our pantry the staples of fruits and vegetables I canned from the previous summer carried us through the winter. We also purchased a wooden barrel full of the salted fish, lutefisk. The lye, also used as a preservative, is what is used in soap. The flavor of the fish was unsavory – like soap. But the lutefisk was sustenance, and we ate what we had. It was difficult for the children, as the lutefisk was not appetizing, but they knew not to show their distaste to Charles. They sat at the table and ate what was presented to them. Years later Walter would remark about having to eat lutefisk as a child, but he never, ever ate it or served it to others as an adult.

As the income earner for our household, Charles needed to have the strength and energy to complete his physical work day. To support that he was served first at meals, then our oldest sons, then the rest of the children and me. Our dining room table was in a room of its own, the one with the big bay window. Those windows in our dining room made me happy to look at; they were an outward sign that our family had afforded a little bit different than what was every day and typical. The table was a heavy oak table with scrolling feet. All twelve of us (including Charles' brother Klaus) sat around this table.

My girls helped me in the kitchen; we worked together to prepare and serve our meals for 12 people. It was quite a production to get that much food properly served at each mealtime, ensuring each dish arrived at the appropriate temperature. Our wood burning stove was tricky to get the oven and cooktop the correct temperature, to not burn or undercook the food. It had to be heated up to a sufficient temperature, which required extra planning. Between going to the garden to collect fruits or vegetables for our meal, bringing in water, running out back for more firewood, stoking the stove, watching the pots simmering on the cooktop, ensuring the food stayed warm until it was time to serve, and setting the table with plates and silverware, there were more than enough tasks to go around. Each girl had a task to complete between food preparation and serving. Even when one of my girls was under age three they helped shelling peas or snapping green beans. I silently worked, occasionally noting to my daughters what task needed to be completed next or if their work wasn't sufficient.

Before the meal started, I rang our dinner bell to notify the family the meal was ready to start. The bell was made of brass, on the top handle was formed in the shape of a horse head. (Many years later this family heirloom would find its way to my great granddaughter's kitchen.) The boys (I include my husband Charles in this group) would all troop in from wherever they'd happened to be – outside working or playing in the barn – and wash their hands in the kitchen. Then they would sit down in the dining room, waiting for the food to be brought to them. Charles sat at the end, farthest away from the kitchen. Either Charles' brother Klaus or my oldest son Herbert sat at the other end. I sat on the long wooden benches on either side of the table, closest to the kitchen.

Mealtime was mostly a business affair of getting calories into our bodies. There was an informal roll call, to make sure everyone was accounted for at the three times per day. During the meal there was some conversation; most often the children might mention something that happened during their day or an item of news from our neighborhood. This was not the forum to complain, though. A very distinct line was drawn for acceptable conversation at the dinner table. It was a somewhat disconnected view of life; topics were mentioned as if we had no personal interest or stake in them. We never discussed the failures we each experienced. Publicly admitting a failure, if it was rather small or large, wasn't a productive idea in front of Charles. He would become irate, thundering at the speaker to keep their concerns or issues to themselves. He just didn't see the need to discuss issues one of us was having- each person was to deal with it on their own, regardless of their age. Because of this I think our children grew up faster than some; our children had to reason for themselves at a young age.

I tried to pass on the gift of family relationships to my children. With there being nine of them, the sheer number of siblings provided multiple possibilities. In the school aged years I encouraged them to look out for each other – during their school day, as they walked to and from school. Their relationships seemed to form mostly around the children closest in age and sex. Herbert, as the oldest and the favored son by Charles, was on his own – set apart from the rest of my children. Elmer and Richard were very close, both in age and temperament. Then Esther, Edith, and Ruth were close, both from being girls and in their ages. Next came Walter, Alice, and Burt. Walter was like the oldest brother to his younger two siblings – he watched out for them, helped them. Alice was the whole family's darling – her cheeks so creamy white and rosy circles on them. She almost looked like a porcelain doll.

One sweet spot in all of my children's lives was when the dairy delivery truck would come through the neighborhood. Charles' sister who lived nearby in Joliet, Sigrid, had married a man who owned the dairy and delivery of milk products to Joliet families. At the turn of the 1900's they delivered the products in a horse drawn buggy. As Mr. Ford's cars became more available, they migrated to use an automobile or 'truck'. When our children saw the dairy delivery vehicle on the way down the street, the message spread quickly like a wild fire amongst our children that were home. "The dairy delivery is coming"! They would pass on the message to the other children.

When the delivery cart stopped in front of our house, the children were almost giddy with excitement. That meant they would likely receive a special treat from Aunt Sigrid's dairy: ice cream. The deliveryman would hand Esther a container of ice cream, frozen solid with ice from the icehouse. Esther would thank him and ask him to let Aunt Sigrid know of their appreciation, then carefully carry the container into the house. She would then scoop out the frozen treat to each child, one scoop each. That would use up the entire contents of the container.

It was like a little bit of heaven for my children to have that ice cream. They so enjoyed the sweetness of the frozen treat. It was "real" ice cream – real cream from the dairy iced into a frozen treat. This made the taste extra sweet and wonderful. Our children didn't often have variations of the staples of what we typically ate. Charles wouldn't spend money on such things or ever think of giving each child money to buy candy. It was a true blessing that his sister gave our children that ice cream, one of the highlights of their childhoods.

Chicago had become a home for the national political process to revisit, as in June of 1908, the Republican National Convention held their meeting to nominate a presidential candidate in Chicago. Their choice was William Howard Taft, as expected resulting from President Roosevelt's urging. As a staunch Republican, Charles watched with great interest the current activities going on in the party.

Life Changes

Not long after the Republican convention, one July day in 1908, my youngest child, Burt, was about eight months old, sitting up but not yet walking. The other children were playing outside. Apparently I had collapsed on the floor of our kitchen. I had been standing at the sink cleaning some green beans for our dinner. Charles had come home from work and found me lying there. He was able to wake me up to consciousness. I sat up in a dazed state. It was like I was groggily awakening after a long night's sleep. After a while I made my way upstairs, put on my nightclothes, and crawled into bed, unable to continue finishing up the day's chores.

Charles contacted the doctor by going to one of our neighbors' homes that had a telephone. (Telephones in the Chicago-area weren't widespread in the early 1900's – in 1900 there were only 34,000. The number grew to one *million* by 1930). He asked the doctor to visit our house the next day to check on me. Dr. Tandis listened to my heart with an object with a cold metal circle that he put up to my chest. He heard some crackling sounds in my lungs. I was a bit uncomfortable with the doctor placing his hands near my chest and on my back. A doctor had never examined me in that area of my body before – the only time I had seen a doctor was a few times when they attended the births of some of my children. My children were afraid and confused by the doctor's visit; he had only been to our home for the births of my youngest children. They knew that wasn't the reason for the doctor's visit.

After the doctor's examination of me, he asked Charles to come into our parlor and sit down. Charles, myself, and the doctor were in the room. We closed the door to the kitchen, which still had air gaps and wasn't soundproof by any means. Doctor Tandis told us that my heart was weakened by the number of pregnancies my body had carried, due to the additional work a mother's heart must do during pregnancy. He stated that if I became pregnant again, it could quite likely kill me. He spoke directly to Charles that I should have no more children, as my heart would not be able to withstand carrying another child. This was the doctor's 'orders' to Charles that we should not have sexual relations in case I subsequently became pregnant. Charles looked stoically at the doctor, showing no outward emotion of this news. Doctor Tandis also stated that to improve my heart condition, we should consider moving to a place that had more open, fresh air than where we lived in Joliet, south of Chicago. The air in Joliet was compromised by the numerous stone quarries, manufacturing businesses and industrial plants.

This conversation changed our lives. It was a pivotal moment from how we'd been living our lives for over fifteen years. In one fell swoop the doctor had stated unless the way my life was dramatically altered, and within a short period of time, my life wouldn't continue. It was stunning news for a family where people didn't have an opportunity to be sick – we all had to get up each day and complete our tasks. I wasn't sure what would happen next, how Charles would react. Would he say I should go live with my sister or that he was leaving our household to go work in another state? Charles reaction frightened me more than what the doctor had said regarding my health.

Dr. Tandis stated he'd be back to check in on me in about a month, and quietly left through the front door. I didn't say anything aloud – I waited for Charles to say something, if he wanted to. He simply said "I'll have to think more about this" and then left the parlor. I remained there for …. it seemed like a long time; it was probably 10 minutes at the most. I sat straight up in my chair and thought about what my health condition meant and what would happen to our family. My children popped into my thoughts first. What would happen if I couldn't continue my duties in our household? Would I be there for them growing up? Herbert was sixteen years old; my youngest, Burt, was less than one year old. I decided I would have to face what came my way and it wouldn't help me to sit there longer just brooding about what might happen. I went back into the kitchen and picked up where I left off of preparing the mid-day meal.

Charles' response to my health news surprised me. He rarely if ever showed any sort of positive emotion or overt act of caring. I wasn't sure, even after being married to him for almost twenty years, he had feelings of genuine love and care for me, or anyone else, with the possible exception of Herbert. He did provide for our family, which was the one primary way he demonstrated his commitment and care. He began looking in earnest for an improved setting for me with fresher air. He gathered information on potential locations by talking with other men he knew from work or in our neighborhood. Some had traveled through different parts of the United States on their way to Illinois, some had only heard about these other places such as the Western Territory, Vermont, or South Carolina.

In the fall of 1908 the Chicago Cubs were in another matchup with the Detroit Tigers in the World Series of Baseball. For the second consecutive year, the Cubs defeated the Tigers to win the Baseball World Series. Chicago Cubs fans were overjoyed – they became the first Major League baseball team to win the Series two years in a row! Unfortunately for the Cubs, they have not been able to win the World Series championship since 1908.

Another invention came literally rolling into the average American's life starting in the fall of 1908. An automobile called the Model T, introduced by the Ford Motor Company, was offered for sale in America. The cost was affordable to many more people, $825, and very simple to drive. Even so that was an enormous amount of money to me. Virtually all drivers were men; women weren't trained to drive these automobiles. It was not the norm in our society for women to drive their horse and buggy; it followed that women weren't typically taught to drive an automobile, either. For our family, Charles had chosen to wait to purchase one. He was saving his money for a bigger purchase: a new home for us that would be better for my health.

Charles walked just over a mile to downtown from our house on many Saturdays to the Joliet Public Library, to look at maps and books on United States geography to assist in the selection of location(s) for our relocation plans. The library building had opened one day after our son Walter was born, which was December 14, 1903. The building is located on Clinton and Ottowa streets, and was designed by D.H. Burnham & Co. (the same architect of the White City we had seen over ten years earlier at the Chicago World's Fair) at a total cost of $175,000. That was an astounding amount of money in 1903 – it is a magnificent building that many citizens are able to utilize. The library still operates out of this building, which has since doubled in size, so that it now occupies more than half a city block! The very first location of the Joliet Public Library had opened in 1876, with the collection from the Joliet historical society led by Captain Phelps.

Through his research, by mid-1909 Charles had narrowed the choices down to the New York or Pennsylvania countryside. He was looking for a non-city based location, without industry smokestacks that added particles to the air making breathing more difficult. The fresher air of the countryside would be ideal, away from the smokestacks billowing their dark black, coal induced smoke.

During these times, we were so caught up in our daily lives we didn't incur the expense and effort of having a family portrait taken. We (Charles, really) were saving every spare penny we had for a new property away from Joliet. In retrospect I wish that we had done so – it would have been nice for my children's children to see all of us together in a photograph.

In November Taft, the Republican nominee, was elected to the Presidency. He had been America's administrator of the Panama

Canal and former Secretary of War. Once he was elected, we would make "Taft" cookies – these were plain molasses cookies, with not much sugar to sweeten them. These cookies were like President Taft himself – not very sweet and very reliable, but not decadent or outlandish in any way.

President Taft took office in 1909. Progressives were pleased with Taft's election. "Roosevelt has cut enough hay," they said; "Taft is the man to put it into the barn." Conservatives, such as our family, were delighted to be rid of Roosevelt—some had called him the "mad messiah." President Taft later said that Roosevelt "ought more often to have admitted the legal way of reaching the same ends" (indicating his distaste with the means Roosevelt employed serving as President).

During his Presidency, Taft had alienated those who were "liberal" Republicans by defending the Payne-Aldrich Act which unexpectedly continued high tariff rates, his opposition to Arizona becoming a state, and his continued support of his Secretary of the Interior, who was accused of failing to carry out conservationism. "Liberal" was not a word that would describe politics in our home at all, it in no way resembled Charles' beliefs. Taft's administration did accomplish many tasks including: initiating 80 antitrust suits against big businesses, submissions to the states for amendments to enable a Federal income tax, and changing the law so that US Senators became directly elected by their states' constituents. His administration also established the United States Postal System and a federal level commission for Interstate Commerce that was directed to set railroad rates.

By 1910, 10% of Chicago's inhabitants were of Swedish decent – over 100,000, keeping its title of the second largest concentration of Swedes in the world. On a national level, 54% of Swedish immigrants and their children lived in the Midwest. Some 10% lived in the West coast, some of whom had migrated there during the depression years of the early 1890's. Charles and I had thus far contributed nine additional Swedish Americans. Chicago had blossomed into a hometown for Swedes in America. Many businesses were run with only Swedish clientele; grocery, livestock, and banks. It was possible to live one's life in America only interacting with other Swedish people.

1910 was the year our family purchased a Model T. We were excited that it was an American made product and that financially we could afford to purchase one. Charles brought it home from the automobile store (or dealer, as I heard they were called), its sleek black tires turning onto our property where previously only our wagon had made its tracks. It was an exciting moment in our household. When not in use, it sidled up alongside our horse and wagon in our barn in the back of our house.

Our new Model T made multiple inaugural drives around Joliet. First Charles took Herbert for a drive, to show him how it ran and be the first to ride in it. Then he returned back home to take our other four boys – even Burt who was just under three years old! Lastly he came back home and took me and our four girls for a drive around Joliet – six of us in the car, the girls all in the back seat together. It was exhilarating to ride in the car, with the air flowing on our faces from the open window. It was truly a treat and a joy for all of us to experience that feeling of freedom.

Charles immediately set to instructing Herbert on how to drive the new automobile, which came in handy for me as Herbert could then take me on a trip downtown. Charles wouldn't instruct our other boys; he held the driving privilege only for Herbert, our oldest son. Riding in our new Model T was a bit like riding in a wagon – one felt every bump in the road – but at a faster pace than a horse drawn wagon. The glass that protected one's face from the wind and bugs was a wonderful improvement over the open air buggy. The ride in the automobile, however, was filled with uncertainty as I was never quite sure if we would make it safely to our destination, constantly wondering if something would go awry.

Downtown Joliet was my primary destination as a passenger in our car – other than one or two Sundays that Charles took me out driving around the country. The Model T added a completely different dimension to life – one could be ten miles away and then back home in a few hours. Herbert came up with multiple reasons for requesting use of the car, including taking a girl friend to the movies. Charles acquiesced. I didn't want to grant Herbert's request, but Charles' word was the rule.

Next Steps

In the winter of 1911 Charles' research for a new home for us ended. He had completed the purchase transaction for a farm near Cortland, New York, sight unseen, which would be our new home. It was a 100 acre farm, somewhat hilly, with good soil for crop growing. There was a house and barn on the property. That was all I knew of it; a place where a new phase of my life would begin. Charles had selected this area due to its similarity to the climate of Sweden and the agricultural possibilities.

Cortland had fairly recently, in 1900, incorporated to become the 41st city in the state of New York. Cortland is known as the "Crown City", as it is the highest in elevation above sea level in New York State at 1130 feet. It sits on a plain at the convergence of seven valleys, making the horizon and scenery very picturesque. Surrounding Cortland are seven valleys, which are made up of and lined by prime farmland.

The area was largely agricultural based. The temperatures and climate of this area are similar to Joliet – cold winters with warm summers, making for fertile growing seasons in the late spring through the early fall. The difference was much more snow in the winter and the humidity in the summer. This area actually receives more snowfall than any other metropolitan area in the United States, due the 'lake effect' from Lake Ontario and the Nor'easter snow pattern. The air was cleaner on the farmland Charles had purchased, which was the primary purpose for our move there.

The industry, established primarily in the mid-1800's, was similar to that near Joliet: rock quarrying, mills to refine various local natural resources, and manufacturing. One additional industry was the mining of salt. Until 1900, the majority of the salt used in the United States came from this area, stretching to Syracuse, 33 miles north of Cortland. The city was also home to a university established in 1868, which would become known as SUNY – Cortland. (State University of New York at Cortland).

The large quantities of limestone deposits around Cortland beckoned Charles to obtain stone masonry work from the limestone quarried from the local area. Many ornate stone buildings are part of Cortland's architecture; two of which are the residential mansions of the Wickwire brothers, Chester and Charles. The latter moved into his magnificent home in 1912, the year we would arrive in Cortland.

Our big event for the summer was for Charles and I to go to New York to look at the property Charles had just purchased. Charles had purchased us tickets on the Pennsylvania Railroad line, which would take us to Cortland to view our newly purchased property. Our minds were filled with thoughts of the great promise for my leading a longer, healthier life, and thus we highly anticipated our trip. We were ready to start new lives in another place, leaving our only home we knew in America for another one not yet known. The feeling I had reminded me of when I had come to America; I had left the only home I had ever known and settled in a different, unfamiliar place.

Near our home in Illinois, in the early summer months of 1912, Chicago repeated its active participation in the presidential candidate nominating process. The Republicans again held their National Convention in Chicago in June, where they renominated Taft as their candidate for President. Theodore Roosevelt, one of the liberal Republicans who now differed with Taft on the issues, literally led his supporters out of the convention. Along with these supporters he formed the Progressive Party, which became known as the "Bull Moose" party. This moniker originated when Roosevelt responded to a reporter's question about his health saying "I feel as strong as a bull moose." Having a third political party candidate running created a division of the Republican votes in the general election, thus handing it to Woodrow Wilson, the Democratic candidate, in the fall election.

There were also new happenings and changes in Joliet that summer as we made our plans to travel East. Joliet's Union Station had just opened prior to us taking the train to New York. Our trip to the station was made easier by the layout of building, made by Chicago railway architect Jarvis Hunt, where the railroads were elevated into and out of the station. This allowed for the automobiles and horse traffic to travel more freely to and from the station. It was a beautiful building, so ornate with its stately arches. It was so beautiful, I really didn't expect the building to house a train station. The Grand Ballroom, which we peered through the windows in the closed doors, was simply breathtaking with its crystal chandeliers and high ceilings. It was a place like I'd never seen before. I was happy that such a wonderful building was in our city of Joliet.

We boarded the train in August of 1912 to go look at our newly purchased property in New York. The first train left from Joliet station, which took us to Chicago's Union Station. From there we transferred our luggage to the next train which would take us out east to New York. The train station was bustling with activity – ladies in their finery (silk dresses, ornate shoes) even within the soot filled air that collected in the train station. I wore my best dress, a dark brown cotton dress that I had made. I was clean and neat, but nowhere near as ornate as some of the wealthy ladies were.

We waited in the station room for a few hours before our train to New York was ready to board. It was somewhat confusing to me to see all the people rushing by – on their way to varied destinations and for varied purposes. It was almost like watching a performance, with all the people and the various subplots going on. Such a variety of life was presented in the train station. Everyone's purposes for being there and their outward presentations of themselves was so different. It became somewhat exhausting seeing all the people moving quickly in various directions. I was quite glad when Charles told me it was time to seek out our train.

He carried our small bags – since we had never travelled by train together, we didn't own any 'luggage' specifically. Our change of clothes and a few other personal items fit into a bag more like a rucksack- or in more modern days like a duffel bag.

We looked up on the great board hanging high over the walkway at the entrance to the train tracks. Written in chalk on the big chalkboard were the day's departure and arrivals, with track numbers assigned. We found our way to the assigned track, number five, and walked down to the car our tickets would permit us entry into. The train was immense; the Broadway Limited had just been placed into service. We were very excited to board this new train which would take us to see the location of where our new lives would begin. This steam engine powered train would become the most famous operated by the Pennsylvania Railroad.

Already the day had become long for me. After awakening early, boarding the train to Chicago, waiting in the station, then boarding yet another train, I was tired. It seemed so long a walk from even the train station waiting area out to the train tracks. I became breathless and several times needed to ask Charles to wait for me. He strode ahead, his pace seeming to quicken with his anticipation of boarding the train. I just couldn't keep up. Being in the summertime, by midday the temperature had heated up with the sun and the steam emanating from the many trains arriving and departing the station. The combination of being warm (in my long brown dress) and the physical exertion it took to move around the train station was taking a toll on me.

I was so grateful to sink into my assigned seat on the train. Charles had stowed our bag underneath the seat and sat down beside me. I took this time to rest and tried to calm my whole body with my thoughts. I focused on my breathing, in then out, and probably even looked like I was asleep to an onlooker, as I had closed my eyes to help myself focus.

After some period of time, probably almost an hour, the train rumbled and began to inch its way out of the station. We were on our way. The journey would take us over 20 hours, which was the fastest way there at the time. It would be a long, jostling trip to New York. We left the tall buildings of Chicago, including the recently completed Insurance Exchange building, the Medinah Temple, and the first 'skyscraper', the Monon building. This building was completed in 1890 by Anders Landquist, a Swede, and was about 170 feet high with 13 floors towering above the ground. Our train rumbled on through the short distance in Illinois to Indiana, then to Ohio, Pennsylvania, and our destination of New York State.

Charles and I ate our supper from a smaller sack I had packed from home. The food was at room temperature, not fresh out of the oven or stove. We chewed slowly and ate in silence, prolonging the time to finish our meal as something to keep ourselves occupied as the train swayed in progress towards our destination. Charles and I hadn't much discussed the trip or our feelings about it. That was not a type of conversation we had during our married life. We each lived in our own little worlds, keeping our feelings, hurts, joys, and sorrows inside ourselves. That was just how it was.

Night fall came and I was lulled asleep by the rocking motion of the train. My heart was tired from having to work harder to pump blood throughout my body. In later years this condition could be diagnosed as high blood pressure. At the time I experienced it, it was not known why or how it happened; it simply happened. Then during my sleep, I simply floated out of the earthly world to another world. I saw my earthly body, leaning in my seat on the side of the railroad car. No longer was I sitting ramrod straight up in my seat, my hands folded neatly in my lap. I had left to go to another place — away from my family and home. I had completed the years of my life on Earth: forty five.

Passing

Charles turned to me at about 6 am after a long night on the train. He was going to see if I was awake, to look out the window at the scenery the dawn was just unfolding. He looked at my chest and realized it wasn't pulling in and then exhaling breaths. He tapped me on the cheek, seeing if I would stir into motion.

When he realized I was no longer alive, he let out a silent cry. He couldn't verbalize or audibly make a disturbance in front of the other passengers in the train car. He wouldn't allow himself to do so. Charles removed his coat, and put it over me, as if to keep my body warm. He then got up to walk to find the car porter to determine next actions for removing my body from the train.

The porter stated it would be best to remove my body at the next stop, which would be Newark, New Jersey. After the train had pulled into the station, the passengers whose destination was Newark departed for wherever their lives would take them. The car manager went to the yard manager and explained my body needed to be removed from the train. A local undertaker was summoned, and my body was placed on a pallet, and taken to his storefront.

Meanwhile, for me, I was floating. That might sound strange; I will explain. My spirit stayed in my body for an hour or so after my heart had stopped beating. I calmed myself and said my silent goodbyes to those I knew on Earth; my children, Charles, my sister Nilla, my family in Sweden. Then I floated. My spirit floated away from my physical body, and I began another phase of existence.

I observed Charles spending the night in Newark alone, sleeping at a boardinghouse nearby the train station. It was the first night in over twenty years he had slept in a bed by himself, without me. He didn't sleep much that night. He was looking for me on the other side of the bed even in his sleep. For the time he did sleep, strangely, he slept soundly. He didn't dream of me or go back over my passing the day before. His mind shut off to all influences even in sleep.

Charles left Newark the next day on the return trip back to Chicago with my body, which was put in a wooden casket. He rode, of course, in a passenger car. My body was now 'cargo' so it rode in one of the freight cars towards the end of the line of cars in the train. My physical body was now merely something that those living would transport to find a resting place on Earth. In those days telegraph was the primary means of long distance communications, which he thought not necessary to send for a one day notice to the children. He completed the trip back to Joliet, and upon his arrival made arrangements for my body to be transported to our undertaker.

He walked the mile or so home from Joliet train station with our bags in his hands. The bags seemed to weigh him down with each step; he was indeed carrying more weight in both physical and emotional dimensions. It was to be a hot summer day, and by mid-morning that was apparent. He sweated somewhat in his suit and from struggling with the bulkiness of our bags.

Once again on William Street, he ascended the steps into the front door of our home. He dropped the bags in the foyer and called out to see which of the children were home. Esther came to greet him with a look of surprise. She looked quizzically at Charles, not understanding why he was home, without me, our trip to New York having just begun.

Upon seeing Esther, who looked like a young version of me, with dark hair, pulled back from her face, Charles' body crumpled a bit. He sat down on the front staircase and choked out the words informing Esther I had passed away. Esther cried out; she was almost in shock and saddened with the news. In one moment her life had crossed over a threshold. One minute she was a fifteen year old girl who helped around the house with her siblings, the next she was called upon to assume the duties of running the household. She knew my passing meant she would now be considered an adult, that any girlish activities or tendencies would have to be suppressed for the motherly decisions she would now assume.

The other children came running when Esther called for them. She told them the news that I had died. Charles had gone silent by this time. All the children stared back at her in first disbelief, then confusion, then sadness. They all knew my passing meant their lives were going to change. Burt was only four and Alice six, so they didn't quite grasp all the meanings and implications. They did understand that I wasn't coming back home.

Walter was eight years old; he was one of those children wise beyond his years. He knew it was going to be even tougher for him in the house without me there to temper Charles' reactions. He stood bravely facing the news, although inside his chest was in great turmoil. He wouldn't cry in front of anyone else; he waited until nightfall when he was in bed (which he shared with Burt). Then he let the tears silently fall into his pillow, grieving his loss of me, his mother. I wanted to reach out to him – I wanted to tell him I was sorry for leaving Earth and that my body had failed me. That was not possible; I was gone and never returning in the form of my physical being.

Two days later, on Saturday, my burial took place at Elmhurst cemetery in Joliet, located about a mile and a half east of downtown. Charles did pay for a large limestone marker to be placed at the head of my grave. His choice of limestone was so appropriate, given he worked with this stone almost every day of his work life. It was somewhat surprising for me to see how generous he was with his hard earned money to pay for something that would be of no further use to him.

There was a graveside service, attended by family (my sister Nilla, Charles' brother and sister, and our children), a few women neighbors and a few other women I knew from church. At the end of the remarks by our church's minister, Charles sprinkled some dirt over my coffin, indicating it was time for the cemetery staff to finish covering up my coffin. Each of my children approached my grave singly, in order of their birth. Each said their goodbyes to me, moments I greatly appreciated and that I will always remember. I heard their thoughts, both unspoken and the words they said aloud. It was comforting to know each of my children wanted to wish me well in the world I had now gone to. I had received my children's messages very clearly. My response to acknowledge and appreciate their sentiments couldn't be delivered verbally. They had to make do with the nonverbal messages I attempted to send them.

I learned in those minutes that sometimes on Earth it is hard to verbalize your love and thoughts to another human being. Then, when someone a person loves passes, the thoughts and words flow. The tragedy being it is then too late for them to audibly hear and understand you. Like my love for them, I knew they loved me, although we didn't say that aloud. I learned how clearly one can see relationships and communication in retrospect.

Watching

The new form of my life was underway, where I could only watch what was happening on Earth. It takes some getting used to. As a mother, I would want to speak up, to say something to correct my children in their behavior or warn them to not forget their lunch pail for the school day. As a spouse, I wanted to tell Charles I was sorry to have left so abruptly, though it was out of my control. My new life felt somewhat like when I was on Earth. In many instances as Charles' wife I was expected to behave per the guidance given to children: "be seen but not heard". My experiences on Earth made my new life somewhat easier to adapt to.

I had to learn to communicate in ways other than verbalizing. This presented quite a challenge to find people who could be receptive to nonverbal communication. Charles' mind was closed to messages; he would not permit his mind to be aware of external messages. I therefore didn't attempt to talk to him directly. During my life on Earth, he never spoke to me about his dreams, but I assumed he had them because he mumbled words during his sleep. I used his subconscious to communicate with him when I felt he was going too far in one direction, such as in disciplining our children. He would wake up as usual and not recognize what had happened. I had planted the seeds during his sleeping hours that would bear fruit in his actions during the daytime hours.

It wasn't a foolproof method, though. Many times he didn't listen to my pleading with him to be kinder to Richard or Walter – Charles was a man who acted, within the realm of his control, as he wished. Sometimes my subtle guidance to Charles did hit the mark, such as the time years later that Esther asked Charles if she could leave home to attend nurse's training. His first inclination was to deny her request; he felt she should remain in our home to help with the household. I lobbied him to let Esther go, as there were many positive benefits for her: help others, learn greater independence and earn money to support herself financially. He subsequently assented to Esther, and she was on her way to nurse's training in Chicago. Charles was also a very practical man, realizing that if Esther could support herself via her work in nursing, he would be released from funding her welfare.

Overall Charles wasn't dealing very well with my absence in the household. He had no experience or interest in running the household matters. He sat Esther down in the living room two days after my funeral and told her she would be taking on my duties – cooking, cleaning, getting the children off to school. She had just turned fifteen years old, and suddenly became a mother figure to her five younger siblings. My oldest three boys were pretty much all grown up by this time – they just needed someone to cook for them and do their laundry.

Walter missed me terribly, although there was no outward way for him to express the loss he felt. He drew into himself, and became more reserved as he grew older. He lost that boyishness exuberance, amidst the gloom Charles settled on the household. When I was alive he was my spunky child – pushing the limits of what he could do, climbing in trees, evading coming in to start his schoolwork. I quietly admired his spark, but also knew he had to fit in with how our household was run. He came to me when Charles was unkind to him, which was quite frequently. He would sit nearby when I was doing a household chore, not saying much. He just wanted to be near me. My presence offered him a measure of safety and calm. That was all gone when I left Earth. There was no longer a buffer between Charles and Walter.

Charles became angrier after I passed away. He couldn't verbally express it, other than imparting his anger towards the children. He barked orders at the girls when the potatoes weren't cooked to his liking, when his laundry wasn't folded exactly as he wanted it to be. With the boys he was more physically violent, punishment was corporal, administered with his belt or his hand.

Walter, understandably, was not that happy in our family home after I passed away. It was a difficult place for him to be, given that he never knew if something he did would release the tide of Charles' anger. Walter wasn't doing all that well in school, even though he was a smart child, as he was trying to weave his way through the minefield of Charles' emotions. He was a child that meant well, but because of his environmental influences, had a tough time connecting with some people and activities. He waited for the day when he could leave home and support himself. Charles waited for that day too; the feeling was mutual.

Walter spent the next nine years trying to avoid Charles' wrath. He found diversion in activities outside, such as climbing trees and concocting games out of tree branches and rocks in the yard. He also came into a love for reading – our Joliet schools had a well-stocked library and he continually checked out books. Unfortunately Walter's reading gave Charles another reason to dislike him; Charles mocked him for always seeming to have his 'nose in a book'.

I am so thankful that Esther was there for my youngest five children, including Walter. She offered a softened view of life as an adult, which she instantly became when I died. She mothered and encouraged the youngest children – imparted what she knew about dealing with school mates and also their father. Her first priority always had to be what Charles asked of her; that was how strong his grip on the household was.

My family's lives continued on with school, church, and chores around the house. All the children had chores especially since I was now gone. To make it through each day someone had to cook meals, do the dishes, clean the house.

Charles never remarried after I had left Earth. He wasn't actively looking for a spouse; there also weren't many women who would want to take on eight children at home and the household. So he remained in our house, conducting his life as he had before I'd passed away. He did hire a cleaning woman to come to our house during the day while Esther was at school. She took care of chores Esther couldn't complete and Alice and Burt, our youngest children who were not yet old enough to attend school.

After I had passed away, a family picture was taken of Charles with the children (see Photo 4 in the Appendix). They were in a new phase of their lives, without me. I wasn't there to help get the children dressed for this formal photo. They were all responsible for their own self-care and grooming now, with the exception of Esther's prodding and assistance to Alice and Burt, who were too young to complete all of the preparations for the photo themselves. In looking at this photograph it is interesting to note my son Walter is in the center of the family. That came to be true in later years; he was the central hub about which family activities revolved in the years to come.

Herbert had moved out of our home to live near the technical college he attended in Chicago. He was the only one of our children Charles would fund education for past high school.

The farm we had purchased in New York sat idle while Charles sorted out matters following my death. He didn't want to move there alone; the purpose for the move was to be for my health. He decided to remain in Joliet and continue working as a stone mason. For him to move to the farm alone with our children would have been a dramatic shift. He decided to send our two sons, Elmer and Richard, to go to the New York farm and establish it. Richard, younger than Elmer by eighteen months, had just graduated from high school in the summer of 1913.

Charles took them to the Joliet train station; both of our sons had suitcase with their clothes and cash in their pocket. This was all they had to start their new lives in New York. They would never live in Illinois again. Their leaving Joliet that day was much like when I left Sweden, they were on their way to a new phase and part of their life's journey.

The boys (young men, really, but as their mother they would always be my boys) arrived on the train in Syracuse at Vanderbilt Square. The station was a grand building, with several floors. It was even more ornate than the Chicago station, as it was named after, and partially funded by, the New York Central railroad magnate, Commodore Cornelius Vanderbilt. It was a regional hub for railroad traffic, bustling with activity. They exited the train station and found their way to where they would catch a ride on a truck bed which was bound for Cortland, thirty three miles away.

The truck jostled my two sons all the way to Cortland. The trip took about three hours, due to the condition of the roads and the speed the truck could achieve. They made their way to a sort of hotel – a place where they could sleep for the night. The next day, walking around Cortland, they began seeking the provisions they would need to start their lives on our farmland. After three days, they were ready to 'move' to the farmland. They packed the supplies on the newly purchased horse and set out for the farmland, which would be their 'great frontier'.

Elmer and Richard became homesteaders – they established the business of the farm and the buildings and equipment to support it. I was quite proud of them, seeing their progress and efforts rewarded via crops and healthy livestock. They did all of this without guidance from an older adult, all on their own. Charles received information on how the farm was doing via letters the boys sent him. He didn't have advice to offer them, though, as he had never owned a business or run a farm.

Meanwhile back in Chicago the city continued to grow and prosper through the "Roaring Twenties". Most of these businesses were legal, while some were not. A criminal element emerged in the city that has continued to the present day. I am sad to report that the criminal 'owner' of Chicago in the 'teens and twenties was a Swedish immigrant named Fred Lundin. Fred had grown up quickly; by age eleven he was a primary supporter of his household, which consisted of only himself and his mother. He did whatever he could to earn money for food and their meager apartment, which was located in a very shabby section of Chicago.

As a young man around twenty years old, he rose to prominence after organizing an effort to prosecute two Irish policemen, who, while off-duty, had killed a similarly intoxicated recent Swedish immigrant. Fred organized meetings of the Swedes and community to bring these two trial. This was his entre into the political world and machine of Chicago. He soon took political control of North and Northwestern Chicago; he enabled Republican candidates to win elections in exchange for jobs and favors. One such delivery occurred when, in 1912 he promised Big Bill Thompson, who was perceived to be an incompetent outsider, victory as mayor of Chicago. Against all predictions, Big Bill was elected mayor in both 1915 and 1919. Fred Lundin, the Swede, held the power over Chicago during these years. Only in 1927 did Mayor Thompson break ties with Fred, instead opting for a newcomer named Al Capone, to organize his victory.

Throughout Fred Lundin's years as a political machine boss, he represented himself to be "just a poor Swede", even though the rich and influential people of Chicago were his contemporaries. He maintained his anonymity, unlike his successor Al Capone. Both of these traits, to underplay one's status and not be outwardly visible to most of society, are typical for Swedes.

On the national politics scene, in late 1912 President Taft seemed to be relieved when he was voted out of office in favor of Woodrow Wilson. Taft delved back into the study of law first as a Professor at Yale University. Later in 1921 President Harding appointed him Chief Justice of the Supreme Court of the United

States, a position he considered his greatest honor. He wrote "I don't remember that I ever was President."

December of 1913 saw the Federal Reserve Act enacted under President Wilson's guidance. This setup a new baseline for the banking system in America, and Federal Reserve Notes (now known as US Dollars) came into usage. This was difficult for Charles to adapt to – he was used to storing his money somewhere in our house, not in a bank. Using paper money seemed very odd to him – he wanted the silver or copper coins which had the metal backing their value.

The United States' Federal Reserve would go on to play a central role in funding World War I, which America was not involved with until 1917. Germany was at war with France and England, having been sparked in June of 1914. The long running trust issue, championed by Roosevelt and then Taft, was resolved with the new Federal Trade Commission, whose role was to issue orders prohibiting "unfair methods of competition".

Another passing occurred in my family in October of 1915. My mother, Pernilla, had completed her years on Earth; she had lived to be 95 years old. That was amazing given the expected lifetime for a woman in Sweden in her age group was forty three. Charles and the children received that information months after mother had passed away; he wasn't one to keep in touch on family news. Nilla had contacted my daughter Esther to let her know. My children had never met my parents, and thus their impact on their lives in Joliet was about nil. They knew the scraps of information I had mentioned to them, which wasn't much as I didn't often reflect or reminisce of my life in Sweden. My children knew my parents had raised me and sent me to America; that was about all.

My parents lived on our family's farm until they died, Mother surviving Father by sixteen years. The farmhouse was not inhabited again following Mother's death; there were no family members in the area to inherit or live there. Johanna and Anna and their families lived at locations in Sweden where their husbands had selected. My brother Lars had passed away at his home in Lund in 1914, living to be over age sixty. He had never married and had no children; he had no heirs. Following Mother's death, with none of us children to live on the family farm, the farmhouse was sold and the land was absorbed into a nearby farmer's plot. Today all that remains is a clearing in the grass where the house once stood.

Mother and I were reunited after all those years since I'd left Sweden for America. We had a lot to catch up on, including what her life had been like after I'd left home. I was able to tell her what my life was like as an adult. It was wonderful to be able to communicate with my mother after such a long time. During our lives on Earth the vast expanse of physical location between us drove our relationship in that same direction – a wide gap in our connection as mother and daughter.

World War I became a harsh reality for Americans on April 6, 1917, when America entered the fray. More than 350,000 American men, most of them either still in their teenage years or just barely out of them, were inducted into the Army and Navy. My sons were not drafted into the effort, as Herbert had a family to support and both Elmer and Richard had both married and were working the farm. Walter was only fourteen, and Burt ten; they were too young to serve. As a mother I was glad to know they weren't in harm's way; as an American I wanted our family to help where we could.

While the World War raged on, a war of another type continued within America my family was not directly involved with either. During this time period a variety of ethnic groups were moving to Chicago, in search of work. Conflict, both verbal and physical, arose amongst the workers who were competing for the jobs in the factories and mills of Chicago. There were riots in the streets in

Illinois protesting the influx of black (as African Americans were referred to at the time) workers from the South. The unions of workers, such as the AFL (American Federation of Labor), continued to strengthen, their membership up to 2.4 million workers. The average American worker wanted representation against the big industrial companies, to have an eight hour workday, safer working conditions, and increased pay.

America's national pastime of baseball provided some respite from the War effort and the domestic labor issues which rippled their effects of concern, some anger, and fear, through society. There was joy in our house in the fall of 1917 as the Chicago White Sox defeated the New York Giants to win the World Series. Charles, Walter and Burt followed the progress of the team hovering over the newspaper. They poured over the details of the game and the statistics, providing a diversion to thinking of the efforts they were making for the War. This was exclusively a male enclave of activity – our daughters were not allowed in these discussions and debates.

The winter of 1917 came, and with it, all Americans had to do with less as much of the national monies and efforts were for the War. Charles and the children living at home, now two sons and four daughters, made do with rations of meat and sugar. This was the first war America had been involved with that our family experienced which had stretched across years and whose impacts were felt on a national and local scale. The winter in Illinois felt especially cold and harsh, but not compared to the reports of the troops in combat living outside and the many diseases and loss of lives that occurred.

Our family wanted to do our part. The girls knitted socks and sewed uniforms for the troops and sent them in care packages via the USO (United Service Organizations). Walter and Burt collected all the scraps of metal they could find to turn in for reuse. Charles contributed monetarily via his workplace and the stonemason union. He also purchased as many "liberty bonds" (which were bonds the US government sold to help finance the War) as he could. Celebrities of the times, including Douglas Fairbanks, Charlie Chaplin, and Mary Pickford, encouraged people to buy the bonds. Even the Boy and Girl Scouts campaigned for bond sales with "Every Scout to Save a Soldier".

In the growing seasons of the year Ruth had assumed the role of garden tender. She grew produce to feed our family in the garden plot in our backyard, called a "victory garden". Ruth was quite a successful gardener, to a greater extent than I. She was careful to watch the progress of each variety of plant and adjust where needed. I wasn't as careful; the tending to my children and my other household duties took higher priority.

All four of the girls would preserve what wasn't eaten fresh by canning the fruits and vegetables. These would be eaten during the months when the garden doesn't produce, October through May. This process would involve most of the day on a few Saturdays in the fall – boiling the water to sterilize the jars, adding the food, ensuring the lids sealed properly. If it happened to be a warm fall day, the heat from the stove, the boiling water, and the ambient temperature could make this an uncomfortably warm job. No matter the weather on canning day, it was a necessary part of our household's well-being during the winter months; the job was undertaken and not complained about. It was something that had to be done. The girls wouldn't dare protest to Charles about the tasks.

Edith thought of opting out, of going golfing or another pastime activity, but she didn't attempt to. Even though she was a young adult, Charles would have reprimanded her for not participating and doing her part for the household. During such a day of canning and gardening, Charles would be either tinkering in the barn or reading inside the house. He did not participate in activities he considered 'women's work' and didn't permit our boys to, either.

In the spring of 1918, American troops arrived on the battlefields of France. By the middle of summer 10,000 young American men were arriving *daily* to help win victory over the German troops and their allies. After the Hundred Days Offensive, victory was achieved on November 11, 1918, and the World War was concluded.

Over 4,200 soldiers from Illinois lost their lives during this year and a half. Some of the boys from our neighborhood that had grown up near my children were included in this number. They had gone to war to serve our country; some would never return. Their mothers were women I knew from the neighborhood or our church. For those homes that had a son serving in the War, a placard was displayed in the front window; a public display of the sacrifice and effort that family was making for our country. If a pair of dark uniformed service men walked down the street, it was understood they were on their way to one of the servicemen's homes to inform the parents of their death. Watching the military men walking down the street caused mothers to pause in fear, wondering which home they would need to visit to deliver the news of a son in the War – either their whereabouts or their death. Many mothers who lost sons in the War heard of their combat wounds, that their sons died in battle, due to the increased accuracy and lethality of the weapons used. Outbreaks of dysentery, typhus and cholera were rampant in the troops during the war, disease killing one third of all casualties. These young men went through unspeakable difficulties and experiences. Many gave the ultimate sacrifice – dying for our country. Parents were greatly saddened by losing their sons so early, after seeing them through to young adulthood.

At the conclusion of the War, Americans were greatly relieved that the loss of life had ended. New hope and enthusiasm spurred economic progress in Illinois and around Joliet. During the election in November, Illinois voters approved the first bond issue ($60 million – a mind boggling number during those days) for the construction of a statewide system of hard roads. This meant commerce could be increased throughout our state via the new automobile and truck proliferation and the improved surfaces for them to travel on. The waterways of Chicago's port and the canal down through Joliet were already a significant means of transporting goods throughout Illinois.

Walter : Becoming a Young Man

In 1919 my son Walter was still in school at Joliet Township High School and sixteen years old. Our country was in turmoil, with many veterans returning from World War I with no work. Many unionized workers went on strike in the steel and meatpacking industries. Downtown Joliet and Chicago saw a resurgence of angry clashes between the union workers and the companies they worked for. The Illinois National Guard was called out to restore order to stop the violence of race riots which raged from July 27 to August 3. Thankfully none of my children were involved in this violence. Angry public outpouring is not the way my children were instructed to express dissatisfaction. Our family would tend to adjust the course of our own actions, then quietly continue in the revised direction. The violent strikes failed and the unions had to be satisfied with their position they'd earlier achieved.

In 1920, the year Walter graduated from high school, the population of Illinois was almost six and a half million people. It amazed me that one state in America had more residents than all of Sweden. He would have loved to have gone to a university to study, but that was not at all possible given the family finances. In that time period, there were no student loans; education after high school must be paid for in cash. Our family, namely Charles, had made it clear that only Herbert would be provided monetary resources for education past high school. So Walter went into a profession where he could earn money immediately after graduating from high school - stone masonry. Charles introduced Walter to some of the foremen on jobs he had previously worked on, and soon enough Walter was steadily working as a brick layer.

Charles and other workers on the brick laying jobs taught Walter the trade. Walter listened and learned the best techniques, one of which was to bend at the knees, so as not to strain his back. He was a quick study and rapidly found himself asked to work other brick laying jobs. He liked the order of the bricks and the repetitive motions of scooping the mortar, layering it on the surface. With his left hand he placed the brick on top of the mortar, next, with a trowel in his right hand, he scraped off any excess mortar. He did that for nine hours a day, five days a week.

Walter was still so young- eighteen years old. He had grown into a tall (six foot three), slim young man. He was the tallest of my boys, certainly taller than Charles which, as another provoking point, didn't endear Walter to Charles. Walter was sometimes playful during his work - playing little jokes on his co-workers. He would turn his cap around backwards on his head and look off to one direction, making him look a bit goofy like some of the actors one could see at the picture shows in the movie theatres. Charles did not appreciate any sort of actions that were not directly related to work and frivolous in his opinion. He didn't understand, and thus disapproved, of Walter.

In spite of Charles' mean streak and cruel words towards Walter, Walter never spoke badly of his father. He might say something about Charles being a tough man, but no more. It was just not the Swedish, or our Anderson family, way to mention any less than desirable characteristics or actions of family members. Walter had a can-do attitude; he tried again when he was knocked down. I loved that about him.

In the summer of 1920, while Walter was pursuing his life in the working world, the Republican National Convention was held in Chicago. Chicago had become quite the political hot spot – with so many national party conventions and Illinois emerging as a state of huge commerce opportunities. The convention nominated Warren G. Harding for President.

Overall the United States experienced a period of great growth in technology and business in the 1920's. It was a boom time after the World War years and earlier recession. Automobiles and electric appliances fueled the economic growth and way of life for more and more Americans. To fund this growth, companies producing these products continued to borrow more and more money from banks. Walter, as a young working man, was absorbing the news of the economy and business experiences.

The nineteen twenties were a nice change from the depression and war years America had experienced for almost twenty years earlier. The agricultural economy's financial bubble collapsed in 1921, driving more and more people to jobs in the cities, expanding the housing and building sectors. Growth in those areas was good news for my family - more opportunities for work were available for Charles and our boys. Oil became more common for heating, instead of coal or wood as we'd had earlier. Our home on William Street had an oil burning furnace installed; a great big steel device that would last for the next ninety years. It was a big step forward in technology for our home.

Progress and modernization continued in our home on William Street when it became 'electrified' in 1922. This made a huge impact on how my family's lives were lived – the kerosene lamps were no longer needed, replaced by Edison's invention in 1879 of the light bulb. Our family could now stay up later in the dark winter evenings, reading or playing cards in the living room.

My sister Nilla joined me in the spring of 1922, passing into the world I had been in for ten years. It was good to be reunited with her. Together we watched Nilla's husband Charles struggle to make decisions as to how to keep their household running. He couldn't do it without her; their remaining daughter at home went to live their oldest daughter's family, in order to finish high school at Joliet Township High School. Nilla was saddened that she had not been able to see her youngest daughter, Sigrid, graduate from high school. She observed Sigrid's graduation ceremony from her new perspective.

After working in Joliet for a few years after his graduation from high school, Walter decided it was time for him to leave home and find work elsewhere. Charles was pressuring Walter to 'go get a job' (even though he was already employed). What he meant was he wanted Walter to move out of our family home. Walter learned of some businesses in the region, ranging in location from Illinois to Michigan state, looking for workers from his brick laying compatriots.

In 1923 Walter accepted employment with a rock quarrying business southern Wisconsin, the Waukesha Lime & Stone Company. These businesses recruited workers from other cities and states to operate. They provided a place to live and basic meals for their workers. Walter's work in this quarry near Milwaukee, Wisconsin was to sort the rocks as they came out of the crusher and run the tractors that broke up the rock. Though there is a heavy drift mantle, there are many outcrops of Niagara limestone in this area. Most of the rock that came out of quarries in this area of Wisconsin was used in roads and concrete work in the nearby city of Milwaukee.

Being away from home, living away from his family, was a new, yet refreshing, experience for Walter. He seemed to feel he could now fully breathe – he wasn't being tamped down by Charles. Walter lived in a room furnished by the quarry company in Lannon, Wisconsin. He shared the living quarters with another young man, also from Illinois. They had little in the way of possessions; meals were provided by the family that ran the boarding house in the dining room on the first floor of the house.

Walter worked hard during the day. The work with the rocks and stone could literally be back breaking. Thankfully the techniques he had learned in his first years of work helped keep him safe and injury free. With the weekdays being completely filled up with the cycle of rising early, working a long day, eating, then going to sleep, the weekends were something to look forward to for Walter.

Friday was payday, and there were many establishments in the area interested in parting the quarrymen from their earnings.

During this time in my son Walter's life, from my viewpoint it seemed he was rebelling against Charles' strictness. Many other adults in America were also rebelling during this timeframe, as in 1920 the 18th Amendment to the US Constitution was passed, which prohibited "the manufacture, sale, barter, transport, import, export, delivery, furnishing or possession of intoxicating liquor". President Hoover believed this new law would eliminate alcohol consumption in the United States. Instead the effect on Americans was to enhance the appeal of alcohol. This situation of people buying liquor made illegally and wanting it all the more continued for over twelve years.

Even women were allowed into places that (illegally) sold alcohol. This was of particular concern to me; I certainly didn't want my daughters in these places. To me it wasn't a proper thing for a woman to do, and it was against my religious beliefs. I was concerned for my daughters' safety and hoped they wouldn't think to go in these establishments. Charles was even more concerned that I was, and he made it clear to our daughters they were not to go into one of these places – ever. Even though the three oldest girls were over age eighteen, Charles still had control of their actions.

During this so called "Prohibition", one means to purchase alcohol was through an illegal business called a "speakeasy". They received this name because of the secrecy that surrounded them – people would speak easy (softly, lightly) about the existence and location of these places to buy alcohol. Once they were discovered, the authorities would shut them down by padlocking the doors. The result of that official government action was another speakeasy would open very quickly nearby. Many were literally underground, without adequate ventilation or sanitary conditions, making them harder to locate by the police.

Wisconsin, the state where Walter was residing in these years of the 1920's, had a large amount of beer (containing alcohol) breweries owing to the large German American population. The Prohibition hit the economies of these areas especially hard, as many of their manufacturing plants and associated jobs for workers depended on alcohol production. Once that became illegal, the breweries tried to convert their production capacity to make other items such as soda, ice cream, even cheese to remain a solvent business. Some were successful; most had to close their business and layoff their workers. Many of these laid off workers sought work where they could find it, sometimes working for the bootleggers (the name referring to people would conceal hip flasks of alcohol in the legs of their boots) who continued to produce alcoholic beverages, despite it being illegal to do so. The alcohol business continued to thrive in Wisconsin, as with the rest of the country, yet through different channels and organizations.

Back home in Illinois in 1924 more funding ($100 million dollars) for road additions and improvements was available, originating from bonds sold by the state. The monies provided for more improvements to the transportation paths for commerce, to transport goods away from the river and Lake Michigan to other destinations inland. The roads weren't called highways, then, because there were very few sections were "high" (as in elevated) roads. The train station did have elevated tracks; roads for automobiles had not yet achieved this level of sophistication or complexity. At the time the concept of Federal government funding for state roads hadn't yet occurred. It was up to each state to fund their roads maintenance and planning.

Prohibition had another unintended effect by moving power over the alcohol distribution to violent gangs. Al Capone, who had taken over as the unofficial manager of Chicago, emerged as a leader of this 'network' , running all 10,000 speakeasies in Chicago, with 700 men involved in the support and enforcement of his businesses. He became one of the most notoriously cruel and vicious criminals in the history of the United States. I am thankful none of our family became involved with this sinister network of corruption. He was in the newspaper quite often, where he donated money to various charitable endeavors. Some viewed him as a modern day Robin Hood – helping those less fortunate than he. In my view how he had obtained his monies and power was not admirable.

Walter was intoxicated by the people, sounds, and activities he experienced at the speakeasies. Growing up in a working class area of Joliet, he rarely saw women with the latest fashions. In the 1920's those that wore them were known as the "flappers" because of the flounciness of the dresses. He became a regular customer at the speakeasies, playing poker, drinking whiskey and smoking cigarettes. Most often he lost money at these poker games, which frustrated him – he thought he had sufficient intelligence to win the card game. The games were getting him in some financial trouble. He couldn't earn enough money fast enough being a quarry worker. As his mother I was cringing at how he was living his life during these years.

Sitting in these underground, cramped quarters with many people didn't provide much fresh air or ventilation. Add to that the smoke from cigarettes that had nowhere to escape, and a significant quantity of contaminants were going into Walter's lungs. I wanted to call out to him – tell him to not put himself in that situation, that the people he was playing cards with were cheating him, that the environment and smoke wasn't good for him. I couldn't – my role now was to watch and wait to see what would happen.

Walter couldn't hear my silent pleas for him to change his behavior. My calls to him were lost somewhere in the expanse between the earth and the sky. He did as he pleased, for the first time in his life, with the exception of having to report to work ready for a full day of labor. He was a hard worker – steady and strong. I watched over him during the hot days of the summer of

1924 and into the winter of 1924/1925. He tried to save some of his money earned from his job, however he wasn't successful with the outpouring going to his losses at the poker table.

Being near Milwaukee, Walter saw many of the motorized bicycles made in that city by Harley Davidson. In the late 1910's, this company sold over 18,000 of the motorized bicycles they'd developed to the military that would be used in World War I. Walter did not purchase one as he did not have enough money left after the poker tables he played. He also feared what Charles would say. Walter wanted to avoid any potential opportunity for further criticism from his father.

In the speakeasies Walter saw women who wore rouge (makeup) and had short hair. He liked listening to the ragtime music, Scott Joplin tunes like those I'd heard mention of from the World's Fair. Walter had learned to smoke cigarettes and cigars, breathing deep on the tobacco, the smoke circulating within his body to come back out his nose. My religious beliefs told me this wasn't a good thing; anything that was not needed for a body's food intake was not necessary and shouldn't be spent hard earned money on. The smoke left a pungent odor on a person's hair and clothing.

While Walter was living in Wisconsin, the state's voters had enough of the Prohibition. In 1926 they approved a referendum which allowed the sale of "near beer" (which has a 2.75 percent alcohol content, where 'typical' beer has an alcohol content of somewhere between 4.5 and 7 percent). This broke with the federal government's all out ban on alcohol sales and allowed some legal alcohol consumption in Wisconsin. Then in 1929 the people of Wisconsin repealed their state law of prohibition enforcement, leaving the Federal government to enforce Prohibition in Wisconsin. This had the effect of dramatically reducing the enforcement of Prohibition in the state of Wisconsin.

After five or so years of going to the speakeasies, and being in those confined, smoky spaces, Walter had developed persistent pains in his chest. He thought it initially from the cold winter air he worked in, or possibly from the cigarettes he smoked at night. He began to be short of breath and was having a difficult time keeping up with his work demands. Then the coughing began, which just wouldn't go away.

The extreme force used amongst the gangsters who controlled the alcohol network was notoriously cruel. Many violent acts occurred over rivalries for control of the monies behind the sale of alcohol. One particularly severe event happened in February of 1929, where Al Capone's gang executed seven men on Chicago's north side. This sparked the country's public outcry to end the corruption caused by Prohibition on a national level.

After all the 'good times' of the 1920's, with the economic and social prosperity, monetary investors began to panic. They wanted their money, the cash they had brought to the bank to deposit, back immediately. This was impossible for the banks to complete, as the theories behind the banking system don't support an all cash basis. The banks had loaned the monies out to many businesses who now were unable to pay it back. Companies also didn't have the money to pay their shareholders back if the money was requested. It all came crashing down on October 29, 1929 when stock prices plummeted, all in one day. Many people who were wealthy (on paper) in the morning of October 29 had nothing left by the afternoon of the same day. It was a bewildering, confusing time. The stock crash caused many people to be unable to pay back their debts, such as loans from the bank to buy their home. Thus money was not able to flow through the system. The Great Depression had been kicked off, which would drag on for twelve years until 1941.

Our family's savings and investments were safe from the loan and stock crisis, as Charles paid cash for everything we purchased. We owned our own home and had no investments in stocks of companies; Charles preferred to see physical evidence of his monies. The difficulty for our family came via employment opportunities, as there were few, if any, building projects, and that meant little work and income for Charles. Even if people had savings in banks that didn't go out of business, they were not able to access the money.

By this time, our four girls were working in various jobs – Esther was a nurse, Edith worked for a judge, Ruth in an office, and Alice in a camera shop. All but Alice were able to hold their jobs through the Depression. The money they made provided for the household's necessities during these challenging economic years of the Depression. Charles had some work, but not consistently, and was nearing the time when he could no longer physically complete the demands of his stone masonry work. Burt was still living at home, seeking a profession he couldn't quite find.

Probably because of the stock market crash in 1929, throughout Walter's life he never invested in the stock market. He, like Charles, wanted to be able to physically see where his invested money was in the form of land, buildings, and businesses. These were where he would focus his investments in the years to come.

Deciding

Walter's coughing and tiredness finally pushed him to see a doctor in Milwaukee in 1930. The doctor listened to Walter's lungs with a stethoscope. He heard what's called 'rattling' in the medical world, especially in Walter's right lung. He turned to Walter and said 'Young man, you have tuberculosis. You need immediate bed rest and to no longer smoke. If you choose to keep living as you are, you will likely find yourself no longer able to breathe; you will die."

Walter listened to the doctor's comments with a mixture of anger, fear, confusion, and tiredness. He wasn't sure what he was going to do with this diagnosis and what his immediate future would be. This was a pivotal moment in his life; his next course of action could very well determine if his life would continue. Walter thanked the doctor for his services, paid the receptionist for his visit, and slowly walked the few blocks back to the apartment building he had stayed in.

He sat on the bed he'd slept on for a few years now for a while, probably an hour or so, mulling over in his mind what he should do. He made his decision, then lay down to rest, a wave of exhaustion overtaking him.

The next morning he woke up at the typical time of his workday, and, at a measured pace, put on his clothes. He walked into the kitchen, poured himself a cup of coffee from the pot simmering on the stove, and ate a small breakfast of bread and some cheese. He washed the food down with the strong coffee, Swedish coffee. We Swedes drink quite a bit of coffee – it may have to do with the long, dark winter days we were used to. Even still in the present day Sweden is the 6th most coffee drinking country per capita – behind our neighbors Finland, Norway, Iceland, Denmark, and the Netherlands.

He went into work as usual with his roommates. Once at the job site, Walter approached the foreman and told him he needed to talk with him for a few minutes. The foreman was busy with the start of the work day and assigning tasks to his workers; he didn't want to take precious minutes to talk to one of them. Seeing the look in Walter's eyes, and reading the intention behind it, he followed Walter into the quarry yard office. They sat at a crude wooden table, two chairs on either side of it. The manager was on one side, the worker on the other.

Walter started the conversation by thanking the foreman for hiring him and being a fair person to work for. He then explained that he had to take an extended period off of work in order to gain his health back. The foreman nodded that he understood and wished Walter a speedy recovery. He also went over to the safe, where the money was kept to pay their workers, and settled the balance of wages owed to Walter in cash.

Speedy recoveries didn't happen during this time with tuberculosis; the recovery, if it did occur, was anything but expedient. Streptomycin, the first antibiotic and bacterial agent effective against tuberculosis, was not discovered until 1944. Until then, fighting the disease was in accomplished by fresh air and light work demands. For those that went into the sanatoria (isolated buildings that were setup to care for those affected with tuberculosis) around 1916, 50% of those people were dead within five years. The average American didn't want to meet up with those odds, preferring to fight through the disease on their own if at all possible.

During this timeframe is when the National Tuberculosis Association promoted Christmas Seals as a means to raise money for tuberculosis programs. These are stickers which can be put on letters, especially focused on the Christmas holiday greetings. This association is now known as the American Lung Association; those seals are still mailed prior to the holiday season.

Walter was truly in for the fight of his life, indeed the fight for his life, which stretched over three years. Walter went back to his apartment and collected his meager amount of possessions, putting them back in the same suitcase he'd brought with him to Wisconsin. He then walked the few blocks to the train station, to take the 12:30 train back to Chicago. He bought a one way ticket. He knew he wasn't coming back to Wisconsin, mostly by the lack of energy and strength he felt clear into his bones. The right side of his chest wasn't feeling at all good, either; it felt like a huge weight was pressing on his chest, even while he was standing upright. Walter thought about sending a telegraph to our family in Joliet; then he dismissed that idea as he would be home probably before the telegraph could be delivered anyway.

The train ride to Chicago took three hours; long enough for Walter to see the scenery flashing by the train window, like the scenery of his life. It was a movie that was going so fast he couldn't keep up with the arresting visual display seen through the train window. He was just so tired….. He woke with a start as the train's whistle let out a long announcement of its arrival in Chicago. Walter tried to compose himself, smoothing out the lapel of the suit he wore; his only suit.

Walter had hit a wall with the state of his health – he had to change his ways or risk further injury or death. He chose to fight the disease on a day by day inch by inch basis. I had watched my sister Elna struggle with this disease, tuberculosis, back in Sweden in 1875. It was a cruel master, finally overtaking her.

Walter crossed the railroad tracks to get to a train that would take him home to Joliet. He boarded the train, sat in a hard wooden seat, and waited for the conductor to come through to collect the fare.

At home on William Street, Esther was cleaning. She was surprised when Walter appeared through the front door window. Why was he there? Her mind flashed back to when Charles had come home alone to deliver the bad news of my passing. She was worried about Walter's appearance. Walter was tired from the trip. Esther had to help him into the house and steered him toward the couch in our living room.

In the next few days Walter saw a doctor in Joliet who told him his right lung had collapsed; it was no longer functioning. He would never regain the ability to breathe deep from that lung; it was truly dead to the rest of his body. Interestingly collapsing a lung surgically was one method doctors during this time period used to 'treat' TB patients. Walter's body did this on its own, and it may have very well been the thing that saved his life from succumbing to TB.

Esther swooped in like a Florence Nightingale for Walter. (Florence Nightingale was an English nurse in the 1860's who was known as "the lady with the lamp" because she would take a lamp around the dark hallways of a hospital at night visiting the sick, making herself available to them when other caregivers did not.) As a nurse, Esther knew what to do to assist tuberculosis patients. Now the patient was her brother, Walter. She set up an outdoor, open air bedroom on our back porch for him to convalesce. This was also to isolate him from the rest of the family, so they would not catch the airborne illness from Walter. It being the summer months, sleeping in the fresh air was refreshing. As fall and winter approached, the temperatures outside plummeted. To combat the cold winter air, Walter was provided additional wool blankets. He endured.

Esther administered her nursing skills to Walter. During the Great Depression, when very few had money to buy even basic groceries, Esther made it a priority to put aside money to buy oranges for Walter, so that the vitamin C in them could help him fight the tuberculosis. Again I was so proud of Esther for helping Walter through this difficult health time. She faced Walter's illness and fought it head on with the tools she had available.

Walter fought tuberculosis for three years. Unable to work, he had to rely on his sisters to help him survive. Charles was of no assistance – he excused himself from being in proximity to Walter by saying he couldn't risk contracting tuberculosis. He seemed to watch dispassionately as Walter had been rendered helpless in his cot where he lay. I watched over Walter, praying, trying to comfort him from another dimension of the world. He feels my presence, I know, but cannot speak aloud of how I enter his thoughts during those long hours spent lying on the cot on the back porch. The seasons went by summer, fall, winter and then spring again – the tuberculosis still there. His body fought against the infection to regain his health. The summers can be stifling hot in Joliet; the winters cruelly cold. Walter survived it all on the back porch of our home on William Street. He read the Bible several times over those years and other books made available to him by Esther.

Esther already had a full time job as a nurse during the daytime. She took care of all of Walter's household needs of laundry, bathing, clothing, and bed making, during her off hours from the hospital. She cared for him like he was her own son. I think Esther's acts of kindness saved Walter's life – both from the vitamins in the orange juice and food and the love that went into purchasing the produce for him.

Interestingly, Viktor Frankl also notes in his book that tuberculosis patients in the sanitariums of this time period faced the similar aspects of mental challenges to those in the World War II concentration camps. Neither of these groups knew a "date for their release – they were without a future and without a goal". Frankl asserts that the most challenging state of being is when either a person who is physically ill or in captivity doesn't have a timeframe of reference for how long their situation will last or hope for the future that their situation will change.

Walter made it through his years of fighting this disease by having a goal of recovery. He chose to let his body rest and heal itself, which was the only remedy to tuberculosis patients available at the time. Isoniazid, the first oral mycobatericidal drug, which was the antibiotic to combat tuberculosis, wasn't available to the general public until 1952. Vaccinations for TB in humans achieved their first successes with BCG (bacilli calmette-Guerin) in 1921, but did not gain widespread acceptance in the United States until the late 1940's (after World War II). Walter's life was enabled by my daughter Esther, an excellent nurse and encourager to Walter. She didn't give up on him.

By the time Walter was able to walk around and begin physical exertion, he was a gaunt six foot three man, weighing about one hundred and forty pounds. Over subsequent months he gained a bit more weight, but still remained very slim. He looked quite like a toothpick walking down the street. The United States was still in the throes of the Great Depression. It was a difficult time; jobs were almost non-existent, especially for many young people, even strong, healthy ones.

Now that Walter had his health back, although not to his former level of strength, he worked hard to find a way to earn money. It was difficult to find work, and, based on his earlier work quality and experience, was able to find work as a stone mason. He had to pace his exertion levels during this workday much more than he did in his early twenties. Soon he fell into the rhythm of work, rising early in the morning, working a long day, returning home at night.

This was 1933. Unemployment was at an all-time high; many didn't have money to buy even the most basic groceries. Banks were failing by the thousands in 1932 and 1933. Loans were impossible to get for a home or new business, even if a person wanted to start anew and had some initial capital to invest. Poverty had stricken

America – millions were unemployed, senior citizens had no means of support, businesses were either bankrupt or unable to act.

With the high unemployment and ongoing Prohibition driving up criminal activity, there were many people unable to make ends meet through a legal work situation. The city of Chicago had several notorious gangs that made dangerous shoot-outs, robberies, and the like. After years of public pressure on the United States government to end the Prohibition of alcohol, in December of 1933, the Federal Government repealed the Prohibition law, the 18th Amendment. This brought most of the control of alcohol back into the government's hands and away from the criminal element. The criminal element was firmly established in America and would not be going away as a result of these laws being repealed.

Edith : A Young Woman

My daughter Edith was working in the legal field as a court reporter. Although she lived in the same household as Walter during his illness, she was unable to slow down the pace of her life to spend time with her brother. It was as if she didn't believe Walter was as ill as he was. She continued on with her daily activities as they were before, refusing to yield to Walter's care needs. She was a tenacious, sometimes obstinate, exacting woman. She was a pioneer in the business world and leisure activities. As an unmarried woman she could never have the social standing that came with being married in the 1920's era. She had to make her social and financial status all on her own.

Like many people in society, Edith's social and financial statuses were tied together. After high school she attended a secretarial course at Chicago Women's Business College. She learned secretarial skills of shorthand, typing, and filing. She was able to leverage that training into working in the court house. She would walk the distance between our home and the courthouse, which was a mile, to report for her work promptly at 8:30am each day. The Joliet courthouse serves as the Will county courthouse, known for having sensational cases from the southern side of the Chicago area tried there.

Edith began her work at the courthouse as a secretary to a judge. After five years of working in that role – typing, shorthand (a language of characters that enabled faster writing), and filing tasks – she was promoted to "court reporter" for Judge Bartley. Being a court reporter meant she was relied on to quickly and accurately record the proceedings of the court. She was entrusted with case records and recording testimonies. This was a prominent role for a woman in those days.

Because of her business acumen, the position of court reporter brought her prestige in the legal and business communities. She heard and recorded the proceedings of all of Judge Bartley's cases. She knew backgrounds, stories, and suppositions about many, many people in the Joliet area. For the time period Edith was in the working world, she truly was a pioneer. She travelled with the Judge whenever he had a case outside of Joliet. They went to other cities or counties in Illinois on a loaned basis – to Kankakee or Elgin. Edith was a founding member of the Joliet Women's Business Club, and very happy to have some of her nieces and grandnieces (my granddaughters and great-granddaughters) participate in the club in later years.

Edith was always a pioneer in every aspect of her life. Regarding her religious practices, as she became an adult she chose a church to attend. She selected the First Presbyterian Church, on the corner of Broadway and Western Avenues. She attended services by herself, briskly walking the four blocks to the beautiful limestone church each Sunday. The congregation mostly consisted of the conservative business people of Joliet, those working in the professional fields, as in relation to our family of laborers. Even though she had a close relationship with her sister, my daughter, Ruth, Edith went alone to her church. Ruth continued to attend the Swedish Bethel Baptist church we had raised her in.

In her personal life, Edith pushed the boundaries of what was socially acceptable for a woman in Joliet. She was an avid golfer – see Photo 5 in the Appendix for a photo of her in her golfing attire. When Edith learned to golf, in the 1920's, this was the time of the flapper, when women wore dresses that flounced with ruffles and didn't extend to their ankles. She breathed oxygen onto the flame of the flapper movement and ran with it. Because the all-male golf clubs wouldn't allow women on the course to play at the same time as men, women golfers were only allowed after all the male golfers had finished for the day. Thus the tee times remaining were in the hottest parts of the day – 3 pm in the afternoon or later. In the middle of summer in Joliet this can be a sweltering, unbearable time to be outside, much less in the direct hot sun walking the golf course with a heavy golf bag. Edith persevered through it – she wanted to golf that badly. Most Sunday afternoons she would play 36 holes of golf – a tough schedule for anyone.

She also pushed social limits when she had a male suitor during her thirties, beginning in 1930. This man was nice enough; he came to our house on William Street to call for Edith. They would sit in the front parlor, talking and playing cards. Other nights they would go out for a drive or possibly to the movies in New Lenox, a nearby town. None of those activities was out of the norm socially. What was out of the realm of 'normal' was that her suitor was married.

This truly was a scandal of some proportion – a married man courting a single young woman. The additional information was that Edith's suitor's wife was alive and well – and living with her parents in Kingston, New York. The marriage had proved the couple to not be compatible, and, rather than divorce, they lived completely separate lives. Nonetheless, the man was married and that was against the rules of society at that time. I am surprised that Charles allowed this relationship to continue. Maybe he thought that at least Edith had no possibility of marrying this man, so what was the harm? By this time Charles was near seventy five years old; it is possible age had made him more ambivalent about controlling our children's lives. In his younger years he would certainly not have allowed Edith to have this relationship. To him it was clear that Edith and Ruth still lived under his roof, and that meant under his rules. Charles had not permitted Ruth to even think of marrying her suitor, who was a nice Catholic boy. He would not allow Ruth to marry outside the Protestant faith.

Esther : A Young Woman

Now that Walter's health had improved, Esther took an opportunity offered to her to work at a hospital on the South Side of Chicago, in the predominately Swedish neighborhood between Twentieth and Twenty-first Streets. Esther moved out of our family home to the nurse's quarters near the hospital in Chicago to begin her new phase of her life there. She shared a room with three other nurses. They cooked their meals in the kitchen of the building.

Housing for the nursing staff was setup in a dormitory style – separate sleeping rooms with common areas of kitchen and sitting room. In the sitting room there was a radio – a magical device where people's voices floated out of. Tuned into the station WLS, which broadcast from Chicago, the nurses and nursing students would listen to the radio shows of Amos N Andy, Eddie Cantor and the Thursday night favorite variety show, the Maxwell House Show Boat as a diversion to their intense work at the hospital tending to patients. In the early 1930's the radio had become people's connection to others across the world – it brought news from faraway lands and humor and comedy to their lives. It transported people away from their woes of the economy to a happier place for those minutes the radio show was on the air.

Esther progressed to become one of the charge nurses, overseeing the newer nursing students. Probably because of her being the oldest girl in our family and tending to her siblings, she was well suited for this role, which including a touch of mothering the younger nurses. Esther would return to Joliet to visit Charles, her father, and Edith, Ruth, and Burt, her siblings, who lived at home on Sundays and occasions she had a few days off in a row.

One of the younger nurses working with Esther in 1934 was named Alice (likely also named after Teddy Roosevelt's daughter). Alice was nine years younger than Esther – almost the same age as my daughter Alice. Alice was new to Chicago as a nursing student and mostly kept to herself. Her parents had died when she was six years old, when she had been spared from living in an orphanage by going to live with her Aunt and Uncle in Indiana. Luckily for Alice, they had chosen to open their home for her to live in. As an orphan in the 1915 timeframe, if extended family didn't become guardians for the child, they would be sent to a boarding house or orphanage. The living conditions there could be crowded, Spartan, hospitable, or hostile; it was never sure which and at what time. In her Aunt and Uncle's home Alice had a place to live that was welcoming to her presence.

Esther and her new protégé Alice would take their lunch at the same time and talk about the newest patients and what activities the nursing staff might be conducting that week. During one of these conversations, Esther asked Alice if she would like to meet one of her brothers. Alice hesitated at first, being wary of being introduced to a man. She then acquiesced to accompany Esther to Joliet for a Fourth of July picnic.

Our family always had a grand celebration on the Fourth of July to celebrate being American. We would send someone, usually one of the young adult family members, to Bush Park early in the morning of July 4th to stake out the picnic spot. This was the same park where Charles and I first met. Grand preparations (on our scale) were made; Edith made her rice pudding (based on our Swedish recipe for risgrynsgrot), which included at least a dozen eggs for richness of taste. We made a special purchase of watermelon, with its sweet juice and seeds that had to be spit out in order to not swallow them. My daughters would make sandwiches and potato salad for everyone.

Alice came to Joliet for the first time on the train, where Esther and my daughter Alice met her at the train station. They went to the park to meet up with the rest of the family. The picnic celebration was in full swing – over 75 people were there. There were games of horseshoe throwing, sack races (where a person runs with a potato sack over their feet and legs), and lawn bowling. The women mainly sat in the shade, talking near the food table.

Esther brought Alice over to meet Walter. Walter, at six foot three, towered over Alice, who was barely five foot four. They exchanged introductions, and Esther faded off to go check on the food. They walked around the park, talking about their pasts and where they had grown up. Walter was thirty years old; Alice was twenty four. Both were of older age for marriage in those days. By the end of the day, they agreed to stay in touch. The plans were for Walter to arrange a subsequent date.

During the summer of 1934 Chicago's criminal world activity continued to percolate, even after the end of Prohibition. These groups and gangs moved in and around the same locations and settings as lawful, tax paying citizens did. John Dillinger, who had robbed great sums from many banks in the Midwest, was living in the Chicago area, unbeknownst to the general public and even the Chicago Police department. He spent time on the Near North side of Chicago, and attended many games of his favorite baseball team, the Chicago Cubs. On July 22 he had attended the movie, Manhattan Melodrama, at the Biograph Theatre, located on Lincoln Avenue, not far from what had been known as the Swedish area "Andersonville". He was accompanied by two women, one of whom was his most current girlfriend. The woman who was not his girlfriend had told the Bureau of Investigation (whose Chief was J. Edgar Hoover), when Dillinger planned to be at the Theatre. She wore an orange dress to identify their group of people, to help the agents single out John Dillinger. (The dress appeared red in the lights of the Theatre; this is where "the woman in red" phrase has become part of American lore). As he was exiting the Theatre, federal agents shot and killed him.

Walter and Alice also saw the movie Manhattan Melodrama that summer, although they went to the Rialto Square Theatre, on Van

Buren Street in downtown Joliet. The building of the theatre is an attraction in and of itself which had opened in 1926; the architecture reflects Greek, Roman, and Byzantine styles. The interior has ornamental terra cotta façade which brings together Classical, Moorish (from Spain), and exotic motifs. Architectural features inside are modeled after the Hall of Mirrors in Palace of Versailles (near Paris, France), the Arc De Triomphe (in Paris, France), and the Pantheon (in Rome, Italy). This was all quite ornate for our city of Joliet.

The remainder of their courtship was brief; they both knew they were looking to find a spouse. Walter and Alice announced their upcoming marriage ceremony on a Wednesday, three days before they were to be married. There wasn't much time (or money) for fussy preparations. They had invited my children living in the Chicago area and their spouses and Alice's only sibling to attend; a total of eight people.

Walter and Alice

Walter and Alice's marriage ceremony was a simple one on the second Saturday in September of 1934. In the imposing and grand building of the Fourth Presbyterian Church of Chicago, their wedding occurred in the small yet beautiful chapel on the right side of the building. The building itself had been finished in 1914 and was constructed of Bedford limestone. The church today presides over Michigan Avenue, and was declared a National landmark in 1975. Their wedding was attended by five people: Esther, Ruth, Alice, Burt, and Alice's sister. Edith had decided not to attend, stating she didn't believe they were getting married. In reality she did not want to give up her tee time at the golf course.

The area surrounding the church was very different in its beginnings. Chicago's now famous "Magnificent Mile" was an underdeveloped street called Pine Street. Thus the neighborhood grew up around the church, and except for the familiar Water Tower (which actually distributed water to the city) two blocks to the south, Fourth Church is in current times the oldest surviving structure on Michigan Avenue north of the river.

Walter and Alice began their lives together in Joliet. Walter continued working as a stone mason, and Alice was to continue nursing, relocating her work to Joliet's Silver Cross Hospital, the hospital funded by the Protestant communities of Joliet. Saint Joseph's was the hospital funded by Joliet's Catholic community. (Hospital patients in Joliet were divided along religious lines in those years.) They settled in to an apartment in town. Happily for them, Alice became pregnant with their first child in late 1934. This ended her nursing career; women weren't allowed to work when they began showing signs of pregnancy. She stayed home at their apartment in Joliet until their child was born.

Sadly for our family, my oldest son, Herbert, suddenly passed away early in 1935 at 42 years of age. The physician at Herbert's death declaration figured the cause of Herbert's death was a heart attack. He followed my footsteps; I fear I passed this on to him. He left behind his wife, Bell, and three daughters. Charles had doted on Herbert; Herbert's death was devastating to Charles.

Charles transferred his affections to Herbert's adorable three daughters – Shirley, Mary Lou, and Doris. Doris would play all day at our house, running up and down the staircase. Charles allowed Doris to do many things our other grandchildren were not allowed to do: sneaking snacks from the kitchen, mussing up the slipcovers on the couch, playing behind the living room curtains. She certainly was a cute little girl; very much a look alike to Charles with bright blond hair and blue eyes. She occupied a piece of Charles' affections that wasn't very spacious, but nonetheless did exist. Edith and Ruth watched after the three girls when they were visiting our home on William Street.

With Herbert's passing he joined me in a place separated from Earth. That was wonderful to have his company again, one of my children to be with me. Of course I would have preferred Herbert to have more time on Earth with his wife and three children. The range of emotion felt by a mother when their child passes into a different world than they are in is extensive. Losing a child is the highest stress that a parent can experience. At least in this situation Herbert had joined me where I now was – we were in the same place once again. The natural order of life, where a parent passes away before a child, was intact for me, but not for Charles.

Another family picture was taken in 1936 in the living room of our home on William Street (see Photo 6 in the Appendix). Interestingly, again Walter is at the center of the photo. My four girls are standing or seated below Walter. They formed the core for the family, where Walter assumed the overseer role, as his place in the photo suggests. Herbert is missing from this group photo, as he had passed away the year prior to when it was photographed.

192

The painting in the background of this picture hangs in my great granddaughter's living room in present day.

Walter's mind was whirring with business ideas. He wanted to own his own business and had developed the idea of owning a chicken farm. He didn't have sufficient funds to purchase the land or chickens, and, as America was just emerging from the Great Depression, a bank loan wasn't feasible. He asked for a private loan from my son Herbert's widow, Bell. She agreed to loan Walter money to start a chicken farm on the outskirts of Joliet.

Walter and Alice moved to the farm in 1936 and began the business of raising the chickens and selling the eggs. It was hard work for both Walter and Alice, rising early in the morning to feed the over 5,000 chickens, gathering eggs, sorting & preparing the eggs for sale. Alice's life was even more challenging with another child due in the summer of 1936 and caring for her son who was only seven months old. She was exhausted at the end of her day. Alice was not used to farm work; she was a nurse by training. Walter didn't have much experience with farm work, either, although he was no stranger to hard work. He had previously helped with the small coop of chickens we had in the back yard of our house on William Street. Nothing close to the scale of the chicken farm he was now running with Alice.

Their business was running smoothly, although it was very difficult to obtain any profit from it to generate income for their family. They were literally scratching out their existence via their chicken farm. Bell panicked about the loan she had agreed to with Walter and asked for full repayment within two years. Since it was a private loan between family members, there was no schedule for payments or interest costs. In any circumstance it can be very tense, stressful times when a loan is called in, demanding repayment. Walter scrambled to repay the loan from Bell, marshaling every last cent out of the chicken farm. He did repay her, although it took him about a year after she'd asked to fully pay the money back. Both he and Alice had no luxuries, and neither did their children. Everything they made went back into their business to pay off the debt to Bell.

After experiencing business ownership with the chicken farm, Walter decided he needed another more lucrative business to support his now growing family. A new baby daughter had followed in the two successive years from the birth of their son. He now had three children and his wife to support. They continued to live on the chicken farm, with Walter seeking additional sources of revenue. The day to day operations of the farm were contracted to another family.

Because of his significant amount of experience on construction sites, Walter opened his construction business in early 1938. He catered to the wealthier families of Joliet, building elegant residential homes primarily constructed out of stone or brick. Walter had a keen eye for design – both exterior and interior. He often selected (or assisted his clients in selecting) the interior design of their living and dining rooms.

The homes Walter began building in the Joliet area featured his exacting stone masonry on both the exterior and interior. Walter did some of the stone masonry himself, focusing on detail to ensure each stone piece fitted together and the overall aesthetic of the work. He hired out carpentry, plumbing, and electrical work. He was a tough employer; he demanded a full day's work of his employees. When asked years later what he would have said if one of his workers asked for an increase in wages, he stated "I'd fire 'em!" On many points he did not negotiate.

As a six foot three tall man, with a shock of dark brown hair, Walter was an imposing figure on the work sites. He was there every morning before the sun came up, waiting for his employees to show up for the work day. He usually also closed up the job site for the day. When he returned home, after eating dinner, he would return to his work, making phone calls or lists of items to be done the next day.

Walter and Alice named their first child Charles, after my husband. Interestingly none of my other children named my grandchildren after either Charles or myself, Christina. Alice was tired with caring for three children under age two. They lived in a farm house that had no running water: no indoor bathrooms, showers, laundry facilities or drinking water. As a nurse who had been transplanted by marriage to a farm outside of Joliet, she was out of her element. After her third child, she asked Walter to move to another room to sleep, the implication being to give her a respite from having more children. He respected her request. Alice was on her own all day to run the house and care for the children.

Then three and a half years later in 1940 a surprise pregnancy occurred for Alice; another daughter arrived. Since the older three children were so close in age, they formed their own play group out of necessity. Alice had four children at home under age five in a home with few amenities. It was exhausting and difficult to wash diapers and clothes, bathe, and use the facilities where water had to be obtained from the well, outside the house – in rain, shine, or snow.

On Saturdays Alice could use the car to drive into town to go to the grocery store. That was her one day to get out of the house by herself. It was her day of relative freedom from the other six days of her life which involved cooking, cleaning, childcare, and farm chores.

Sundays the family went to the Swedish Bethel Baptist church, the same church Charles and I raised our children in. Walter and Alice's oldest three children sang together in church in front of the congregation at a young age. Their cherubic, clear voices entertained the congregation. After Charles was about nine years old he declined to participate in the singing group. Then my youngest granddaughter joined in, so that they were now an all-girl group. All four children had beautiful singing voices, fascinating the congregation.

There was love in Walter and Alice's house. They were also very busy with the demands of their lives. The love in their relationship was not as much romantic love as more of a quiet, serene love that sustains a family and its associated business. And they, like Charles and I, were reserved in demonstrating their love for their children. Alice and I were alike in the sense that we were both so busy with household demands when our children were young, we didn't have much time to talk with or focus individually on our children. We both understood our role and jobs within our families; it was part of being married to our spouses.

Walter and Charles were not the same kind of father. Walter was kind, but firm and stern with discipline. Gradually over time Walter's business success allowed him to provide extravagances for his children; all four children had their own pony, which they were free to take to whichever direction they wished. Walter was not a demonstrative person of his love; he didn't say "I love you" out loud to his children, but they knew it; it was unspoken. This way of parenting is probably attributable to his Swedish heritage of reserve and understatement. Alice had no role model for being a mother; her custodians were reserved in their interactions with her. She utilized her innate talent of nursing and caring for others in her role as a mother.

When Walter and Alice's children were very young, there was little money for anything extra, and at times even the basics of newer clothing. My daughters Edith and Ruth each took on providing school supplies and clothing for Walter and Alice's oldest two daughters. Edith and Ruth both worked downtown Joliet and lived at our family home, resulting in some discretionary monies for themselves. Walter and Alice's two older girls were so close in age they were like "Irish twins". (This is a colloquial term used to indicate that caring for children who are so close in age, less than a year and a half apart, is like having twins.) Having different personalities and interests, their growing up years were sometimes contentious. The way Edith and Ruth conducted their relationships with their little protégés also contributed to the fray.

Edith was one daughter's special aunt, Ruth another. Difficulty entered these relationships because of the differences in Edith and Ruth's individual styles. Edith spent much of her money on clothing and looking stylish, and transferred this approach to her niece she was connected with. Edith's independent, driving personality was better suited to her niece who she was charged with. She was more compliant than Walter's other daughter and went along with Edith's wishes. Ruth was more of a saver and investor. She had nice, clean clothes but not as elegant (or expensive) as Edith's choices. Ruth followed that pattern in her purchases for her designated niece, purchasing nice things but not the most luxurious or decorative. Ruth didn't have the gift of style that Edith had - some of her purchases were just not as desirable. Walter's girls had to learn to live with this difference of focus. Edith and Ruth did provide them with luxuries their parents didn't, such as matching clothing or a dressy winter coat.

One of the traditions Edith and Ruth established was to take their little charges to the Marshall Field's store downtown Chicago. (A fellow Joliet resident was Marshall Field's founder, Harlow Higinbotham, who had overseen the Chicago World's Fair). They would ride the train from Joliet station to Chicago. From there they would walk to the store on State Street, with its grand windows and cavernous floor space. For a special treat they would go to lunch at the Walnut Room, so named because of the walnut wood that lines the walls. (The dining area first opened in 1907). It was an opportunity for my young granddaughters to show their good manners in public. The table had crisp white linens and a full service of silverware. This was sometimes challenging for the young girls. They might not prefer what Edith and Ruth had ordered for them to eat. One of my granddaughters would go along with whatever Edith had set out for them. The other, Ruth's charge, would find ways to dispose of food she didn't like. (Oh how the wait staff's work was complicated by the napkin containing the offending items.) My granddaughter held fast to her belief in what she would eat, and wouldn't give in to what Edith had asked her to do.

Walter's business venture of building upper end homes and businesses in Joliet was thriving, despite the financial challenges the chicken farm had presented. His clients included many doctors and lawyers, the upper echelons of Joliet society. He was the foreman, architect, and designer for their residences. Stone was a central focus of his buildings, prominent in the fireplaces, interior walls and exteriors. He also constructed many brick houses, which looked neat, tidy and orderly, mirroring the way he ran his business. He had a penchant for accuracy and neatness. All of these factors contributed to his establishing an excellent reputation in the Joliet building community.

Walter's financial success began to make life more comfortable for his family. The challenge was the income varied over the year, as different projects finished at different times, thus the payments were somewhat unpredictable. Alice had to budget (just as I did) to not spend everything in the "up" months of income, and save some for the lighter income months. A special event occurred when she would take all four children up to Chicago for the day, riding the train in the morning and back in the early evening. They went to Michigan Avenue, looking at the tall buildings and shopping in the department stores. Marshall Field's, with its dark green logo, was a particular favorite. Walter took them to White Sox baseball games at Comiskey Park.

Walter again experienced a business setback on one particular construction deal. A client, for whom he was building an extensively large residence, kept changing the building requirements, after the initial bid and agreement had been made. Financially it had become a runaway train. The client verbally promised to pay, and Walter tried to keep up with the increasing work requests. After months of the costs escalating dramatically upward, Walter had to make a tough call of whether to continue the project. He was paying the subcontractors out of his pocket, while the client was not making payments for work completed. He finished the home, but at a great loss to his company.

Instead of foisting the financial burden onto his subcontractors, he chose to pay them completely for the work they had performed. This decision caused a significant change in his personal life. He had to sell his family's home and land near Plainfield, and moved to a much older home farther out of Joliet. Their recreation times were cut short, due to the sale of their vacation home on Lake Delavan in Southern Wisconsin. His children weren't aware that the sour business deal was why they had to move so suddenly to another home. Walter had made his decision how he and his family would adjust to the situation and navigated through it.

I felt so proud watching him going through that difficult time in giving up material items he had worked so hard for. He acted honorably, making the situation right according to his own internal compass, which directed him to do much more than others in the same situation might have. Walter put down his pride and did not become self-centered, focused only on his own financial status. He cleaned his financial house, making good on the cost of the work the subcontractors performed and accepting the loss entirely himself.

Not that he was happy about this situation. It was a rough time for him to persevere through. But he did it and kept his head held high. His decision had greatly affected his family's life style and position in the Joliet community.

After this great setback, Walter slowly and steadily continued to progress back up the ladder of the business world. He approached business as he did his brick laying and stone masonry; slow and steady. Lift one, trowel, place the stone, then clean the excess. Keep repeating the process until the wall is finished. That approach served Walter well in his business life: keep repeating until finished. He had an excellent reputation in Joliet and businessmen respected him.

New Business

With the advent of the more reliable automobile for more of the population in the late 1940's, Americans became more mobile than ever. Walter saw an opportunity to open another business, capitalizing on the American vacation and travelling lifestyle. He literally built a motel, with the assistance of many laborers. Walter's stone masonry skills came back into use, where he laid limestone for parts of the building. The limestone he had worked with most of his life was a significant part of the entryway and walls of the motel.

In Joliet there is a street, two over from our family home on William Street, called Manor Street. Walter incorporated the name into the businesses he would run for the next forty years.

The motel, the Manor Motel, became a fixture on I-55, a major north south route between Chicago and downstate Illinois. It is located on the historic Route 66, one of the first highways in the United States, which was established in November of 1926. All totaled the route covered almost 2,500 miles. Originally it ran from Chicago to Los Angeles, California. By this time Walter's three oldest children were teenagers. His son, Charles, helped out by maintaining the grounds of the property and farm chores with the tractor. His two older girls helped in the motel office, checking in guests.

He also 'took in' his younger brother, Burt, my youngest son. Burt was married, in his forties, without a specific purpose or trade. Walter let him live in the duplex he'd built behind the motel for the motel management and handed some of the motel management duties to Burt and his wife. Burt's personality did not fit into typical society. Walter sheltered him, giving Burt a safe place to live and contribute. Walter was like a social service agency that didn't exist at that time in America. He helped others by providing them work and a place to live. Sometimes Walter was generous to a fault;

he gave Burt many opportunities and chances that Burt received because Walter was his brother. Walter sometimes had a blind spot for actions our family members made that he wouldn't have tolerated in an unrelated person. I think he wanted to believe the best in people, especially if they were related to us. It was truly a family business, with Walter at the helm.

Additional business opportunity came from the overnight travelers and guests at the motel indicating they wanted a good restaurant to eat dinner or breakfast before they resumed their journey. Thus Walter investigated opening a restaurant in 1953. He constructed this building across Route 6 from his motel, and called it the Manor Inn. His hard work grew this business into an icon for miles around. Most travelers on I-55 knew of the Manor Inn and the excellent food and service.

Walter insisted on quality and high standards for the services his businesses provided, and also for those who worked for him. This was learned from his Swedish heritage. He expected a full day's work for a full day's pay. If an employee was found to be not working or not working hard enough, they were let go. He didn't tolerate employees who weren't diligent workers. On the other hand, he was good to his employees. He paid them at competitive rates, and provided holiday gifts and remembrances to them. If he heard an employee's child was ill or needed help, he would slip a bonus amount of money into their paycheck. He didn't ask for or even want public recognition for his acts of kindness. He went on in his quiet, persistent manner, preferring to stay out of the public eye.

In a version of his own personal society aid, at the back of the restaurant, Walter authorized the cooks to provide hot coffee and toast to any person who was unable to pay for food. He would feed a homeless person a meal in exchange for a work task, such as sweeping or mopping the floor. He was a tough boss, to be sure, but he was fair.

My husband Charles lived a long life, and died in March, 1955, in our home. Our daughters Ruth and Edith were by his bedside. They had cared for him all of the years since I had left Earth – including the tasks of grocery shopping, laundry, meal preparation, house cleaning, and yard maintenance. They were both devoted to their father, although most of the devotion was demanded by Charles.

Walter had moved into becoming the central figure in our family's life. He felt it was important for family to be together- even if not everyone was getting along. He encouraged, prodded, and provided for family get togethers, particularly on holidays or special events such as Ruth's eightieth birthday party. Unannounced he would send money for relatives to travel to where the gathering was, which was most often in Joliet. He was an organizer, a person who pulled people together. If the participants weren't too excited about being there, he would take them aside and cajole them into participating with the family group. Sometimes the money he sent wasn't used for the purpose he'd intended. He didn't confront the relative about it. He just learned from the experience and adjusted his actions at a later time.

From the motel business, Walter and Alice travelled to Quality Inn conventions which were held at various locations in the United States. In 1962 the yearly convention coincided with the World's Fair being held in Seattle. A landmark built for the Fair was the Space Needle, a 605 feet high structure that looks like what most people would describe as a space saucer on a stick. The top portion of the building rotates around approximately every hour – providing diners at the restaurant an ever changing view. It was, and is, a unique building and setting. During Walter and Alice's trip to Seattle, where they had driven in their car the two thousand miles, they visited the restaurant and saw the Seattle skyline. My daughters Edith and Ruth had also come out to Seattle specifically for the World's Fair. This was a trip of independence for them; they were two women who struck out on the cross-country trip on their own. They took the train, their journey stretching over five days. They also went up in the Space Needle to the observation deck. As Edith and Ruth were cost conscious, they chose not to spend their money on a meal at the restaurant.

Walter's wife Alice died at age 53, from an apparent heart attack. (Years later it was learned that it was a massive stroke that killed her, resulting from a blood clot in her brain). He was saddened by her death. She had been with him through difficult times and was just now enjoying some of the benefits of all the hard work they'd completed. Now alone, he moved into an apartment over the lobby of his restaurant. The family home where their children had finished their high school years was too big for just him, and he didn't want to be reminded every day of the exact spot where Alice had passed away.

This began a new chapter in his life: eligible bachelor. He was a successful businessman and therefore offered financial security to a potential wife or girlfriend. In his grief, dealing with Alice's death, he travelled the world extensively with the motel convention tours, which took him to places such as Hong Kong and Portugal. He went to many different geographic regions that I couldn't imagine travelling to. He was by far the most well-traveled of anyone in our family.

Walter and Alice's four children produced twelve grandchildren, six boys and six girls. Alice was only alive to see the first four born; the remaining eight were born after she had passed away.

Walter was generous to children, including his own and his grandchildren. He may have been compensating somewhat for his own youth, where he had nothing extra and received little if any positive reinforcement from his father, my husband Charles. Walter made a habit of giving his grandchildren ten dollars each on their birthdays. That was an extravagant sum for a child in the 1950's, 1960's and later the 1970's!

Given that he was extremely busy with his work during the years his children grew up, Walter wasn't a father who was present all the time. He, however, was a superb grandfather. His business' demands were such that he had more free time to go on excursions to Chicago and around the Midwest. He also made a point to travel to see his children and grandchildren who didn't live nearby.

Those heyday years of the 1970's were when Walter's businesses of the restaurant, motel, and new liquor store were running at full tilt. Walter had high standards for how his business was run — cleanliness, high quality, and customer service. He set an example for people miles and miles around as a tough, but fair and kind hearted employer.

Favorites

The habit of 'playing favorites' was passed on from Charles to Walter. Walter appreciated certain traits in people that he felt aligned with his personality. He admired adventurous, inquisitive, intelligent people are tried to surround himself with those types of people. This selection process even applied to his grandchildren (my great-great grandchildren). The situation really wasn't fair, but it was understood across his family how Walter felt about each person. I would have advised Walter to let his grandchildren know they were all loved in an equal manner. Sometimes specific children's personalities are more pleasing or suitable to older relatives. But imparting an adult's inequities of feeling to children isn't a healthy feeling for them. Adults should have the self-restraint and awareness of others' feelings to not show favoritism. However, in my husband Charles' case, he just simply couldn't do that – he did let his preferences be obvious, speaking them aloud frequently.

Nonetheless, in spite of my feelings on this topic, Walter also did have his favorites in his grandchildren: a grandson, who coincidentally resembles my husband Charles (blond, tall), and a granddaughter, Julia (who more resembles me – darker hair and features). Julia has the family facial feature of the "Anderson eyebrows". These are a natural eyebrow shape that resembles an upside down V – pointy in the middle, dramatic slants down on either side. They present an imposing look to others, especially when scrunched together in concern.

Walter established a tradition when he took Julia to the Space Needle in Seattle for dinner on her fifth birthday. He loved to take people out for dinner, enjoying especially seeing children have some special treats. The first was a "Shirley Temple" a beverage named after the actress from the 1930's. This consisted of grenadine (cherry) syrup and Seven Up (a lemon lime flavored carbonated soda). It was served with a maraschino cherry on a plastic spear (like those served with grownups' drinks). For the children, this drink was extra special because it was something they only drank when Grandpa had taken them out. They knew it cost more than a 'regular' drink of milk or water, and realized Grandpa was doing something nice for them.

At the end of the meal Walter always suggested the children order ice cream for dessert. Sometimes the children were so full from dinner, it was difficult to eat the ice cream. Most often the dessert was a special treat, as, again, their parents wouldn't have suggested dessert, due to the additional cost. Walter just wanted them to enjoy the meal and have a special treat at the end of the meal. He didn't measure the cost of the dessert; for him the enjoyment of seeing the children's faces was a reward.

Walter appreciated the spark in Julia. She was inquisitive even as a small child – she wanted to understand and see the world around her. She loved being around her grandfather Walter. She would sit in his store with him for hours, helping with the customers, putting items in bags, organizing shelves. Julia got so much enjoyment from 'helping' Grandpa in his store. She was fascinated by the cash register, counting money at the end of the day, preparing the store for the next business day.

Oh how fun it was to order in their meal from Grandpa's restaurant next door. It was so exciting to Julia as an eight year old to be able to order whatever she wanted from the café menu – a hamburger, a melted cheese sandwich, or a French Dip. She felt so grownup and responsible when she 'signed' the check, writing her name in cursive letters on the green lined order check. Since my son Walter owned the restaurant, the 'check' was written off into the restaurant's receipts. Probably not the best business lesson that she didn't have to pay for the meal – but it was a thrill for an eight year old for her signature to be requested on a check!

During summer visits, Julia would love to sit with Walter in the liquor store while he tended the store. It was all so fascinating to Julia – the cash register, the plastic numbers that displayed the cost of a particular item, the store room of inventory. Also at Julia's eye level was the candy shelf – a treasure trove for an eight year old. Walter allowed her to have the candy – although Julia rarely asked for it. It didn't occur to Julia to eat something without asking or hide some of the candy. It was enough for Julia to know that shelf full of candy was right there, within her reach.

She loved helping put the items their brown paper bags. Being eight years old, Julia had a vague notion of what alcohol was. To her it was just something grownups wanted. She didn't understand why they wanted it or what it offered them. It never occurred to her to open one of the bottles and drink some of the liquid contained inside. The cash register was also an item of fascination – with its LED light displaying the cost and seemingly endless buttons to push. That was advanced technology in 1973.

On one hot summer day that year, the twelve cousins (Walter's grandchildren) were hanging around together as a small herd of children. They went to the swimming pool at the motel, where they swam until they tired. Walter had permitted the local children access to the swimming pool. It was a gathering place for the area's children on the hot Illinois summer days. His grandchildren visited the vending machines located near the pool, to buy a soda and a candy bar, with the change their Grandpa Walter had given them. Once they'd made their selection, they would pull hard on the metal rod that would release the selected candy from the machine. What a treat for them to select items of their choosing from the vending machines!

After showering and getting dressed again in rooms of the motel checked out to them, the herd of children wandered over across Route 6 to the restaurant. The coffee shop was open fourteen hours a day; the dining room was open at dinner time and lunch only on the weekends. The kids went into the darkened dining room, where there was an adjoining bar. It was distinctively decorated, the dark wood paneling providing an enveloping, familiar feeling. Since neither the bar nor the dining room was open for business in the middle of the afternoon, no staff was present or lights on.

One of the cousins got the idea to go behind the bar (which they were instructed not to do) and start playing with all the colorful liquids and devices. This was a fascinating place in the world to the children. The hand held soda machine squirted out five different kinds of soda, depending on which color button was pushed. The bottles of liquor lined up underneath the bar – whiskeys, vodkas, gins, vermouths - with the tops on them that allowed the liquid inside to flow out in a steady, even stream. There were lots of colors there too: amber brown, white, yellow, bright red. They offered a creative challenge to see the colors swirling together in a glass.

The children added the extra touches to their creations from the condiment tray – the green olives with the red pimento inside, the orange and lemon slices that would sit so nicely on the side of the glass or the juice squeezed into the glass' liquid and then dropped in. There were little plastic spears that looked like a pirate's sword and used to spear olives or fruit. Grandpa's bar even had the mini-paper umbrellas to provide a tropical feel for the drink.

This activity was approached all in fun. The cousins were pretending customers were sitting on the other side of the bar. They chatted with their imaginary customers, asking how their day was, what the news was at their workplace, if they'd like another beverage. They took the glasses off the counter, poured out the contents, and turned them upside down on the bristly, soapy machine that washed the glasses. With their foot on the floor pedal to activate the washing, the sudsy soap and the warm water came squirting out into the upside down glass, swirling and whirling to clean its target.

All of this buzzing activity came to a screeching halt when someone entered the heavy glass doors to the bar area. It was Walter – who called out 'who's there?'

The grandchildren froze for a second – they were unsure of what to do with their activities being discovered. Then they ran in panic towards the restrooms, which were completely in darkness due to no openings for natural light to enter. It was scary for children to be in a windowless, dark room. They waited in the darkness, breathing quietly so as not to be discovered. For them it would have been far scarier to face their Grandpa Walter when he discovered they'd been playing around with all the expensive liquor from his bar!

The children waited in the dark bathroom until their Grandpa had left – like a bear who had come to see what was going on, and seeing nothing in particular, wandered off to complete some other task. To them it seemed like forever. They cautiously peered out to see if the 'coast was clear'. The afternoon bartender was just coming in for his shift. He wordlessly helped the children clean up the glasses and napkins.

Interestingly it never occurred to the children to try and drink any of the liquor they'd poured. They knew it was alright to drink the soda, but the liquor was off limits. Their game was a quite expensive one; they had no understanding of how much money they were pouring out.

Walter didn't get angry about the money – in many respects he thought it humorous. He was too busy with other demands of his businesses to worry about this incident. He didn't get too excited about events when the grandchildren were doing things they shouldn't have; he didn't overreact. He just made sure they knew that might not have been the best thing to do and then moved on.

Around this time Julia, as an eight and nine year old girl, loved reading – Pippi Longstocking by the Swedish author Astrid Lindgren was a particular favorite. She loved the thought of an independent, spunky girl who made her own decisions and wasn't afraid of anything. On this summer visit to Joliet, she went with her cousins to see the movie adaption movie of the book.

In the mid 1970's, big things were happening in America that would greatly affect my future descendants. In 1975 a Federal Law was enacted, called IDEA, which governs all special education services for children in the United States. It provides for an "appropriate" education for all children, regardless of their disability level. Section 504, a civil rights statue, requires that schools not discriminate against children with disabilities and provide them with reasonable accommodations in the school environment. These laws guaranteed, at least legally, a place in the public school systems for children with disabilities. It gave them the chance to attend school, with appropriate supports, and be able to get out with others in the community - socialization.

Walter was generous to many people, holding huge banquet parties in his restaurant's large room. Being in the restaurant business allowed Walter access to the cooking staff of his kitchen, who prepared the tables full of food for Walter's guests. He meticulously planned the meals, writing down on yellow legal lined paper the layout and diagram of which food dishes would go where. Two ten foot long tables were full of a variety of food for his guests.

The food offered extravagances to his guests of family and friends. There was the huge bowlful of large shrimp, which had been flown in from the East Coast. For the Midwest, this was truly a luxury. He served many of our Swedish heritage foods – limpa bread, meatballs, ham, rice pudding, oyster casserole/stew, pickled or creamed herring and stuffed dates. Not everyone who attended the gatherings ate all of these items, but he thought them important enough to serve.

One of the biggest parties of the year was held on Christmas Eve. Walter's restaurant closed earlier than usual on that one night of the year, and then the banquet room in the dining room was opened for family and friends. He paid his wait and kitchen staff extra for working on the holiday. Everyone seemed to enjoy these parties, where the long buffet tables were laid out with a large variety of foods including ham, shrimp, prime rib, vegetables, desserts, breads. Since the party was held in his restaurant, he could direct what dishes were prepared and served. The resources of the bar were there, too, with two bartenders hired for the night. The drinks were flowing; the food was plentiful.

The children had a great time at these events too, where their parents made sure they were dressed up sufficiently to attend the event. Walter expected the boys to have ties on, and the girls wear dresses. The 'pack' of his twelve grandchildren would prepare a Christmas play and perform their enactment for the attendees.

One of the special items on the menu for the Christmas Eve party was an alcoholic beverage called a Brandy Alexander. As per the name, brandy is a key component of the mixture. That is blended with vanilla ice cream and crème de cocoa, then served chilled. Given the two alcohols included in this beverage, it was for adults only. The kids thought it a bit of a game to try to get an adult to give them a taste or one of the Brandy Alexanders. Amazingly, no adult did give one of Walter's grandchildren even a taste of these alcoholic beverages, despite the children's pleadings and best efforts. Maybe they tasted so good the adults didn't want to share!?! The children were prepared milkshakes, with the vanilla ice cream.

Julia

Over the years Walter had made it a point to be in attendance for milestones in his granddaughter Julia's life, including her high school graduation. He was an important figure in her life, providing guidance from a distance, at times thousands of miles. He would drive over two hundred miles to the university she attended to take Julia out to dinner or to the football game. On some of these occasions, he would press some money into her hand, saying it was for spending money. Walter's thoughtfulness meant a lot to Julia; she didn't have any extra money to spend on food or entertainment. Her eyes welled up with tears – she really didn't want to depend on another person's 'charity' and had (as she does now) a difficult time accepting assistance. On the other hand she knew Walter gave the money freely and wanted her to have it. The money was nice to have as "spending money" during her school week, as her student loans were accumulating in her later years of college. She worked both during the school year and each summer to earn more money to pay for college tuition, with not much left over for anything extra.

Julia lived in downtown Chicago for two years following her college graduation. Walter was advancing in years; he was over eighty at this time. He would drive up to Chicago to meet Julia for dinner. This may not sound out of the ordinary, but by this point Walter's eyesight was not what it had been. On a few earlier occasions he had run into one of the stone driveway markers at the edge of his driveway. He knew well of the marker's existence, having literally built it there himself. He simply had not seen it. He wasn't ready to relinquish his driving license and the associated independence, however he probably should have done so to protect other drivers. He had made up his mind he was going to visit Julia in Chicago, and somehow safely transported himself on the busy freeway there and back.

On one occasion, Walter had somehow navigated Interstate-55 (known as the Stevenson Expressway) Chicago freeway traffic and was characteristically early to see Julia that day. Walter made it a point to be at least thirty minutes early to all appointments, calling it "Lombardi time", after the Green Bay Packers football coach Vince Lombardi (1959 – 1967 seasons). Lombardi had insisted his team be ready early for their time commitments. Walter adopted this idea into his own life, and subsequently all the others around him who went places with him. Being thirty minutes early was a challenge for many of his grandchildren, especially on days they would drive down to the University of Illinois football games. This meant waking up extra minutes early on a Saturday, when his high school and college age grandchildren would struggle to keep up with him.

That day Julia had walked home the mile or so from her workplace on the Chicago River to find Walter standing on the front stoop of her third floor, walkup apartment building on Delaware street. He was unable to ascend the three flights of stairs to her apartment, so he waited at the doorstep. He had stood there for over forty five minutes, awaiting Julia's arrival. (He was not known for being patient.) Seeing her grandfather standing on the doorstep, waiting for her to arrive, touched Julia's heart. She appreciated his effort to see her and be present in her life.

Julia still had a longing to live back in Seattle, where she had lived for a total of ten years during her growing up years. She decided to move back to the Seattle area when she was twenty three years old. She packed up her burgundy Ford Escort to drive out Interstate 90 to Seattle alone. Walter came up to Chicago and literally followed her car until near Minneapolis, where they parted ways on the roadway. He had wanted her to stay in Chicago, so that they could see each other more frequently. Walter didn't try to guilt her into staying or make disparaging comments about her choice; he saw her off on the next phase of her life. He respected Julia's decision, but was still watchful and concerned for her future.

Julia's Ford Escort delivered her to Seattle in October of 1989. She continued carving out her adult life, now based in Seattle. She was focused on her career and finishing her graduate school degree. During one of her classes, she saw a man she'd not seen before seated across the aisle from her. She looked over and surveyed this new person. As for dating prospects one of the first criteria was that the man be tall – Julia, at five feet ten inches, had inherited much of Walter's height. This new man had an intriguing attitude about him. His motorcycle helmet was sitting at his feet, his leather motorcycle jacket slung across the back of the chair. Just who was this person, anyway, a fellow student in the MBA program?

The intrigue would continue for two and half years, as Julia could never think of any words to say to this man – she was speechless. Finally she saw him in one of the last classes she would take before graduating in the spring of 1993. The man and Julia happened to meet in the hallway before class. Julia worked up her courage to comment on something they were both looking at posted on the wall.

The man's name was Bill – they began to talk easily before and after class. One night after class they went together to a local bar and had some dinner. Julia was in a business suit, having arrived at school straight from her work day. They played pool and ate dinner. I cringed as I saw her laying across the pool table in her nice work suit, aiming a shot for a corner pocket. Nothing about this situation was something Charles and I would have permitted for one of our daughters or, in this case, our great- granddaughter.

Graduation day came in mid-June of 1993. Bill, Julia, and several other of their classmates sat together in the large stadium during the ceremony. It was kind of humorous to watch women classmates vie for a seat next to Bill. He was loving the attention of these young women, knowing there was a competition amongst them to sit next to him. Julia played the situation coolly, figuring if

Bill wanted her to sit next to him he'd find a way to make that happen. He did.

Walter made the effort, at eighty eight years old, to attend Julia's graduation. His youngest daughter, my youngest grandchild, had driven him out to Seattle from Chicago for the event. He wanted to be there to show his support of Julia. His age and mobility didn't permit him to walk into the large stadium with the narrow stairways, and he remained in his hotel room for the actual graduation ceremony. As was his custom, he hosted a big gathering of family for a dinner at an elegant restaurant. He accepted Julia's request of inviting Bill to attend, where Walter met Bill for the first time.

Bill and Julia went on to date for about a year when they had flown back to Chicago to visit with Walter in the summer of 1994. Julia was thinking this would be a great opportunity for her grandfather to get to know more about Bill. As they walked into to Walter's home, he was sitting at his kitchen table, surveying the landscape his daytime caregiver had laid out for their lunchtime meal. At this stage of his life he needed someone to be at home with him during the long daytime hours that his family members were away from their homes. Two of his children were also his neighbors – one next door, another across the street. They worked at jobs in Chicago during the daytimes, rising early each morning to catch the 6am Metra train to downtown Chicago. The caregiver ensured Walter ate lunch, took his medication for high blood pressure (inherited from me), and rested sufficiently.

During their stay at Walter's, Bill and Julia helped him with household tasks that had yet to find an owner. Bill, being adept at fixing and repairing all sorts of items, addressed a few things that needed attention: the door to the garage needed adjustment, the washing machine needed a hose repaired. He also helped Walter with his personal care, shaving Walter's face and hoping fervently not to nick his skin with the razor. He was nervous that he would accidentally nick Walter's face and anger him. It was the first time in Bill's life he had helped another person take care of their bathing and personal care needs. The action was out of his comfort zone, but he surged forward.

The activity went fairly smoothly, resulting in Walter's whisker stubble removed. Walter was such a proud man, he didn't like others to help him. He wanted to do the tasks himself. On this occasion he allowed his guard to drop; he knew he needed assistance with this task. His hand wasn't steady enough with the shaver to avoid nicking his face or neck. Walter wouldn't say this aloud, but he trusted Bill. He liked having a man around his home and a fresh perspective to discuss politics or the latest sports game with.

Bill and Walter would sit in front of Walter's television, in two Lazy Boy chairs, watching the beloved Chicago White Sox's baseball games. Julia brought in snacks – peanuts, cheese and crackers – and left them on the table between the chairs. She retreated to the kitchen; the television room was a man's domain for the time being. Walter and Bill watched TV and conversed about what was happening. These times were theirs alone. Walter would comment every so often on the game as to who was doing what or if an error was made. Bill, who had never watched sports previously in his life, didn't necessarily know what Walter was indicating. Towards the start of these sports watching episodes, Bill mostly just agreed with Walter's comments. After a few days, he had learned some to offer comments and suggestions of his own. Walter loved that; he loved conversing on an intellectual level with this younger man Julia had brought to his home.

At one point Julia and Walter were sitting around the kitchen table talking. Julia asked her grandfather, whom she had nicknamed "Gramps", what he thought about Bill. Bill, as a Roman Catholic, practices a different religion than our family. I recalled that my husband Charles had denied our daughter Ruth from even dating a

Catholic man, as his family back in Sweden had experienced religious persecution in the seventeen hundreds from Catholics. Walter put his index finger on his thumb, making a round circle with his fingers. This signified "OK" – he was indicating his approval of Bill as a spouse to Julia. That was what she needed to know from Walter. Walter didn't make an issue of the difference in their religions. He liked and trusted Bill as a person. He chose to not proliferate views from earlier generations and times.

Julia is a person who meticulously plans – dates, timing, activities. Her plans had included a list of names that she was considering for any future children she might have, tucked in her daytime organizer, hidden auspiciously in the reference section. She didn't want anyone else to read this piece of paper with her thoughts written on it. First on her list was the name Anna Christina for a first born daughter. She chose this name from my first name, Christina, and Anna being my daughter Edith's middle name. I was pleased with the possibility of having a great-great grandchild named after me and honored that I had been remembered three generations later. Julia wasn't planning on following the pattern Charles & I had of giving our children American names. She wanted her children's names to remember and honor our Swedish origins.

Bill and Julia were married in the late summer of 1995, after two years of dating. Walter wasn't able, due to his health status at age ninety two, to make the 2,000 mile trip to Seattle for the wedding. Julia understood that, although she so wanted to share this special time in her life with her grandfather. He had been there for many other important events in Julia's life. He would have to miss being there in person for this one.

Bill and Julia had a big, church wedding at St. Joseph's Catholic Church on Seattle's Capitol Hill. This church is in an area of Seattle referred to as "Catholicville" as for the past hundred years, a great number of St. Joseph's parishioners lived within walking distance of their church. At their wedding both a Catholic priest and a Presbyterian minister officiated. It was a joining of their lives and two religions in the ceremony.

Their wedding reception was at the Swedish Cultural Center (formerly the "Swedish Club") on Seattle's Lake Union. This was Julia's nod to her cultural heritage of our family's Swedish origin. The Center was established in 1892 (the year my first son, Herbert, was born) by Swedes in Seattle, including Nels Nelson (of Fredrick & Nelson, the Seattle retail business later bought out by Marshall Fields of Chicago) and John Nordstrom (of the department store Nordstrom's). Their wedding guests were offered some of the traditional Swedish foods: meatballs, fish, and ligonberries. The food was laid out on a long, buffet table, reminiscent of those that Walter had planned so many times.

Julia and Bill had conversations prior to their marriage regarding having children and how many they might want to have. This was astounding to me; in my day we women had little choice in the matter of how many children we would have. It was primarily the husband in a marriage that decided how much to pursue having children. We women were mostly left to go along with whatever path our husbands decided. In my lifetime if a woman wasn't able to produce a child, where they would not be looked upon unfavorably (most often) by their husband and/or society. It was thought to be the woman's 'fault' if a couple was unable to conceive a child. This was a holdover idea from times where having sons meant your family had a greater chance for survival. By 1995 it was medically well known that inability to conceive a child could result from either (or both) of the partners in the couple.

Julia and Bill discussed having several children and what the timing might be. In the 1990's the average age of a first time mother in the United States was about twenty five. Julia was five years older than that "average" age when she and Bill were married. Julia was aware that as a woman ages the chances for conceiving a child decrease, even more so rapidly after age thirty five. They decided to try to have children not long after they were married, so that Julia's age would not present a greater issue in conceiving a child.

Great-Great New Life

My great-great granddaughter's story begins long before she took her first breath of air on Earth. It's amazing to me how much information is now available to parents about their children, even while unborn. Julia knew when she was pregnant for the first time within a few weeks of conception. Many women in the 1990's wanting to become pregnant would be aware of the best times for them to become pregnant with all the information modern medicine had discovered and published. In my day most often women weren't optimizing the timing to become pregnant. More likely we were hoping for not too many pregnancies close together.

One step towards Bill and Julia's dream of a child was realized in the fall of 1996 by a doctor's visit confirming Julia's pregnancy. Julia went home to tell Bill the news; they were elated. Both were ready to be parents and so wanted this child. Julia was focused on having a healthy child. All indicating factors were positive. There was no known family history of miscarriage or children's health issues. Every expectation was that this pregnancy would be a typical one, with a typical birth.

Julia followed the 'rules' and guidance for pre-pregnancy and during pregnancy. She read the "pregnancy books", took the recommended vitamins, decaffeinated, never drank alcohol – everything to have the best possible health for the baby. The amount of recommendations and guidelines for a pregnant woman was astounding. Just one generation earlier, in the 1960's, one of my granddaughters, who was a nurse, was expecting a baby. Her obstetrician recommended expectant mothers drink beer to calm themselves. Medical recommendations for pregnant mothers had certainly changed.

During the times of my pregnancies, the late 1800's through the early 1900's, we often didn't confirm our pregnancy until our bellies bulged carrying a baby. This would have been in the fourth or fifth month of pregnancy. Back then mothers didn't get too attached to a specific pregnancy and sometimes even to our infants, because of the frequency of miscarriage and infant mortality. As late as 1911, there were 135 infant deaths of 1,000 live births in the United States. We just couldn't let ourselves get too focused on one child, because of the likelihood they might not survive childhood.

After that initial month of elation and excitement of pregnancy, scraps of information began to flow in regarding Julia and Bill's baby's status. The typical tests run in the 1990's in the United States included the "triple screen", a blood test which indicated a higher risk for specific birth defects in the fetus. The results came back of an elevated risk of neural tube defects in their baby. That didn't seem to be a huge concern, as the doctor explained that there are some false positives with this test, and the percentages are small (less than 3%) for children born with the condition associated with the indicated elevated risk factor. The test was repeated; this time the results showed an increased risk for Down's syndrome (a genetic chromosomal condition).

The term "birth defect" has been in use for many decades in medical vernacular, established in the early 1900's. It is, in present day, an archaic term, more current is the term "congenital abnormality". The term "defect" implies that something isn't flawless, that somehow a standard of measurement is not being met. Many, many, probably most, people on the Earth have some sort of 'defect' – maybe their feet are two shoe sizes different or maybe they have a 'lazy eye' which wanders off of center. Or maybe a person isn't socially adept. "Defect" seems too strong of a word for those situations – although they all could be differences among people as individuals. Two to three percent of all people born have one or more of the known 3,000 congenital abnormalities that are known in the present day. People are not 'defective' – their physical selves possess a variation from what is the physical makeup of the majority of people.

With the elevated results of the second blood test, Julia was referred to get a higher resolution ultrasound than could be performed in an obstetrician's office. This was to be conducted at Swedish Hospital in Seattle, the hospital in the area at the time that had this technology. This hospital was known as Svenska Lasarettet when it opened for operation in 1910 with twenty four beds, intending to provide health care for Seattle's Swedish residents. Dr. Nils Johanson convinced other Swedish-American immigrants to fund the opening of the hospital, comprised of members of the Swedish Club (presently referred to as the Swedish Cultural Center, where Bill and Julia had hosted their wedding reception). Almost ninety years later these Swedes' actions would help my great-granddaughter and her family. Two years after opening, in 1912, the hospital moved to a new location on Summit and Columbia streets in Seattle's First Hill neighborhood, where it remains. First Hill makes up one of the seven Hills in Seattle; it's nickname is "Pill Hill" referring to all the medical facilities on the hill.

In 1880, only 190 people of Scandinavian decent lived in all of King County (where Seattle is located). The subsequent immigration of Swedes, Norwegians, and Finns to Seattle in the late 1800's increased this number to around 8,000 by 1910. By then, on the entire West Coast (including the cities of Los Angeles, San Francisco and Portland), these three countries were represented by 100,000 people. Many came to Seattle for the similarities to our homeland, such as the lumber and fishing industries. The difficult economy experienced in Chicago and other industrial cities in America of the late 1800's contributed to a migration West, when people again were in search of work and a better life. As in Chicago, Swedes would make their imprint on Seattle lasting for generations to come.

Julia's belly was slightly 'fluttery' on the rainy, Cat-in-the-Hat fall day in 1996 – she was nervous about the potential risks to her baby that might be identified. This would be the first time she walked into a hospital as an adult patient. The ultrasound results yielded three indications of the baby's status. The first was that the baby was female. The next showed a slight decrease in blood flow to the baby in utereo. The third indicator was the measurements of the baby's limbs and head circumference. The measurements estimated the baby's gestation age two weeks younger than previously thought, if conception had occurred on the dates Julia had provided of her monthly cycle.

In the discussion room following the ultrasound, the medical team explained the two potential medically impacting indicators and summarized the results of the ultrasound just conducted. No alarm bells were sounded as a cause for concern for the baby's health. The two indicators were explained as likely the baby's position at the time the ultrasound was conducted and that the due date had probably been miscalculated, due to menstruation cycle inaccuracy. It seemed a rational conclusion to the medical team to adjust the baby's due date, based on the measurements of gestation found during the ultrasound test.

The information was seeping into Julia's brain as she sought to understand what she was hearing and what it might mean to the baby in her womb. She fought the words being presented to her. She believed in her heart the conception timing of the baby was correct based on her cycle dates. The medical team, at this point who was led by a genetic counselor, interrupted Julia's thought stream. She advised Julia that if she did wish to terminate this pregnancy that she needed to do so within one and a half weeks. Julia's thoughts were thrown back into a pool of mire trying to absorb and process this new option and piece of information. The closing of the day presented much different options and information than the start had promised. Julia was confronted with making life changing decisions for her baby, within the timeframe of a few days.

I observed, tense from what was transpiring on the Swedish Hospital campus that afternoon in November. The detailed information made available regarding the baby's status was of concern. The second point of my concern was that the medical team deemed it important to mention the option of not delivering the baby. I waited in anticipation of what Julia might say – how she would react – and trusted in her ability to think through the situation she found herself in. Those of us looking on to this situation knew what the baby's status was, although we could only watch what was transpiring.

After thinking over the options with the information available, Julia responded to the suggestion of termination of the pregnancy with dogged determination. She reasoned the medical team hadn't presented any significant quantity of risk that the baby's health could be compromised; the percentages of any impact that *might* affect the baby were quite small (less than five percent). Even if the baby had a 'birth defect', the possibility of which was pushed to the far reaches of Julia's mind, she chose to continue. She was going to move forward with the pregnancy and life, creating the best possible environment for this new child. Julia blocked out the possibility of her baby having a serious issue at birth, thinking positively and pushing her fears, concern, and worry aside. She knew their baby would have a loving home provided for her in their home.

At home that evening, Julia mentioned to Bill the medical team had offered the option to terminate the pregnancy. Even the suggestion of termination rattled their thoughts and hopes for their baby. They hadn't considered the possibility of terminating the pregnancy – they were the parents of this baby in utereo and so much wanted its arrival into the world. Termination was an overwhelming thought. They were intent on giving life, to whatever the form the baby would eventually become.

Julia thought back to other events in her life where if she worked hard and did the right things, the outcome she wanted would come to pass. She thought about facing adversity and staying strong in the face of it. She didn't want to let a small risk factor, a chance, deter her from delivering a healthy baby. The lack of conclusive indicators and no identified family history risk identified allayed Julia and Bill's concerns. They decided to move forward with positive actions to do everything possible to have a healthy baby. However, as life's experiences show, what a person thinks and plans in their head doesn't necessarily always come to be in Earthly life.

In many ways it was probably for the best Julia and Bill didn't know all the decision points that awaited them. Even if they had some idea of what their future would be like, it wouldn't have changed their decision to continue their pregnancy. The ultrasound had shown the baby to be a girl. This girl, my great-great granddaughter, was to have a different course than others on earth; no one on Earth knew what the future would hold. Only those of us watching from afar knew of the circumstances of the baby's development and the foretelling of the future.

Julia's pregnancy continued into the fourth, fifth, and sixth months. She was more tired in the second trimester, as is typical in most pregnancies. All seemed to be 'normal' with her pregnancy. She really didn't know what 'should' be happening or how things would feel, this being her first. She went to the scheduled doctor's visits, ate the foods recommended by the doctors, read the pregnancy books, and continued her typical schedule of work. Julia did much more to care for her baby in uetreo than I could even imagine when I was on Earth. When I was pregnant, I ate what was available, only for a few of my children's births had an actual doctor attending to me, and worked with little time to rest in my home. Our circumstances were strikingly different.

While the outside world continued on, the baby had a different pace and trajectory she was living with. She had sent indicators in the form of data measured by the advanced technology available in the late 1990's: ultrasounds and blood tests. Her signals for attention or assistance were explained by medical professionals in the outside world by probable cause and reasoning. The statistics were presented, analyzed, and rationalized. The baby continued on in her pursuit of life and development, without anyone in the outside world picking up on the cues she was sending to come to her aid.

In her dark, warm world, the baby forged ahead; her heart beat strong and her body continuing to grow. She was fighting in utereo for her chance in the outside world; given what she was going through and had to overcome, her persistence and tenacity were vital for her to continue to develop. This baby was tough. She had survived much already - events that the outside world didn't know she had experienced.

I observed Julia wondering why the baby didn't seem to move all that much in utereo. She consulted the books she had describing the stages of pregnancy and how each month would likely progress (amazing to me, as in my day we relied on what other mothers told us) which said to take a few minutes and measure the baby's movements after drinking some juice to 'wake the baby up'. She tried that, drank some orange juice, and thought it seemed to work.

After a few more days, Julia worked up her courage to call the obstetrician to ask what the baby's movements should be like at this stage of development. Was it typical for a baby to not have much movement the mother could feel? Julia felt rushed through the process of doctor's visits. Her obstetrician always seemed busy, without time to answer questions. Julia didn't want to 'bother' the doctor or be embarrassed by an obvious answer which someone else would think she should know already. The doctor's office responded with the advice that the pregnancy book had offered, to drink some juice, then see if more movement occurred. Julia wanted to believe the baby was just being quiet, that the lack of movement didn't indicate anything in regards to the baby's health. She drank the juice. There were no measurable signs of distress, so life continued on. In my day that was all you could do; you just had to keep going on.

Looking back on this time, Julia would have changed how she responded to this situation. With knowledge and experience that she didn't yet have or know, she would have asked for further testing of the baby and increased monitoring of the baby's movements. Julia didn't know those were choices open to her at this point. She didn't know what she didn't know. She would have challenged the doctor to monitor the baby's progress more closely, to ensure the discovered indicators were tracked and resolved. In retrospect she would have continued to ask questions of the medical team until her understanding was satisfied and agreed on a plan of health care, which included her inputs, to move forward.

The baby decided to announce her readiness for entering the world in early April of 1997. According to the due date adjusted by the doctor, this was one week ahead of her due date. Julia believed, according to her cycle calculations, the baby was one week late. She didn't waver in her resolve regarding the calculation of the due date. The medical team didn't appear concerned about the baby's due date being changed.

Julia's water broke at about midnight, signaling the baby's readiness for birth. Her nightgown was stained dark yellow/slightly brownish. Julia wasn't sure if that was typical; she didn't think so. She had read a paragraph in the pregnancy book about what color fluid to expect. Upon their arrival at the hospital the medical team identified the color of the amniotic fluid signified meconium staining. This situation indicates that the baby had already begun eliminating waste through their own bodily channels, their waste being output into the amniotic fluid. The danger to the baby comes in if they inhale some of that waste into their lungs. This condition occurs in up to 20% of all births, actual aspiration (inhalation) into the baby's lungs occurs less than 5% of the time. The odds were even smaller for this to be a major impact to the baby's ongoing health, and thus didn't cause Julia a great level of concern during her labor prior to delivery. It seemed to be a factor that could be explained away, to be successfully dealt with to cause no impact to the baby's development.

The delivery was fast for a mother's first baby, just eight hours. In the last few hours before delivery, the fetal monitor showed the baby's heart rate was depressed (lower than typical). Because of that indicator and the meconium staining, a specialized baby delivery doctor, called a neonatologist, was called to be present at the birth. Julia was informed the specialist would attend the baby's delivery, although she was not fully cognizant of what all was happening in the room around her and what the various indicators meant. Julia was trusting the medical staff to help her and the baby.

Anna Christina – April, 1997

Very close to eight thirty in the morning, Anna Christina arrived into the world. My namesake. I digress for a moment to say I was very honored to have one of my descendants named after me. Until this time I did not have a namesake on Earth. After Anna Christina was delivered, she didn't cry – the room was strangely quiet. A suspension of time occurred – the seconds and minutes after Anna's birth were precious. Only the space of a few seconds existed for Anna to learn to breathe in oxygen on her own. The neonatologist swooped Anna up and took her to the opposite side of the delivery room, where a team of four to five doctors was hovering over Anna. They were working to get Anna's breathing going, for her to draw in breaths from the room's air. Anna's skin was blue tinged. Her Apgar score at birth was two. (The Apgar scale was invented in 1952 for the purpose of assessing a baby's health immediately after they are born. Typically healthy babies have Apgar scores of seven or more, where the criteria include their ability to breathe on their own, muscle tone, reflexes, pulse rate, and skin color.)

Julia remained on the bed Anna had just been delivered on. She was wondering what was going on across the room. All she could see was the doctors hovering over Anna. Julia tried to twist around in the hospital bed to better view what was happening with her baby. Her view was like looking through a fence, between the slats. The doctors stood side by side, with little space to see what actions were being taken. They were performing some sort of assistance to Anna. Anna wasn't crying or making any noise. She was occupied with trying to breathe in oxygen in the world, having difficulty with this task.

It became apparent in the few minutes after Anna's delivery that she wasn't doing well. The doctor's voices were hushed. They came over to Julia to explain there was no time to put Anna on her mother's chest for them to bond, per the custom at this time in

America. Anna needed to be transported to another room where she could be best assisted by being put in an incubator, providing her an increased level of oxygen. It was later identified that she was missing every seventh breath. She struggled to breathe and was fighting for her place on the earth

The nurses attending to Anna took a Polaroid photo (a camera where the photo prints immediately from the camera) of her and brought the photo to Julia. They wanted Anna's mother to have at least a picture of her while she was alive, in case she wasn't able to hang on and survive. Julia looked at the photo, it being the first view of what was happening with her new daughter Anna at one hour after she was born. She wanted to cry, not tears of joy but tears of concern, worry, fear, dread. She saw her daughter looking limp with her head craned towards her right side.

I watched over Anna, seeing her continuing to struggle to breathe. I sent some of my breath to her – to keep her going during the challenging times. I wanted her to keep going, breathing, surviving and sent my wishes and strength to her. I knew she was close to not being able to sustain her life on Earth; I willed her strength to stay. Her time wasn't done yet for her life on Earth. It had just started.

After a few hours of Julia waiting, sometimes alone, in the delivery room, ambulance technicians came into the delivery room to tell Julia that Anna was being taken to Seattle Children's Hospital by ambulance. They brought Anna by in the portable incubator for a few minutes so Julia could see her baby Anna before she was transported 15 miles away to the specialized hospital for infants and children located in Seattle.

Julia lay in her hospital bed, alone, with no infant and no husband. They were being whisked away to the Intensive Care Unit (ICU) at Seattle Children's Hospital, across Lake Washington from the hospital where Anna had been born. Julia was tired from the delivery, but even more tired from the worry and confusion of not knowing where her baby was and how she was doing. She spent a very long, confusing, painful, and mostly sleepless night without her newborn. Being twenty miles away from her newborn daughter, Julia felt a very lonely sense of isolation. Hers was not the situation where her baby was in a bassinette right next to her hospital bed; her baby was twenty miles away in an ICU.

The morning after Anna's birth, Bill had left Anna's hospital bedside to go pick up Julia from hers. Upon their arrival at the Children's Hospital, Julia was escorted into a wheelchair, given that she didn't have the strength to walk down the seemingly endless hallway to the wing of the building where Anna was. (In actuality the hallway is a hundred yards or so – it seems endless if you are not able bodied.) She was pushed in the wheelchair to the Intensive Care Unit, where she was signed in at the desk to be admitted through the wide entrance doorway. As Anna's mother, carrying her for nine months, Julia had the closest relationship of any other human being to Anna. It seemed ironic (yet understandable given the safety concerns for infants) to identify herself before being allowed to see Anna. Circumstances of a child's birth and available medical care had sure changed since the late 1800's/early 1900's.

Julia was wheeled into the large open room of the ICU, shared by about forty patients in incubators or beds. (This was the layout of the ICU in 1997. It changed significantly in subsequent years where each patient has either their own room or shares with one other patient). Some of the children were no larger than an adult human's hand, tubing and wires entering their incubators and/or bodies to help sustain their lives. There were also older children with adult sized bodies with varying complex medical needs.

Taking the scene in, Julia navigated her wheelchair to focus on Anna, where she lay in an incubator, tubes inserted in her nose to assist her in breathing. Julia's brain was trying to process why Anna was compatriots with the other children in ICU. It wasn't making any sense. Where was the healthy baby that was expected? At Anna's bedside, Julia reached her hand through one of the openings to touch Anna's body for the second time. Wires were connected all over Anna's head, the signals sending Anna's brain impulses to a nearby machine displaying the results. It was a maze of wiring, electrical signals, and monitoring devices.

Anna was not alert and her body was limp. It was confusing and crushing for Julia to see Anna. Julia wasn't sure what was really happening with Anna's health status, and all of the monitors and machines didn't present positive signs. This situation wasn't the cheerful, joyous circumstances when a baby is one day old. It was fraught with tension, concern, and unknowns. One of the ICU nurses appeared, clearing away some of the tangle of wires so that Julia could hold Anna in her arms for the first time. This was the first earthly connection of their two separate bodies, over twenty four hours after Anna's birth. Omnipresent to the moments were Julia's concern, fear and confusion for Anna's well-being. Even as Anna's mother she didn't know what Anna was going through and wasn't sure what all of these medical devices and attention would specifically mean for Anna's future. Julia's mind swirled with confusion and fear of what was happening and what would come next.

At this point in her life Julia didn't really know what it meant to be cared for in ICU, the unspoken implications all tied up inside the words. She had heard of it related to very serious medical situations, but couldn't recall anyone cared for there she knew personally. It's the nature of the human brain to block out situations and circumstances that are uncomfortable and cause us stress. For Julia it was truly confusing to see her newborn, who had meconium staining (which is most often a very recoverable circumstance), in ICU next to preemie babies little more than the size of an adult human hand. Why was Anna in ICU, when meconium staining was a complication that typically is recovered from fairly quickly? What questions should Julia ask and of whom to get the level of care that her daughter Anna needed?

These thoughts flowed through Julia's head, loosely formed and unanswered, causing an ongoing level of confusion and concern that wouldn't go away. Julia learned later that Intensive Care Units are reserved for the most complex, most in need of around the clock monitoring patients in a hospital. Both Julia and Bill, unbeknownst to them, had been inducted into a society they knew nothing about; caring for a child with intense medical needs. They were members without joining this group themselves; it was automatic given Anna's medical situation.

In the subsequent hours and days there would be more information identified, analyzed and delivered to Bill and Julia regarding Anna's medical status. Many doctors, so many they all couldn't be recalled, would appear to discuss Anna with Bill and Julia. They were afraid to leave Anna's bedside in case they missed a doctor's visit, additional information regarding Anna's status, or Anna needed some sort of medical attention. Medicine names they had no clue what they meant or the implications surrounding them would be floated by them. At this point, when Anna was one day old, they knew little to none of those baseline building blocks.

I have to thank the women, led by Anna Clise, who founded Seattle Children's Hospital in 1907, after gathering support from her friends and local business leaders. The hospital Mrs. Clise founded would, some ninety years later, save my namesake great, great-granddaughter's life. From one mother to another, I am so thankful for these mothers' perseverance and thought for others in establishing the hospital. A driving factor for the hospital's founding was that the Clise family had lost a son to inflammatory rheumatism in 1898. By Anna Clise's ability to see beyond herself and grief in the loss of her own son, she enabled a great number of other parents to see their sons or daughters live and gain health. And, coincidentally, her first name was in common with several of my family members, including my great-great-granddaughter who so desperately needed the hospital's assistance.

Anna was outwardly calm for most of the second day of her life. At times she would break into crying spells; some might think typical for a newborn. Anna's high pitched cries were really signaling her pain, hurt, and difficulty. Inside Anna's brain, a circus of activity was going on that caused her great anguish. Her synapses weren't connecting as in a typical human brain; the electrical signals weren't able to traverse the intended path. The feeling has been described by others able to verbalize as having to rethink each thought every 2 seconds – very upsetting and disturbing. The only means Anna had to let others know of her discomfort was to cry and hope the machines that were reading her body's signals provided sufficient information for the medical team to react.

Multiple doctors introduced themselves to Bill and Julia by stating their name and medical specialization. Bill and Julia had no idea about what these specializations were or why Anna was receiving care from them: Neurologist, Pulmonologist, Gastroenterologist, Radiologist, Attending, Resident, Supervising, Medical Team, Surgical Team, and Occupational Therapist. What did all these terms mean? What was the difference between them and which one(s) was the authoritative, most accurate source for information?

Humans avoid situations where their brain becomes confused or cannot process all the information that is being delivered to it. The confusion creates stress within a person's body, stress being something that the body naturally wants to avoid. This was the state Bill and Julia found themselves in, unable to dismiss or avoid it. They had to face the information the medical teams were providing to them. The scientific facts were presented that were indeed realities. They couldn't pretend all was well with Anna, and that all the issues would somehow go away.

The nights in Intensive Care led to Anna's bed being moved to a ward in the hospital. Before she was moved, the team of doctors had prepared an exit report from Intensive Care. The attending physician talked through the report with Bill and Julia.

They heard many medical terms:

seizures….hypoxic….ischemic….encephalopathy…..meconium….. fetal distress…..

None of which indicated anything positive, that Anna would 'recover' and be a typical baby. Bill and Julia were in a daze of terminology – they didn't know what the terms meant as to what specifically had happened to Anna and what it meant for her future. They just knew Anna was to remain in the hospital until some future time.

Later they would learn, from research of their own, the following terms:

- Hypoxic : the absence of oxygen

- Ischemic: Blood deficiency in an organ or tissue caused by a constriction or obstruction of its blood vessels

- Encephalopathy: a disease of the brain, one involving alterations of brain structure

- Meconium staining: a fetus' elimination of waste into the amniotic fluid. Two of the top three reasons for this occurring are the baby's response to an acute hypoxic event or a chronic intrauterine hypoxia

The War for Anna to remain on Earth had begun when she left her mother's body. Anna had survived the challenges that were presented to her in utereo. The loss of oxygen to her brain could have completely ceased her brain's function or her body's ability to obtain oxygen. She won that battle, surviving, fighting for her life every minute, every day. She survived to be born and learned to breathe on Earth. She was now in the next stage: fighting every moment for her next breath.

The puzzle of Anna's initial medical status took three weeks of hospitalization to figure out if and when she could go home with her parents. The first task was for the medical team to stabilize the seizures Anna was having. A seizure occurs when the brain misfires an electrical signal. Anna was experiencing continual seizures, resulting from the injury to Anna's brain from a lack of oxygen. Their occurrence was verified by a test measuring the electrical impulses in the brain, an EEG (Electroencephalogram). Medical studies show that if an infant's EEG returns to near typical levels within 24 hours after birth, they have a fairly high chance of following a typical human development path. Anna's EEG at 24 hours of life remained in the highly abnormal range. Indications of the future didn't look at all good, from the scientific measurement perspective, although this information was not delivered to Bill and Julia. The medical team seemed to want to 'leave the door open' in case Anna's neurological status improved.

Julia was in a daze of hormones, shock, anger, fear, confusion, and exhaustion all at once. Most of those emotions are common to new mothers, given the stress a mother's body goes through in the birth process and the subsequent significant changes to their lifestyle. Julia had additional helpings of some of these with her newborn's major health crisis. Despite all of her best efforts to plan, schedule, and prepare, the circumstances of Anna's birth were outside of her – and any – earthly control. Anna was forging her own way, in her own style, in her own time.

Thus began weeks of determination of how Anna would be able to survive when she went home from the hospital with her parents. Anna struggled, trying to learn how to feed from the bottle. She just couldn't master the challenge of feeding through the rubber tip. Julia was asked to provide breast milk so that Anna could be fed at any hour of the day or night. The process of obtaining the milk was not like the picture of calm; a mother bonding with her nursing child, sitting by a sunlit window. Julia did as was requested for Ann. She remembers feeling like she was in a daze, stumbling around the hospital looking for the lactation room.

After a few weeks of trying the bottle, that plan was abandoned for going with what was working. Julia was called to breastfeed at any given time, when Anna indicated. This presented its own challenges, as this meant Julia was "on call" at all times during the day and night by Anna's bedside. Anna's seizures continued, causing disruption to her thoughts and moods. She would cry out as if in pain. Anna's outbursts also disrupted her roommates – there were three other hospital beds in the same room. These children were going through their own medical issues requiring hospitalization. It was stressful for Anna's parents, not wanting their child to disturb others, but unable to control what was going on with Anna.

Learning

At three weeks of age, Anna was released from the hospital. They brought Anna home and began to try to settle in, to regain some sort of normalcy to having their newborn at home. 'Normalcy' and 'newborn' might not seem to be compatible terms. Many new parents go through an adjustment period, especially with their first newborn baby. With Anna experiencing continual seizures throughout the day and night, causing her thoughts, moods, and sleep to be disrupted, Bill and Julia were on constant alert to Anna's cries and need for action to be taken. Bill and Julia were also adjusting to their child requiring a very high level of care, much more than a typical infant.

Another aspect of their lives changed when Bill and Julia were given a prescription medicine for Anna to be administered two times a day, 7 am and 7pm. These times would be burned into their memory. Every day wherever each of them happened to be an alarm bell went off in their heads – time to give Anna her medicine. One of them had to be near Anna at these exact hours to give her the prescribed medicine, which was to try to reduce Anna's seizure activity. The time sensitivity of the administration of the medicine created another underlying stress for Bill and Julia. The medicine was that important to Anna's life. When it was time to give Anna the medicine, they would tilt her head sideways and use a small syringe to squirt the bitter liquid on the side of Anna's mouth. Anna both didn't like the taste or the additional liquid in her mouth – she would thrust her tongue out, trying to push it out of her mouth. Her parents would be working the other side of the equation, trying to get the medicine in. Bill and Julia felt a minor surge of victory when the medication administration was successful, knowing how crucial it was for Anna's existence. They also experienced a bit of sadness knowing they were asking Anna to swallow the bitter liquid which she didn't want in her mouth.

Now that Anna was in her own home and the family of three were getting settled in, Julia attempted to follow the pattern of typical activities, including sending out birth announcements. Some of the information included the baby's name, birth weight, and birth date. Anna's name, my daughter Edith's middle name, was chosen to honor her and our family. Julia admired Edith's strength and independence, and hoped for these qualities in her daughter. Edith had long said that she would give money to any family member who would name their daughter after her. Thus far no one had taken Edith up on the offer – Edith not being a name that was typically given to girls after about 1920. Upon receiving Anna's birth announcement, Edith sent money to Anna, realizing Anna's middle name was named after her.

In selecting her daughter's name, Julia was not aware that we Swedes had a holiday called Anna Day, which occurs in the season of Advent. This day, the 9th of December, marks the first day Swedes are to prepare the lutefisk to be consumed on Christmas Eve. Starting in the early 1900's in Sweden there have been many more "name days" added for celebration during the calendar year. Adding to the celebration of Anna Day was for all people named Anna. Over one third of females in Sweden are named Anna, encompassing many people to celebrate on this day!

I had been watching out over Julia and Anna throughout this process of Anna's new life. At this point Julia wasn't aware of my spirit's presence; she knew little about me, having not heard much, if any, verbal discussion about me or my life. She knew only scraps of my history: that I was a cook, that I came to America from Sweden. I knew eventually she would find me and hear my voice. To me it seemed like it was taking Julia quite a long time to listen for it and to understand my meanings. Anna and I were able to communicate almost immediately, since her communication is all non-verbal. She came into the world with a heightened awareness of nonverbal communication, the portion of the right brain that sends nonverbal communication to others and processes responses to non-verbal cues received. This part of her brain learned much during the coming months.

About a month after Anna had left the hospital to come home with her parents, they returned to the clinic for a visit with a neurologist. Neurologists are doctors that study the brain. Bill and Julia had a vague notion of what a neurologist does. At this point they were mostly going through the steps directed to them by the hospital's doctors. The steps included follow-up visits with various specialties of doctors, multiple types of therapists, and a nutritionist. It was like living through a foggy day. They didn't know what was through the fog of all these follow-up actions taken on Anna's behalf. Her parents' big focus was to monitor Anna almost twenty four hours a day: checking on her breathing, making sure she was eating, making sure she was able to eliminate. They learned what it felt like to be exhausted, all the way to the core of their bodies, after this rollercoaster ride of only a month.

The clinics (appointments during the day with a medical specialist) are conducted within the building of the hospital. The very fact that the doctor's appointment is literally "in the hospital" stirs up anxiety, worry, and, yes, some dread. At a subconscious level, Bill and Julia knew it wasn't a 'good' thing to be walking into the hospital. A hospital is where you need help from trained medical staff; they perform actions and are aware of information for your child that you as the parent do not have.

Bill and Julia felt it like a public statement walking into the hospital with their child saying "we're here because we need help." Julia has always had a difficult time asking for help. She is one of those people that figures she can do it on her own, if she just tries harder, studies harder, trains harder. This quality is like many Swedish people I knew – they are independent and try to work harder to solve an issue. She wants to fight through it, read the material on a topic to figure situations out on her own. Unfortunately she has found herself in the challenge of her life; she must ask for help at the Hospital because she doesn't possess all the medical knowledge to best help Anna. As Anna's mother, she wants to be the ultimate caregiver, the authority caregiver. But she simply cannot be in all situations relating to Anna. Julia has to give up some of the control and direction of Anna's care to specially trained medical staff that can bring their years of study to bear on Anna's life.

Carrying their newborn back to the hospital, unspoken concerns and expectations swirled in Julia and Bill's heads, thinking this visit meant there would be more information delivered to them about Anna's medical condition. At that point in the Hospital's history, the patient and their family had to locate the correct clinic, among the over twenty, to check in. Just finding their way to the correct waiting room and check in desk was a task – trying to decipher the long, confusing words of the clinic titles – "Endocrinology" "Craniofacial". Observing them reminded me of when I was trying to find my train to Chicago in New York's Grand Central station – so many paths, so many people, so confusing.

Their little family of three was guided into the exam room, which was small and windowless. They sat and waited for the doctor to enter the room. Anna began to cry, a high pitched wail. Julia tried to comfort Anna and attempted to feed her. The door opened with a crisp snap and in walked two younger, fresh-faced looking hospital staff. They introduced themselves as doctors who were assisting the attending physician. Bill and Julia didn't know exactly what these role labels were or meant; they didn't know the difference between an intern, a resident, or an attending doctor. They answered the questions posed to them about Anna. The team wrote some of the information down in notes, and then stated they'd return as they left the room.

Bill, Julia and Anna waited again for some indeterminable number of minutes before the door would open again to the next encounter with the neurology team. At last the door opened and in walked an older man with a black leather doctor bag, most often described as a satchel. Bill and Julia figured he must be some sort of specialist or higher ranking doctor. The bag had hinges that snap open to reveal a significant amount of storage space. I recognized the bag as similar to the type doctors carried with them in my days on Earth. This doctor stated his name and that he was going to conduct an examination of Anna.

The dark, mysterious black bag was opened. The doctor reached in and pulled out a bright red patterned fabric swatch, about four inches tall and three feet long. He folded it in half and then moved it back and forth in front of Anna's face. After completing that he put the fabric back into the deep recesses of the bag, and then pulled out another item. This process seemed to Julia like watching a magic show – what would come out of the bag next? This time it was a reflex tester – the cold metal handle supporting the beige colored triangular stone. The doctor tapped the tester just below Anna's knees and observed her reaction. He repeated the taps on her hands and arms. Back into the bag went the reflex tester. Next out came a small toy that made a sound when the crank was turned. He turned the crank, then held the toy on one side of Anna's head. After about 15 seconds, he moved the toy to the other side of Anna's head. The doctor didn't speak during this examination.

Bill and Julia were not sure what the doctor was looking for or what the results would indicate. They sat, watched, and waited for more information to be delivered. The doctor put the toy back into his black bag. He stood up, closed the bag, locked the clasp, said two words.

"Brain Damage"

He then turned and left the room. The two resident doctors scurried after him, probably not wanting to be left in the room with Anna's family to receive the kick back from the bullet of information that had just been delivered.

Bill and Julia sat in stunned silence, alone in the room with Anna. They were not sure what had just happened, other than hearing the two words the neurologist had stated, and tried to absorb the information. The manner in which the words were spoken by the doctor/neurologist felt like a slap across the face and a verbal body hit, punching into their abdomens. Their expectation for the appointment was to learn more about Anna's development and progression; they didn't know they'd be given a diagnosis in such a blunt form. Brain Damage – probably one of the worst combinations of words they could have heard. They looked at each other and tried not to cry tears of confusion, anger, hurt and fear. They didn't know what to say to each other. Each was trying to process what had just occurred. Anna wailed in confusion and probable hurt from what was going on inside her brain at the time.

After some period of time, time seeming suspended, Bill and Julia were anticipating what would happen next. The two residents returned to the room. They attempted to provide more details regarding the diagnosis the neurologist had stated – what the tests meant and how Anna appeared to be impacted. There were many unknowns such as what the tests could predict, what the tests specifically could mean for Anna and what Anna's future might be like. They explained that Anna wasn't tracking – where a person's eyes follow a visual stimulus, such as the red patterned cloth the neurologist had shown Anna. Another example of how to test that is holding up a finger and moving it slowly back and forth about a foot away from an infant's face. Anna's eyes couldn't fix on the item and then stopped following it soon after it had started moving.

The other unknowns still lingered in the air, and were left dangling like a participle in an English language class – hovering, unspoken, yet ever present. Bill and Julia's minds struggled to think of what questions to ask, given the precious period of time they had access to these specialized doctors. There weren't answers for every question – there was no way to know exactly what Anna's developmental trajectory would look like. Bill, Julia, and Anna would have to forge out of the examination room, out of the hospital, back into 'civilian' life – everyday life, living with these huge unknowns, at least for the time being. They were thrust back into the world of typical people, including other new parents and infants. But they were now identified, at least to themselves, as different than most other people. Anna had been given a diagnosis that made her forever different than a typically developing child. Her trajectory was on a very different course than a typical child's. How would they fit in to the typical world, while knowing Anna's medical needs made them atypical?

They left the clinic room understanding that there would be more follow up visits with other specialists. Specialists were additional layers of doctors who would need to be consulted about Anna's life. Gastroenterology, Neurodevelopmental, Pulmonary, Orthopedics, Surgery, Occupational Therapy, Physical Therapy – the list of specialists seemed to go on and on. There would be much time spent arranging, transporting, documenting, and implementing with each of these specialists. Anna was two months old. The next major battle of the War was outlined : how to get the needed medical resources to help Anna as best as possible. Bill and Julia had to come up with their game plan to combat the enemy of Anna's various medical needs which seemed to be approaching on all fronts.

Thus began their realization the journey with Anna through her life would continually involve medical teams – specialists of many varieties – to sustain Anna's life. Lao Tzu said "a journey of a thousand miles begins with a single step." As they stepped out of the hospital, this was a very big step on the beginning of their thousand mile journey. Bill and Julia were unknowing participants, booked on this journey that would be part of their future. They both had thought having a child was pretty much like one typically hears of – "mother and baby are doing fine." Many times that is true. This time, with Anna, she wasn't "doing fine" – she had been diagnosed with lifelong medical issues that would need to be closely monitored and managed.

The journey for Bill and Julia had begun of lost hopes and dreams. Their dreams for a healthy, typical daughter faded, as if the sun of each day was missing parts of the color of life's rainbow. The realization of what Anna's life might become seeped in slowly. It brought the awareness that Anna would not be anywhere near a typical child or human being. The extent of the injury to her brain was great. The only choice they felt comfortable with to choose was to rise to meet Anna's needs. The other option presented by the medical team was to give Anna over to the care of the state of Washington, thereby terminating their parental rights to Anna. That was a difficult thought for Julia to even think – give up her child? It was devastating to even hear that presented as a possibility.

Anna's days and nights were filled with trying to keep up with the basics of life – eating, sleeping, eliminating, breathing. Many times even these tasks were difficult for her. She would wake crying at night – like a "colicky" baby. Although Anna's crying was more like screaming from the disruptions going on in her brain and the difficulty of nutrition moving through her gastrointestinal system.

Sleep deprivation came to Bill and Julia's life like an uninvited guest that wouldn't ever leave. It remains a part of how they function in their daily life. It has etched its mark on their lives, from the way they conduct them, including activities they participate in (or not) and what types of people they choose to be around. It has robbed them of unencumbered free time, for if there was an opportunity to sleep that would be their first order preference and need for their bodies. It has forced vacations to be one sided for each spouse – so that one could go away for a night to get more sleep. The other would stay and continue lacking continuous sleep to support the other spouse.

The family tried to establish normalcy, given the knowledge they had of Anna's medical issues. Bill had gone back to his day time job. Julia had planned to take three months off after having Anna and then return to her workplace. Julia tried to go about engaging in activities that her peers did following the birth of their child. She joined a mother and baby group and began following up on infant care possibilities for when she had planned to go back to work. It seemed many of these encounters with others were anxiety and fear provoking efforts. During the mother and baby group Anna might become inconsolable, crying a high pitched cry as if something was hurting her. Julia tried to comfort Anna any way she could think of, often to no avail. Then it was either embarrassing or at the least uncomfortable that Anna couldn't be part of a typical group, where the babies happily fed on their bottles, looked at the world around them or slept quietly in their strollers. Once again the feelings of being isolated, of not sharing a similar experience, welled up in Julia.

In their search to find others to help care for Anna during the daytime, since there were so many unknowns as to what was going on within Anna's body and what reactions this would cause Anna to have, it was difficult to relay information to others on how to care for Anna. Much of the time Julia herself didn't know, as the issues Anna was experiencing were outside of what a mother could do for her child. Julia did know she needed a break in the twenty four hour cycle of caring for Anna. It was proving to be challenging and uncertain as to how that respite could be safely accomplished. It was a battle of how much information to provide without overwhelming a caregiver while maintaining Anna's safety.

As I see Bill and Julia's care for their daughter Anna, they hold themselves responsible for always knowing the next action to be taken and what is best for their child. The problem with that rationale is, for a medically complex child like Anna Christina, always knowing what next action to be taken is a completely unrealistic expectation to live up to. To say nothing of the thought that in my day, with the high mortality rate of children in general, it wasn't possible to hold ourselves to that high of a standard of care.

The physical demands on a caregiver from a child with complex medical needs such as Anna cannot be met by one, or even two parents. Anna's medical status requires a person to be on alert to provide care twenty four hours a day. One person simply cannot be on alert all the time to provide care for another. A person can't live at that elevated level of effort for an extended period of time. The caregiver's body needs to have sleep, rest, exercise, and proper nutrition. All those go by the wayside when, as a parent, you are in 'battle' mode caring for your child. This makes rational sense to Bill and Julia; they understand. The rational thought still doesn't balance out their protectiveness and need to care for their daughter Anna. Every molecule in their body wants to do whatever it takes to assist their daughter.

Going Back Home - Joliet

Before Julia's planned return to work, when Anna was three months old, Julia brought Anna back to Joliet to introduce her to her extended family. The airplane ride from Seattle to Chicago was filled with anxiety. Julia was tense, worried if Anna would start crying uncontrollably in the small space on the airplane or airport. She made sure to have Anna eating during takeoff and landing, so that Anna would be both distracted and that her inner ears would not get too much air pressure built up in them with the change in altitude.

They landed at Chicago's O'Hare airport, then took a shuttle bus to my son Walter's home near Joliet. Walter was now ninety three years old. He was experiencing congestive heart failure, which is the condition that contributed to my death. I am thankful that Walter had survived into his nineties; my heart had failed me in my early forties. His symptoms included poor circulation to his feet and dizziness, which became more exacerbated in his last ten years of his life. He rarely if ever spoke of what was hurting him. He was very stoic about his physical pain and concerns. He endured. At this stage of his life, it was difficult for him to keep his thoughts in order, with his brain not receiving as much oxygen through his blood as optimal. Yet his mind was still very sharp.

Walter was very happy to see Julia and Anna. He was glad Julia had a child, which added to her life's journey. He appreciated Julia's effort to visit him. His health had declined to where he wasn't able to travel as he had so loved to do during earlier years of his life.

Walter had literally built his home outside of Joliet when he was seventy seven years old, laying the Joliet limestone for the foundation and interior finishing work of the fireplaces and living room wall. Over the past twenty plus years there were many conversations held around Walter's kitchen table. Walter, Walter's daughter in law (Julia's Aunt), Julia and Anna were sitting at the table one late morning finishing breakfast. Walter was quiet, his eyes bright observing what was going on. Julia and her Aunt were conversing, when suddenly Walter boomed out "Get another one" while pointing to Anna. Julia's eyes widened and looked at her Aunt, wondering if her Grandfather really meant what he had indicated, hoping that maybe what he had said didn't apply to the current situation or was comprehendible. They agreed that indeed Walter had issued a mandate for Julia to have more children.

Walter was trying to encourage family; he liked children, especially those with spark and curiosity. He was very generous in providing them treats, restaurant dinners, spending money, trips to sporting events, vacations, and lavish holiday parties. None of those were made possible for inclusion in his own childhood. He chose to change the pattern from his life growing up into something totally different for both his children and grandchildren.

Julia and Anna returned home to Seattle, after their visit with Walter and other relatives. Julia said goodbye to Walter, feeling tinges of sadness while thinking it might be the last time she saw him. Upon their return to Seattle, Julia again tried to form a routine – work, daycare for Anna, feeding. Julia sought out the most current developmental baby toys, trying to find some external objects that could help Anna with her vision and development. They were still desperately trying to fit in to the world of typical newborns and typical new parents, to go through the paces of activities that one does with a new baby.

One day in mid-October Anna was having a particularly difficult morning. Julia was driving on the freeway to take Anna to the home based daycare she attended. In rush hour traffic Anna was screaming – a high pitched cry indicating something inside her wasn't going very well. Cars next to them on the freeway could hear Anna scream; it was very stressful for Julia to effectively drive the car, try to comfort Anna, and focus on what she should be doing next. Julia realized this wasn't what most parents were going through. She and Anna were literally in their own little world of their car, dealing with a very atypical situation. Despite Julia's best efforts to keep things running on some kind of schedule with some brand of 'normalcy' the path of their lives just wasn't fitting into a typical groove.

Grieving

The fall continued in Seattle with its rainy, cloudy days. On a stormy Thursday in late fall of 1997, the 20th of November, Anna had another follow-up visit with a neurologist who was located in their city. Julia drove Anna to the doctor's office. It was difficult to wait in the space amongst the other patients with Anna screaming uncontrollably. No amount of motherly comforting worked to calm Anna. Other patients looked over at them uncomfortably, sometimes combined with irritation, their reactions rising with each successive minute of Anna's crying. Julia's anxiety rose also with not being able to calm Anna and avoid the irksome glances from other patients.

After what seemed a never ending time of waiting, Julia and Anna were summoned from the lobby of the neurologist's office. They were shown to an examination room, where they waited for the doctor. He appeared after about twenty minutes and asked Julia questions about Anna – if she slept through the night, if she had rolled over, etc. Anna was seven months old and had not rolled over, sat up, or smiled. It was a difficult conversation – partly because of the topic and status of Anna's health and development, and, most immediately, Anna's discomfort and continued crying. Julia was trying everything to diminish Anna's crying. The neurologist seemed oblivious to his patient's discomfort.

The doctor stuck to his script of questions. After running through them, the neurologist calmly stated Anna had "brain damage", that she had continued seizure activity, and that Julia and Bill should consider putting Anna in a residential facility for her care. Those words were a triple whammy delivered within a minute's time. Julia was almost frozen in shock, struggling to understand what this all would mean for their future. This was the second neurologist to deliver their analysis of Anna's issues in such a blunt, matter of fact way.

Julia gathered up their things – the diaper bag filled with supplies Anna might need, including her medicine that always needed to be nearby and Julia's purse. She put Anna in her car seat, to carry her out to the car. Julia's eyes were welling up with tears – tears for Anna, tears for herself. She wasn't going to cry in front of the neurologist, though. She wouldn't let him see how much his words had caused her anguish. She left the doctor's office in a fog; waves of fear, concern, and anxiety washed over her.

Julia buckled the seat belt through Anna's car seat, sat down in the driver's seat, buckled her own seat belt, and began driving towards home. It felt somewhat comforting to be in the cocoon of the car. She and Anna were alone in the small space of the world they were occupying. The windows of the car were a barrier to the rest of the world. Julia didn't care if others saw her crying – she was so upset with the news of Anna's medical status. Sobs literally racked her body – the door of Anna's potential had been slammed shut by what the doctor had just said.

Julia, being so distraught, was in one of those situations a person probably shouldn't drive a car. The news that her daughter Anna was not meeting developmental milestones and would have significant issues throughout her life was devastating. How could she even think of her daughter living the rest of her life in an institution – away from home, with unknown caregivers? How could she fathom what Anna's seizures would mean for her life?

They somehow arrived at their home safely, the road looking mighty blurry between the rain of Julia's tears and the downpour on the Seattle area. Julia relayed the news to Bill when he arrived home from work. They both grieved for the loss of Anna's potential in life and fell exhaustedly to sleep that night from the stress of hearing this news. A few hours later Anna awoke, screaming, summoning Julia to get up and tend to Anna.

Sleep for Julia since Anna was born occurred only in intervals – a full night, a deep sleep was a thing of the past. Anna was comforted, fed, and put back to lie down in her crib. The crisis was over for the moment; the next would be on its way soon. Sleep deprivation, emotional turmoil and worry of the past few months had weakened their bodies' resolve to fight off infections. It seemed like every cold and flu bug circulating found a home with them that fall.

Walter passed away that December, less than two weeks after the crushing news delivered during Anna's neurologist visit. He died just a week before his ninety fourth birthday. Bill, Julia and Anna flew to Illinois to attend his funeral. It was difficult for Julia to lose her Grandfather. He had been such an important, life shaping person to her. Two forms of death had arrived within two weeks. First came the death of some of the hopes and dreams Julia had for Anna, then the physical death of her grandfather who was so important to her.

Walter's physical death closed out his time on Earth. Given the medical issues he endured, he was fortunate to live a long, full life. Ironically his caretaker, my daughter Esther, who nursed him through those difficult years of tuberculosis in the early 1930's, died at age fifty four. This was about the expected lifetime for an American born in the late 1890's. Walter had beaten those estimations and lived to almost ninety four, in large part due to Esther's care for him.

Walter was acquainted with many people around Joliet, either through his businesses or civic activities. Most of them had long since passed away. Very few of Walter's contemporaries were either alive or able to attend his funeral. Most of the attendees were younger people he'd employed in his businesses during the 1960's or family members. My daughter Edith was the last remaining of my children able to attend Walter's funeral. She lived to the age of ninety nine, passing away two years after Walter. Julia and another of my great grandchildren gave the eulogies at their Grandfather's funeral. She was glad to have the opportunity to honor her Grandfather with those that attended his funeral that day.

1997 was a difficult to say the least for Bill and Julia's family. The difficulties had nothing to do with the world around them of work, the economy, or their residence. Their anguish was centered on the world surrounding their family – Anna's medical news and Walter's death. They experienced two rounds of grief – first for their daughter, Anna, and then Walter, following his death. One of the highest stress factors on a person is when caring for a chronically ill family member. Another great stress is a death of a close loved one. Both of these occurred for Julia in a short amount of time. She was struggling to keep going – keep the bills paid, keep the laundry done, keep food in the refrigerator – keep Anna as comfortable as possible. She felt so tired all the time, like a big, heavy weight was focused on her every movement.

Well-meaning visitors and friends asked about the typical child milestones: when Anna had rolled over, when she had spoken her first word. Those events never came. The answers choked in Bill and Julia's throats. They couldn't answer in one quick line how Anna was doing "great" and meeting all of her developmental milestones. On the other hand the questioner likely didn't *really* want to hear the reality of Anna's situation: she wasn't meeting any of the typical childhood milestones, experienced seizures every day, and cried uncontrollably for hours. They both learned to not engage in conversations about children's development – any child's. Pointing out how other typically developing children were doing swelled up the hurt, concerned, still angry feelings within Bill and Julia. They became social outcasts in some ways – unable to commiserate with other parents on the experiences of a typical newborn. They didn't feel like they had much, if anything, in common with other new parents.

It is odd watching humans on Earth think there is a reason or a "cure" to every dilemma that a human encounters and every deviation from what is a 'typical' human development. They don't seem to understand the deviations are part of the plan. That's the way it was intended to happen. The deviations are what make each human unique, the person they are. For example, shoe sizes. Some people have large feet for their height, some have small. The physiological reason for a human's feet to be of a certain size is so that a person can use them to stand up (if the rest of their body enables this) and not fall over. Their feet allow a person to walk, run, or swim effectively. If the size of a human foot had not been planned for, humans couldn't walk. There is more information and thoughtfulness behind human development and their physical differences than most realize.

The anger aspect of the collage of feelings Bill and Julia went through was different for both of them. Bill's anger was focused on the God that would allow his child to be so injured. He didn't understand how God could seemingly leave him, with all of Anna's complications, medical care, and needs. When he attended church, he would hold Anna in his arms, close to the door in the event Anna started crying and couldn't be stopped. Anna, being held close to Bill's chest, could feel Bill's heart rate quicken with the escalation of her cry, involuntarily reacting to her distress. She then included that concern in an ever higher, tenser cry.

Julia's anger at the time was lost in the confusion over what took place with Anna's condition and the sleep deprivation of caring for Anna at any hour of the day (or night). Her constant state of worry caused her to be more irritable, less patient than she might have been. (Julia is not known for being patient, even when she is not sleep deprived). For Anna's first year, she was tethered to Anna due to being Anna's primary feeding source. Julia's anger was submarined in her protectiveness for Anna.

Her feelings of hurt and loss would surface when another mother told of their typical child's temporary skin condition (such as eczema) or requirement for a bottle feeding formula change. These were not life threatening, untreatable conditions. Julia, coping with the prognosis for Anna's lifelong disabilities, didn't have the patience or energy to absorb what seemed to be a small issue.

It angered her when she heard others use words like "idiot" or "retard" in their everyday conversation. These words were originally labels on the scale of intelligence, to indicate people who are in the lower numbers of the commonly quoted IQ (Intelligence Quotient) scale of brain reasoning function. The words have become a means to slander or put down another person – such as "you idiot!" or "he's such a retard!". There are real people on Earth these words do technically apply to, such as Anna Christina. They are not any less of a person worthy of respect than any other person on this planet, even if their intelligence is measured by a different number on a scale invented by other people. Recall that a measurement scale is only what is outwardly observable by another person on Earth, such as via verbal language or intentional movement. They cannot measure or calculate what a person is actually thinking. They may not have the same reasoning ability as others, but that doesn't mean they should be made fun of or mocked for that aspect of themselves.

The battle of sleep deprivation raged on for Anna's parents. Every night saw a see-saw, back and forth movement in the fronts – one hour Anna would be sleeping and quiet, then a few hours or minutes later she would be awake crying out in either pain, confusion, fear, or all three. Bill and Julia tried every sleep trick in the book with Anna – rocking, soothing noises, swaddling. Some nights she would drift off to sleep, her parents thankful for the quiet, restful time. Most often she would jolt them out of their slumber a few hours later, by crying a sharp cry. Anna's cry sounded like something was hurting her, that she was in pain. That is the most excruciating sound for a parent, when their child is calling out in pain or fear.

Most parents look forward to the day when their infant can sleep through the night – some it happens very early, at one month of age, and others it can take up to two years, sometimes longer. Many other people realize it's difficult for a new parent, where they are waking up at night several times to either feed or change their infant. The parent not being able to get to the REM (Rapid Eye Movement) stage of deep sleep can cause them to be more tired, irritable, and less patient in their waking hours.

For Bill and Julia the day that Anna consistently sleeps through the night will never arrive. They were waiting at a train station where the train just isn't coming – it was rerouted at some other point upstream before reaching them. Their path is altered....different. For them it is another battle in the War, to get restful sleep, to let themselves put aside their fears for Anna's wellbeing and safety. This is an impossible task for Anna's parents; they cannot push the needs of their child out of their mind. There isn't an off switch to stop the concern for your child.

The denial of restful sleep has been the most wearing for Julia throughout Anna's life. As a mother, Julia's senses are functioning almost twenty four hours a day, listening for a sound from Anna that indicates she needs something. For months at a time Julia isn't able to sleep deeply enough to get to REM to sufficiently restore herself. In Julia's sleep she worries about Anna, her unconscious not letting her relax during the night.

Bill and Julia went through the motions of life – going to work, caring for Anna, paying the bills. They don't remember many details of the entire next year. Their brains blotted out the difficult memories of trying to sustain Anna's life on a moment to moment basis. They became somewhat disconnected from other people. They didn't invite people over to their house to socializing because they were so wrapped up in trying to keep Anna going and were literally exhausted from those efforts. They also weren't facing the same issues as other new parents. Anna never did (or would in the future) meet the standard infant developmental milestones of rolling over, sitting up, babbling or tracking an object with her eyes. Each week and month seemed to have some other news about Anna's development which was falling further and further behind her peer group.

Julia had gone to her doctor for a checkup, and told her of the tiredness and exhaustion she felt, both physical and emotional. The doctor prescribed an anti-depressant medication. She asked Julia to try it for a few weeks to see if it didn't help Julia sleep better and feel better emotionally. All the medicine did was make Julia more tired during the day – that wasn't going to work for her keeping up with her schedule of caring for Anna, working, taking care of her house. Julia simply didn't have time to sleep more during the day and feel sluggish when she was awake. She stopped taking the medication; she decided she could "tough it out" with her Swedish resolve. (Footnote: that approach doesn't always work.)

In retrospect Julia realized she wasn't depressed in the clinical sense of the word. She was going through grief – extreme grief. Working through those feelings of loss and grief had to happen. She couldn't go around them, avoid them, or circumvent them. There is no medicine for grief; it cannot be removed chemically from one's mind and body. Grief simply takes time, differing amounts for each individual, for a person to resolve. Then hopefully there comes a day where they can pick up and go on. Julia's grief for Anna was the loss of a healthy baby – it was now clear that Anna would have ongoing medical issues for the rest of her life. It was also grief for herself that in spite of Julia's best efforts, her child was not 'typically healthy'. The impacts to Anna were outside of what her parents could possibly control.

Julia discovered that her worst fear, held deep in her subconscious mind, as a parent had been realized – her child had serious health issues that would last her entire life. Her daughter's development was not typical, not anywhere close. They were in another world, almost, not tracking with the different stages of childhood. Julia tried to learn more about Anna by reading books on epilepsy, developmental delay, and "mental retardation". Even picking up a book that has any of those words in title was hard to do. It was a realization that the information contained within the book is of interest and/or needed by the reader. In a bookstore Julia would wait until no others were around the "Special Needs" section. She then would scan the shelves for titles that related to what Anna was going through. There were general books on disabilities, few, if any, books written on Anna's specific diagnosis.

Julia and Bill had to get over their initial discomfort of seeking out the information in those topics. It was frustrating to not have tools for being able to understand what Anna's future would be like, and associated needs she would likely encounter. No scientific study could be documented by a person for Anna's path in her life – she is on her own, unique path. She doesn't fall into a specific, well-known 'birth defect' where her future needs could be well understood and planned for in advance.

One chapter of a book with the words "Mental Retardation" in its title outlined the bell curve of development and impact to the brain of microcephaly. The bell curve hit a nerve with Julia, as all throughout her education she was aware of the idea of the curve – that very few are in the top percentages and very few are in the bottom, most are in the middle. Julia was used to maximizing the possibilities to be at the top of the percentiles – by working hard, studying, doing the 'right' things. With Anna's medical status their task would be to maximize the possibilities in the bottom percentiles of the curve – no 'get out of jail free' card to improve Anna's standings on the curve. No herbs, medicines, prayers, or hopes could repair the damage that had occurred to Anna's brain.

There was an unknown culprit – nowhere or one to go after, chase, convict, punish. They were fighting against a nameless, faceless opponent for Anna's health and life.

Adjusting

Giving up control is difficult to do. As part of that process there comes a realization that we as people on Earth cannot be in control of everything that occurs to us or those we love. Julia had tried to positively influence all that she could for Anna. Anna's medical needs had long since superseded Julia's control and expertise. They needed specialized medical assistance to help Anna in the best possible ways.

The grief Julia experienced allowed her adjustment to the new reality of how Anna's life would differ from others'. What happened to Anna just happened – there was no rational explanation for why it happened to her. Why, for those instants in Anna's development, did her brain lose oxygen for some period of time to cause that great of an impact to her brain? There is no answer to that question. Julia rejected the notion that it's because God is giving only what someone on Earth can handle. She doesn't think God could be that mean, that God would select negative events to inflict on people on Earth.

The difficult thing for Bill and Julia to come to terms with is that what can be done for Anna is to manage what she does have, to positively influence her life experience and maximize her capabilities. Then again, taking a small step back to view this situation, that is what any parent should do for any child. Anna is no different in that regard. Bill and Julia are not shrinking from accepting and helping Anna have the best life she possibly can. The path they are on will be long and arduous, full of tasks to do, complete, ensure happened, and follow up on.

The next steps in their lives didn't come easy – to make the best of the cards they were dealt. Julia was motivated to make the best of the external factors of Anna's life – to enable the best possible situation for Anna to live in. Like most parents Julia wanted Anna to grow up to be happy, healthy and strong. She was facing the reality that Anna wouldn't be able to achieve all the hopes and dreams she'd had for her. Those hopes included graduating from a four year college, having a successful career, being a loving person. Fragments of those hopes would be possible given Anna's functionality limitations. They would have to be happy with whatever successes Anna did have. Bill and Julia came to realize that Anna was doing the best she can. That's all that can be asked of anyone. Anna is going to be who she is, on her own scale. They accept and love Anna for who she is; not who she might have been.

Anna battled through what was going on inside her brain and body these rough months and into years. She endured the seizures that happen frequently throughout the day. Sometimes she would cry out, a painful cry, because of the confusion and interruption going on inside her brain. Other times she simply waited for the seizure to cease – not vocalizing, but her pupils twitching back and forth. These are called "absence seizures" , where the person is seemingly absent/not cognizant of what is happening around them during that timeframe. Anna also would experience these when she appeared to be staring off into space, especially when her head would turn toward the left side of her body.

Bill and Julia also realized that Anna wasn't going to have a 'cure' – where her capabilities could improve in skill and breadth to become a typically functioning child. Her injury is one that cannot be repaired, sewn up, medicated or radiated to remove. It will always be with her; it just is. The impact of her brain injury is forever a part of her history. It cannot be erased, written over, or supplemented. This was difficult for some others to understand – that there wasn't some therapy or pill or rehabilitation that Anna could go through to become a typically functioning child. Bill and Julia had a difficult time addressing others' questions as to why Anna couldn't "get better". Many people said "they (meaning the medical community) can do so much now". Medical science has leapt forward and helped so many more people overcome their issues. Cancer can be beaten back into remission, backs can be straightened to facilitate a child to walk, diabetes and blood sugar can be controlled to live a mostly typical life. Medicine and medical technology cannot right *every* injury. For Anna's brain injury all that is left to provide is supportive care – helping her body perform the daily functions it needs to for her survival.

In the spring of 1998, at almost one year of age, Anna was still able to breastfeed. Julia made herself available at any opportunity to Anna to nurse, which was difficult for an entire year, given that Julia was trying to work during the daytimes. The long hours of attempting to feed Anna soft foods via spoon were not yielding growth results. Anna's nutritionist and occupational therapist had put Anna on a diet of high calorie foods – mayonnaise, avocados, full butterfat cream cheese. Any possibility for adding to Anna's calorie intake was made. The frustrating part, and uncomfortable part for Anna, was that Anna's stomach oftentimes couldn't absorb the food and she would reflux it all back up after having swallowed it. It rapidly became a futile situation trying to get calories in Anna's system.

It was more apparent that Anna needed more help in the form of intervention by trained medical staff to add in determinations of how to best help her. Julia did not yet fully realize how much their daily lives would be impacted by medical staff. The choices for Anna's health future were outside the purview of her parents. An ever increasing number of specialists were called on for assistance to help Anna. Anna's needs could not be met by any parent. They had long since surpassed what a typical child would require.

Infants can be affected by 'colic', where a small child is irritable, may have reflux, and has a tough time sleeping. Anna's symptoms were like those of a colicky infant, however they persisted and became more severe in nature. They were part of her daily life. She constantly woke up crying throughout the night, at two to three hour increments. She refluxed (threw up) her food and had difficulty keeping the food in her stomach. Anna's behavior didn't settle down into a routine or typical pattern. Bill and Julia, and of course Anna, were stuck in a continual loop of living with the care demands similar to that of a newborn infant, where all life needs must be met by a caregiver.

Comparing Julia's situation to mine, I, too cared for my children who were infants over the course of fifteen years; the time of consecutive care would have been nine years. The differences in our situations were my children were all 'typical' – they outgrew their night wakefulness, were able to feed typically, and didn't cry very often (learning that in our house, a baby crying was not tolerated). I saw that Julia was going through a completely different experience as a mother than I had. She didn't know what she didn't know, that the majority of babies become much easier to care for after about three months.

Bill and Julia spent many nights waking up and walking across the hall to see if Anna was breathing. The worry of SIDS (Sudden Infant Death Syndrome) and Anna's seizures literally kept Julia awake at night. Julia had never experienced difficulty sleeping before in her life, until this experience with Anna.

The whole first year of Anna's life was difficult for everyone, primarily Anna. Anna tried so hard to keep up with what was being asked of her; the feedings of baby food that she tried to swallow as fast as she could, which would take several hours to complete. The sense of defeat her parents felt after working so hard to slowly portion the food into Anna's mouth, only to have the food refluxed and her stomach emptied again. The reflux started causing Anna to aspirate fluid into her lungs, and she developed pneumonia a few times before she'd even seen her first birthday. These bouts of illness landed Anna in the hospital, to administer IV fluids and oxygen support for her breathing. The vicious cycle continued.

The follow-up visit with Anna's pediatrician, when Anna was one year old, offered the newest insights into Anna's status and progress. Anna's weight gain was not keeping pace with her gains in height – she was long (tall) for a one year old. Another progress measure is the measurement of the circumference of a baby's head. This is an indicator of brain development in young children. Anna's head circumference had grown only 2 centimeters since birth – way below what is typical for a one year old. Most of the human brain development occurs before age two; half of that timeframe had slipped by for Anna.

Again the bell curves of statistical analysis popped back into the picture – where was Anna on the growth charts for her weight and head circumference? She was in the bottom 5%, actually bottom 1%. Julia felt the sting of the knowledge that Anna's developmental progress ranked in the lowest percentiles. She felt powerless to help Anna develop and move up into higher percentiles. She couldn't *will* Anna's brain to grow. Anna's progress showed she was slipping, slipping, slipping further and further behind her peer group; she just couldn't keep up the pace of growth and development.

Diagnosis

Diagnosis : Failure to Thrive

After reviewing Anna's data, the doctor informed Julia that Failure to Thrive was Anna's diagnosis for her development. This term has been around for decades in the medical field – it is meant to indicate situations where children are not meeting developmental milestones. As a parent this diagnosis can be devastating – first of all the word "Failure". Who aspires to "Failure"? Certainly Julia and Bill had worked so hard for Anna, spending countless hours in support of Anna's needs. They had reorganized their lives around what Anna needed – work schedules, leisure activities shelved for some time in the future. Even with all that effort, "Failure" was the label applied to Anna.

Next the word "Thrive" – Thrive indicates flourishing – growing – achieving – doing well. None of which applied to Anna. Another blow to Anna's parents – she wasn't 'thriving' – she wasn't keeping up with typical human development in her abilities or weight. This label applied to Anna's status felt like it implicated Anna's parents for Anna not 'thriving', even though they provided as much of an ideal environment for Anna as possible and had worked so hard.

Up until this time, the door to Anna's prognosis was left open. No doctor would specifically tell Julia or Bill what Anna's future might be like. They kept thinking and hoping that maybe things would work out alright for Anna – even if she had some impairments she may have a fairly typical life. The doors were now slamming closed, right in her parents' faces. Julia gathered up her courage to specifically ask the pediatrician, her voice shaking with fear of the response, "What is Anna's life expectancy?" The pediatrician replied, giving her best estimate, that Anna would be lucky to make it into her teenage years.

All this in one visit when Anna was one year old. Not the quick, routine yearly checkup for a one year old – the visit was a long, drawn out, painful few hours. It dragged on with more data and negative news. The doctor had thrown her allotted time limit aside for this visit; there was much difficult news to deliver to Anna's parents about her prognosis and life expectation.

Being science focused people, Bill and Julia still wanted to figure out how to 'fix' Anna's issues. Parts of the problem included that they didn't know what all of Anna's issues were and they weren't medically trained to know what certain factors indicated or meant. Julia went to the University of Washington's medical library – a place she had gone to study while an undergraduate at the University of Washington – and copied off (on one of those "Xerox" machines from the 1970's) all seven articles relating to Anna's diagnosis. They all said "outcome is poor" for children with Anna's symptoms, certainly not encouraging information. Why were there only seven articles? Julia surmised later that once the damage has been done to the brain, the only course of 'treatment' is 'management'. This basically means living with what you have at that point. There is no miracle cure; no medicine or operation that can repair the damage that had occurred to Anna's brain. It seemed they were at an end of progress and information.

Bill and Julia were asked by well-meaning people "what could be done" for Anna. (What others didn't realize is they were hitting on the nerve of Bill and Julia's efforts for Anna – they were desperately trying to figure this out, with all the information and medical assistance they could find.) To be fair to the 'well meaning' others, it is difficult to know what to say to a parent of a child with disabilities. No one wants to hear that there is no miracle, no cure. The only hope for improving children's quality of life is to diagnose as early as possible in a mother's pregnancy, and then manage any aberrations the baby experiences. And sometimes any of the factors that humans wish to 'manage' or think they could 'control' are simply not within their grasp. There are circumstances and factors in human development and gestation that no human can explain or 'correct'.

Anna meanwhile was experiencing pain, confusion, and seizures in her brain every hour of the day. She fought hard to maintain during the waking hours – she didn't mean to cry out sharply – she just had no other way to indicate the storm that was going on inside her. Most all of her bodily functions needed assistance. Since she wasn't able to purposefully move her body, she couldn't move food through her gut efficiently. Pain and hurt seeped in to her life from a variety of sources.

Anna tried to focus on the red, black and white baby toys her parents sought out for her. (Red, white and black are the easiest colors to see for a baby). She couldn't focus on the particular shapes – Anna held her head and looked off to her right. (This was because her brain was more injured on its left side, thus impacting the muscles on the right side of her body). She really was looking at an object somewhat to the left of her. She had to adjust to see what she could out of her peripheral vision. Anna's vision was measured by putting leads all over Anna's head and measuring the electrical impulses going to Anna's eyes from her brain. This indicated that Anna was legally blind – she most likely sees in shades of gray. In communications with me Anna expressed her frustrations of not being able to clearly see and look at her surroundings.

Anna began to further develop her sense of sound to supplement her lack of visual acuity. She learned to discern different people's voices and identify who they belonged to. She knew her mother, Julia's, voice, she knew her father, Bill's, voice. She seemed to prefer female voices, as many babies do, with the higher octave being more pleasing and comforting.

The neocortex of a human's brain provides higher level reasoning and functioning. The systems supporting that are the limbic and brain stem. The brain stem provides basic bodily functions such as regulating the heart's rate, blood pressure, and breathing. It is quite sensitive to the "fight or flight" response of identifying environmental dangers. This portion of Anna's awareness is what she utilizes to alert herself to a perceived danger. The limbic system is the next layer, providing recognition and memory of fear and pleasure. This also generates and moderates emotions, along with attention to internal and external stimuli. Anna demonstrated her use of these systems when she was just over a year old. The family was watching the Chicago Bulls (and Michael Jordan) play in the NBA finals. The game was exciting, and Julia yelled encouragement for her hometown team, the Bulls. Anna cried in response and became so upset Julia had to move her to another room. Anna read her mother's loud voice as an influence disturbing or harming her mother, and cried out in response.

Anna also knows when a person is not a calm, loving influence around her. This function of sensing when a 'danger' is near is centered in the sympathetic system. It readies the body for defensive action. Anna's was triggered during a group with other special needs children that met once per week. This was a group of one to two year olds – some children had Down's syndrome, some were developmentally delayed for an unspecified reason. Another child's mom in the group was a loud, brash woman. This woman probably meant well – she was just loud and boisterous, bursting out with comments or loud laughter during the hour long session. Anna began to cry in response to the volume of this woman's voice. Julia finally realized the noise stimulus was upsetting Anna. She picked Anna up and moved out to the quiet hallway, where Anna almost immediately calmed down and stopped crying. Anna knew what environment she was comfortable in and expressed her preferences in the way that she could.

Her parents and others involved in Anna's life on Earth have to learn Anna's language – what does she mean when she takes a certain action? Is it intentional – or merely coincidental? For example she can swat things away with her right hand – as if to say get the item away from me, it is irritating me. Or, sometimes she yawns while someone is talking, in apparent boredom. While this would not be socially 'correct' behavior – it is unfiltered feeling for Anna; her behavior is not modulated by the right side of her brain that governs nonverbal communication and the holistic sense of the scene a person is experiencing.

It became apparent that Anna is difficult to care for, as her crying seemed unexplained and agitating to others around her. Many people gave up in frustration and didn't want to be around her. Bill and Julia had tried to find a daycare facility that Anna could attend. The problem came in due to the attention level Anna required from a caregiver. Attending to Anna's needs took more time than with typical children – she couldn't be quieted quickly with a bottle or a toy.

After several instances of being asked to remove Anna from a daycare facility, Bill and Julia felt the sting of rejection. Anna just didn't fit in with a typical classroom with typical children. Another battle lost; their hopes tamped down by the overt words that Anna "just didn't fit in".

They had to take charge of the care plan for Anna. The determination ensued that Anna needed another person who could be attuned to her specific needs. Her parents arranged for Anna's care in their own home. They either adjusted their work schedule so one of them would be home with Anna, or Anna's grandmother, my granddaughter, sat with Anna while her parents were away. Anna needed people around her who were focused on her needs and available to meet them where possible. She required one on one attention.

Breathing, maintaining an open airway, is a very real, specific concern for Anna. This continues throughout her years. Because of Anna's brain injury, her ability to breathe is an ongoing, moment to moment risk. Her parents' high level of concern remains part of their brains' focus at all times. Out of necessity for their own mental health, their concern may have been temporarily pushed out of the forefront, but never stops. Julia thinks it is like a runaway process on a computer; it just keeps looping and looping, never ending.

The concern for Anna's life brings the day to day into focus. Bill and Julia try to center on the question "is the situation alright right now?". If there is no major crisis, that is counted as a success in the continual progress against the War. The enemy has been held off one more moment, hour or day.

To effectively cope with living at a high state of alert, a person must learn to let go of some of the worry a bit at a time. If one is not able to release some of the stress, the body begins to erode its healthy state. People who work in emergency rooms, military service, and jobs that require constant monitoring where a loss of service could result in a high level of loss of money or people are especially vulnerable to the symptoms of stress.

The effect within the human body when a stressor occurs, such as a child crying, is for the body to protect itself from the stressor or aggressor. This is a visceral reaction – a person's body automatically goes through these steps to protect itself from whatever is the perceived threat. We aren't even aware that our brain has responded – it just does. First the heart rate increases sharply, to supply oxygen to the muscles. The respiration (breathing) rate increases. A person's liver discharges glucose to provide more nutrients to the muscles. Lastly blood pressure rises as adrenaline and cortisone like hormones are delivered into the bloodstream. All of that happens without the brain being able to control it.

There is an additive effect on a person's body if stress is a frequent, repetitive process. It's like continually jolting a person's system with an electrical impulse. Stress can quickly wear down a person's system to the point of exhaustion. Other symptoms may appear such as weight gain, inability to sleep, indigestion/reflux and loss of social connectedness.

As a parent we'd like to be able to fight off any dangers or threats to our children's health – to whack all predatory factors away. For Julia and Bill the factors that might attack Anna just cannot be removed – they are always out there, lurking. These enemy attackers don't have a face, identity or name. They are held off by caring for Anna and bringing resources to bear when needed.

No parent would choose Anna's experience for their child – a lifetime of various cycles of pain and being totally dependent on others for all needs. Yet parents are called (sometimes literally – either by phone or their child) to rise to meet these challenges. Many, many times thus far in Anna's life she could have given up – not able to go on. Many times Bill or Julia could have given up – not able to go on caring for Anna due to the intense time and emotional demands for her care. Each finds a way to continue; to take more steps in their journey and not yield to the War for Anna's life. I am helping where I can – by bringing peace to Julia's subconscious mind, soothing her as only a mother can do.

Each person on Earth must persevere to keep their place every day. Every day everyone living has to figure out how they are going to live through the day, whether they realize it or not. For some that might mean going to work to earn money for their household's living needs. For others that might mean how they are going to survive on the street of a large city for one more day. For Anna it means how she can take enough breaths to see the next morning. We all have various levels of effort we need to expend to live; Anna's are sourced from the most basic human needs – breathing, digestion, caloric intake.

After another occurrence of pneumonia, which required Anna to be hospitalized for her breathing and caloric intake needs, the medical team approached Bill and Julia about placing a gastrostomy tube (g-tube) in Anna's stomach. This is a tube that is outwardly prominent where (liquid) food can be inserted directly into the stomach, thereby circumventing the mouth and throat. G-tubes placed in a person's stomach for longer term, constant use have only been possible since the late 1980's. In my day if a child was unable to eat typically, there were very few steps that could be taken. That would have been a cause of their demise.

Anna endured a three hour surgery to place the g-tube. The risks of the surgery were elevated due to Anna's breathing and respiratory status. Thankfully her heart has always been strong – beating at a regular, steady pace. Anna recovered from the surgery, after difficulties with the effect of the general anesthesia and pain medications administered in the hospital. She eventually began to gain weight and grow at a much healthier rate. The g-tube, her doctors and nurses saved her life. Without this specific technology, Anna would not have been able to continue growing.

There were some crystal clear moments of joy, also. When Anna was a year and 3 months old, she went with her parents to Berea, Kentucky. Bill, Julia, and Anna had flown to Kentucky to visit Julia's aunt, my granddaughter. In the picture taken on that day in June, Anna had a happy expression, the smiling eyes. The picture shows the beautiful person Anna is, her spirit emanating out through her smile and her eyes. (See Photo 7 in the Appendix). It captured a special moment where circumstances were good for Anna – she is happy. In the background, what you cannot observe in the picture, is Anna was taking a steroid that was meant to help reduce her seizure activity. It did help somewhat, although the seizures persist. And, at the time the picture was taken, the medicine made her face somewhat puffy looking.

Along the path of Anna's life there have been some funnier occurrences, too. One such occasion was when Anna was about a year and a half old Bill and Julia had taken Anna to see one of the specialists on her care team at the Hospital. The day was spent "in clinic", seeing the variety of specialists that Anna needed. They were in a clinic room for most of the day, starting when they checked in at 10 am in the morning.

The clinic building at that time was from the construction that had occurred in the 1950's – the walls looked very much 'hospital' – flat, white cement painted walls. The radiator was steaming its contents out to heat the room. The small family sat in the room, awaiting the next specialist's entry while caring for Anna's needs. They waited and waited for what seemed like a long time – over an hour. By this time it was 4pm, and Bill and Julia were thinking about the traffic that would await them to get back across the bridge to home. Finally Julia couldn't take sitting there waiting any longer. She opened the windowless door and looked out into a deserted hallway. Where had everyone gone?

Julia walked down to the closest reception desk and asked about the status for Anna's next provider appointment. The person led Julia to the scheduling board and reviewed what the plan was for Anna. She informed Julia that she was surprised they were still there, as the last scheduled provider had visited them 2 hours earlier. Bill, Julia and Anna were sitting in the clinic room for almost 2 hours, when they could have left to go home, the visit being concluded.

This experience taught Julia a very important lesson – always ask what the next step in the process is. And, if waiting for more than 20 minutes, be sure to ask someone how the progress is going. As frustrating as this was, it illustrated to her to always ask questions when you are not sure of the status, don't leave your destiny as an unknown. Take charge.

To attempt to answer the question of "why did Anna's brain injury occur?", Bill and Julia had been referred to a genetic counselor, a medical expert who researched the potential genetic causes for Anna's brain injury. After analyzing blood tests, family history, and risk indicators, the counselor told Bill and Julia their chances of having another child with similar impacts were one in a million – the same chances as any other new parents'. While this was good news for any future pregnancy risks, it also invoked the feeling that Anna had just had terrible odds – her 'number' had come up to have this impact happen. Based on this information, they decided to proceed with the potential expansion of their family.

Julia's second pregnancy occurred in the summer of 1998. She was monitored by a high risk pregnancy obstetrician, based on the history with Anna. Weekly tests monitored the baby's heart rate, many ultrasounds were conducted to see the progress of the baby's development. Bill and Julia worried the whole pregnancy – what if what had occurred to Anna happened again, despite all the efforts being made? Julia and the baby remained healthy during the pregnancy – the baby was delivered, completely healthy, almost two years to the day after Anna was born.

Anna continued to grow. She gained weight and grew taller, with the aid of a feeding tube inserted into her stomach. At least the liquid food was absorbed into her body and the nutrients could be used to help her grow. Her personality became more apparent, also, as her pain level decreased and her seizures became closer to being managed. She often laughs at a socially appropriate time, seeming to indicate to others around her she understood what was said and found the humor in it. She smiles and laughs when a sound or sensation is pleasing to her. She knows when she likes something or someone, and verbalizes that via sounds or laughing.

Anna's brain did develop some skills based in the right portion of her brain – the skills of knowing and sensing when something isn't right or someone isn't acting in a positive manner towards her. She becomes agitated when around loud people or noises, indicating she wants that thing or person to go away from her. She knows – without being able to verbalize her discomfort or unease. She vocalizes those emotions. Even though her brain is the size of a newborn infant's, she thinks most thoughts that others do. She just cannot speak aloud and her reasoning capability is limited by the physical size of her brain. She has all the emotions and feelings of any other human being. Anna can clearly communicate with those of us not on Earth – although those on Earth don't have visibility into this communication.

An example of the ability of a person to understand what is going on around them, without themselves being able to verbalize, is seen in the narrative from a woman who survived her growing up and young adult years in an institution in Melbourne, Australia. In that country in the years between 1961 and 1979 disabled people were warehoused into facilities, and often not given sufficient food, nutrition, or appropriate stimuli. This woman, Anne McDonald, was non-verbal, yet she can describe in detail the events that happened around her, via the technologies now available that can transmit her communications via computer. What a tragedy to think that just because a person is non-verbal means they cannot think or be aware of what is happening around them.

Julia had read this article, published in the Seattle Times newspaper in June of 2007, and realized that Anna could be quite like the author – very much aware of what was going on around her, yet unable to affect changes in her living and care situation. As Anne stated in her article, "No child should be presumed to be profoundly retarded because she can't talk." "The only possible way to find out how much a child who cannot talk actually understands is to develop an alternative means of communication for that child." Anne survived her experience to persevere in her ability to communicate with others, through a means other than verbally. She so accurately illustrates that those who can verbalize likely have no idea what is going on in a non-verbal person's brain.

A nonverbal person literally doesn't speak the same language as a person who is able to verbalize. It does not mean, however, that a nonverbal person doesn't have a language – they have their own.

There are others on Earth who are typically functioning who take the time to care and show concern for those who are not typically functioning. They meet the person where they are in the spectrum of human development, and thus make another person's life better for it. Some take the opportunity to practice this every day via either their work or daily life. The key is taking the time to understand the most appropriate means to reach out to another. This might be helping a person struggling with their grocery bags or paying for the next person in line's coffee. And there are people who can push the effort to help others to a whole new level -- game changers. They are literally changing the game so that others can live the most fulfilling lives possible.

Two people who have been game changers for Anna came into her life as her Neuro-Developmental doctors. This specialty of doctor focuses on the study of how an individual's neurological development impacts their physical development. It is a specialty that looks at the whole picture of a child's health, of their growth as a person and the physical aspects of being human. This is especially critical in a person's first years of life, as the brain (neuro) develops the most in the first two years of life. These doctors took the time to understand Anna and brought their expertise to improve the circumstances of her daily life. They pointed out to others, including Anna's parents and other doctors, how Anna was understanding the conversations going on and voicing her opinion. And they were right. When Anna was included in the conversation, she would quiet down to listen. When she seemed to feel no one was listening to her, she would vocalize more. Her reactions and behavior make perfect sense, if others take the time and effort to understand what the intent of her expressions are.

Connecting

My daughter Edith passed away in February of 1999; she would have been one hundred years old in December of that year. She lived a long, healthy life. She was the last of my children remaining on Earth, the eight others had already joined me. Being the competitive, driven person she was lasted until the very end of her life. She wanted to live the longest of any of my children, her siblings.

With Edith's passing, our house on William Street now stood empty. All of the voices of our family who had lived there were now silent; we all had left. Edith had asked one of my grandchildren to be the executor of her estate, which included our family's home. Now what would be done with our home which contained the memories of our lives? It was a formidable task to approach the house, turning the spider key in the front lock, to attempt to sort out the contents that had amassed from over one hundred years of lives being lived in it. Edith was a good caretaker of our home, structurally it was sound. During the last ten years of her life it had become difficult for her to keep up with its caretaking demands, both inside and out.

There were many treasures and memories in the house, most of insignificant monetary value. The furniture from when Charles and I were living there remained, from the couch in the living room to the huge, solid wood dining room table that seated fourteen. The house sheltered lives worth of history in boxes, trunks, shoe boxes, and (later on in time) plastic bags. One example was the huge pots for boiling water were still sitting on their shelves in the kitchen where I had spent so much time working for my family. There were also boxes of tools from the barn (which had to be torn down in the 1980's, since it was sagging from its own weight) that Charles and our boys used.

My daughters' belongings made up a significant portion of our home's contents. All of my four daughters had lived in the Joliet area their entire lives (only Esther having moved to Chicago for a few years to pursue her nursing career) and none had children to pass things on to. Only one of my daughters, Alice, had married, which lasted only five years. Thus most of their possessions remained in our home on William Street following their passing. As Edith and Ruth had lived in our home their entire lives, any property they had accumulated was there. That included the car that only Ruth was able to drive and Edith's golf clubs, which were so important to her.

For almost fifty years the treasures of Esther and Alice's lives were there, weathering the cold, dark, slightly moist basement. When both of them had passed away (before 1960), Edith and Ruth were living in the main floors of the home. Esther's and Alice's things were put in the cellar, including their cedar trunks that were part of their wedding trousseau. (Trousseau is probably too strong of a word – our family had few things to pass on to follow them into their marriage homes.) Esther, having never married, had never used her 'trousseau', although she had set up a household for herself living in a house on my son Walter's property. Alice's personal items were there, also, as she had returned to live on William Street after her divorce from her husband, which was a difficult action in our family. Alice was the first and only one of anyone in our family to divorce. It wasn't something that was even a remote possibility when a marriage was undergoing difficulty. Usually a female relative would try to console the woman in the relationship, and a male would approach the husband to offer suggestions for resolving the conflict. Circumstances had to be extremely extenuating for a divorce to even be considered. Her husband, who had been a roofer who was exposed to high temperatures during the hot summer days in Joliet on the tar rooftops, had suffered a mental breakdown, and was committed to a mental hospital.

In the late summer of 1999 Julia, Bill and their two daughters had come back to Illinois to introduce the extended family to their second daughter, who was then five months old. The four of them went to our home on William Street to ascertain what items they might wish to keep as remembrances. They ascended the narrow steps, turned the metal 'spider' key in the lock, and crossed into the world within the walls of our home.

Three of my granddaughters had spent months of time sifting through most of the contents of our home. This task was a huge undertaking, requiring many hours of effort and emotional upheaval in sorting and discerning all of the items that held memories of our family. They purposefully sorted and laid items out on tables and surfaces that were remnants of my children's lives; photographs, souvenirs from travels, china sets, and our furniture were all set out for display. After several weeks and months of work, other family members were invited to come by the house and select items they would take to their own homes as remembrances.

I am happy to say all of my grandchildren and great grandchildren were respectful of each other. Each one that visited our family home took some items for remembering our family. No one gorged themselves at this buffet of remembrances of our family's lives. Those that came to our house during those months of 1999 took what they could comfortably absorb and left some for others that would follow.

Standing in the entryway of our home was a poignant moment for Julia. Her eyes scanned the rooms where so many events in our family's lives had been lived. So many memories were now locked up and contained in times past. Now all was silent. My children's presence was only possible in their spirits, no longer their physical selves. The house looked so unfamiliar with all of the contents laid out on tables and furniture. It was like a store where all the items were of no cost. Yet the stories and history behind each of the items were of priceless value to Julia. She was overwhelmed with the volume of history that was contained in our home and sad at the time she couldn't do anything more to capture it than to select a few objects as remembrances.

The items were artifacts from my children's lives, a display for younger generations to review. Some of the items were common, everyday items not worth much – green marbled glasses purchased from a dime store (a store so named because, at its origin, most items cost under a dime – hard to even imagine in present day times!) in the 1960's. Some of the items were priceless for the memories and significance they stood for – Edith's letter holder purchased on her trip to the World's Fair held in Seattle in 1962. (This was one of the items Julia selected to take to her home on that day). Every time Julia looks at it she remembers our family and Edith's independence. Other items lay there in wait for a new custodian, for example a set of china that Alice had acquired during her marriage.

Julia entered the kitchen. Bill was watching over their daughters, both were in their car seats taking a nap. The kitchen was quiet; no one else is in the room. Julia looked around, surveying the walls, the sink, the stove. She reflected on what my life must have been like – preparing food, washing, cleaning. She thought of my daughters standing there, helping me with tasks. She thought of conversations between me and my daughters, of my boys running through the kitchen to try to pick up a quick snack, and how I might have looked out the window while I was working.

As she stood there, the room looked much different than when my children were young. Now there were objects covering almost every surface, on display for family members. The 'new' stove, installed in the 1960's, was white, sturdy and not giving up almost forty years later. Our porcelain white sink was still in use, its width big enough to fit multiple uses – washing vegetables, dishes, or babies. The wooden countertops had been covered with some sort of material I don't recognize – this was done long after I had passed away.

The sun streamed through the south facing window; natural light that I could transmit messages through bathed the room. Julia spied a rectangular glass butter dish on the countertop, the light glinting off of it in a kaleidoscope of colors. It was made of thick glass, patterns cut on its outside, in the days where efficiency and reuse were not as much a part of producing a product. Julia picked up the dish, choosing it from among the items to take with her. She held it in her hand, thinking of how it must have been in everyday use at our house. Her thoughts were hurried along by her family's impending departure for their next destination. She stood at the doorway of the kitchen and for an unknown reason, for the first time in her life, began talking to me aloud:

> Hello Grandma Christina – I know you worked in this kitchen many hours. Your daughters were probably here helping you with your tasks. There's the sink where the dishes were washed. The sink was also probably where you washed your children when they were babies.

Julia was directly talking to me – asking me what my life was like when I worked in my kitchen with my daughters. I sent her a picture of Esther standing beside me, her long hair braided back from her face and falling down her back, us working side by side.

To let her know I heard her and that I was there, I sent Julia another signal, this time one she could hear. The glass of the butter dish clinked in Julia's hand. Julia stared down at the dish in wonder; she knew it was me communicating to her. Julia hadn't moved her hand; she realized it must be some other form of communication. It was a moment of great success for me. Julia realized I could send her messages and was aware of my virtual presence. It was a beginning of her awareness of me.

I wish I could tell Julia more: that I'm with her every step of the way, that I went through hardships too, that she can handle what will come her way. There isn't anything else I can relay to her at this time to allay her fears and concerns about Anna's future. Only my spiritual presence is in my kitchen, not my earthly body to audibly communicate.

She almost literally backed up in amazement at what had just happened. She was astounded by the connection between us. Then Julia's rational mind took over - thinking of the next place she needed to go, how she would transport her daughters in their baby carriers to the car (those machines were called automobiles in my day). Our communication had ended its two way messaging. The moment was over.

Their family of four departed the house. Julia picked up Anna and walked to the front entryway. They passed over the threshold of our home, closed the door and turned the "old fashioned" iron key in the lock. That was the ending of Julia's interaction with our family home – she walked down the narrow porch steps in the front of the house (as in Photo 3 of Alice, Walter, and Ruth in the Appendix). She walked toward her life, leaving our family home behind. With the intensity of the moment she and I had just shared, Julia was drained from the emotion we had exchanged.

The next day Bill and Julia's family decided to visit our family's grave markers at Elmhurst cemetery on East Washington Street. Julia did not remember ever visiting our gravesites; this would be her first time. Visiting our gravesites was not something that my children and grandchildren did very often, if at all. I knew when they thought about me, and I appreciated that.

The cemetery is located in a part of town that was not on a pathway she'd taken before. I am glad she chose to visit. (Unknown to her, I had called to her during her sleeping hours to take her time and energy to visit my gravesite.) Bill drove them in their rented car into the cemetery, the limestone walls enveloping them, navigating to where our grave markers are located.

Julia stepped out of the car, carrying Anna in her car seat. As she approached our family's grave markers, a sick, nauseous feeling washed over her, unlike anything that's happened to her before so suddenly. She felt like when a person is riding in a car or merry go round, where the world seems to be rushing by you and one's stomach is churning from the motion. This is not a feeling or experience I wanted for her, however my spirit wasn't as powerful as Charles'. His gravesite is to the right of mine, and he could see this visit unfolding. If Charles had met Julia in person, he wouldn't have liked her. She would have reminded him of our son Walter (her grandfather) and her personality would have been too much for Charles – they would have conflicted at every turn. He chose to send Julia a message to turn back, to go away.

As she approached our markers, Julia tried to squelch the nausea she so suddenly felt. The purpose of her visit was to think, reflect, and pay tribute to us. The malaise that had washed over her body was making this difficult for her. I saw her there; I am so glad she came to visit. She located our grave markers and softly said "Hello Grandma Christina". She looked over at Charles' headstone, which is larger and more ornate than mine. Charles' energy overwhelmed the situation. Julia felt increasingly nauseous, as if she might reflux her lunch. Anna Christina wailed from her car seat – she was uncomfortable, also, feeling the spiritual energy around her.

They both made a hasty retreat to the car. Julia was not sure she had the strength to get back to it, some forty feet away. When they arrived at the car, Julia put Anna and her car seat in the back seat and sank herself onto the seat beside Anna. She didn't have the energy to buckle Anna's seat belt, the feeling of nausea overwhelming her. Bill assisted by securing Anna's car seat via the seat belt and returned to the driver's seat to drive them away from the cemetery.

Julia asked if they might locate the restroom within the cemetery walls, fearing the effect of the nausea. Bill drove them back down the winding cemetery road to the front entrance, looking to see if the caretaker's building was open and might have an accessible restroom. By the time their car had reached the building and the front gates of the cemetery, Julia was relieved of the negative energy she felt and seemingly instantaneously was no longer nauseous or feeling ill. A huge weight was lifted; the cloud that had settled onto her was removed by leaving our gravesites. She has never had that feeling any other time in her thirty two years of her life and hasn't since that day. At the time Julia did not know what was likely occurring during her visit. Her level of awareness of the power of the human spirit had just recently been ignited.

They concluded their visit to Joliet, and their family of four returned home to Seattle, to continue on with their daily lives. They were able to pack some of the items they retrieved from our home on William Street on the plane; some books, other memorabilia. One of the items was a limestone brick that was near the back door of our house. The brick was stored there in the event one needed replacing on our home. They packed the brick into a carryon bag, to transport it back to their home in Seattle. Bill lugged the brick in his carryon bag on the airplane ride home. As I watched them carrying this brick on their trip back to their home, I thought it somewhat silly of them to transport this heavy stone brick. But Bill and Julia thought it important to have a physical memory of the building that had been our family's home for over one hundred years.

Unknowns

Julia and Bill's family life continued on, filled with more doctor's visits and additions to the pieces of the information puzzle of Anna's life. One of the puzzle pieces was ascertained by indicators of how Anna's brain was developing. A physical means to indicate brain development is to measure the circumference of a child's head. If it is increasing, this indicates that the brain inside is growing. At each doctor visit the paper measuring tape would be brought out. Measurement of Anna's head at the visits showed a fraction of a centimeter in growth. She diverged from the typical growth curve after her first two months of life. The trajectory continued throughout her first years. An X-ray of Anna's head was taken to see if the sutures, that are soft when a baby is born, had prematurely fused together, causing the skull to not be able to expand. That possibility was ruled out. It was clear that Anna's brain wasn't developing as typical for her age. A new word is added to Anna's list of diagnoses: microcephaly. This literally means "small brain".

The foundation of the walls of isolation from other parents was laid when Anna was born. Day by day, brick by brick they increased in size and strength with each new revelation of Anna's differences from typical children. There is loneliness in having a child with special needs – by definition the situation and circumstances are different. To further this effect Anna Christina's diagnosis separated her from the typically developing population. This diagnosis doesn't have a well mapped out plan and trajectory – microcephaly ("small head") only occurs once in every 80,000 births. Even amongst those with this diagnosis there is a wide range of developmental functionalities possible.

Bill and Julia were faced with the unknown on many levels with the diagnoses Anna was receiving. There were a few diagnoses that were ruled out, which was comforting on some level. Anna didn't have a heart defect and her skull was not prematurely fused.

However by this time it had become apparent that the impact of her brain injury was limiting her brain's ability to continue to develop. It was still unexplained to Bill and Julia what the lack of development would mean for Anna's future. Will she have a major ("grand mal") seizure in the next ten minutes? Will she reflux and aspirate fluid into her lungs in the next day? Will she be able to learn to read?

The unknown can be difficult for anyone to live with. Everyone on Earth has some element of the unknown in their lives - what will tomorrow be like? Will a person still have their possessions? Will the boy a teenage girl likes ask her to the school dance? Most every human would like to think we can plan, schedule and organize the details of our lives. Some appear to be successful at maintaining rigor and order in their lives, keeping the unknowns at bay.

For Bill and Julia, all of the unknowns swirling around Anna make it difficult to come up with what would even resemble a plan for their day or week. Would Anna get sick in two days, causing Bill and Julia to need to reschedule a family get together or a rare evening out? Would Anna be able to be cared for by someone else so that Bill and Julia could go to work the next day? Will Anna ever be able to live away from her parents?

At times all of these questions and pressures become overwhelming. Everyone deals with unknowns and uncertainty. For Bill and Julia Anna's very life is of unknown status and uncertain. It's a very difficult place for a parent to be. Their concerns of the unknowns for Anna are perpetually circling around the basic functions of life: 'is she breathing?' or "is Anna feeding and eliminating effectively?" Experiencing these unknowns feels like not graduating, not completing a challenge to move on to the next. Anna continually repeats and retakes the same basic tests each and every day.

In order to continue functioning in their day to day responsibilities, Bill & Julia needed to reach a point where they could be happy for the here and now. Today is another day of life. It has become reality, Anna is still here, still living on Earth. They enjoy that day for what it is. They cannot do anything about yesterday – it has already passed. They can make attempts at positively influencing tomorrow, but it hasn't happened yet.

Don't let me lead you to think that Julia is walking around, bouncing in her step from happiness every second of her days. Some days Julia is so exhausted from hearing and caring for Anna at night she is appears to be walking around in a fog. She fumbles with trying to remember the details of her life for that day – tasks to be completed, monitoring status. The sleep deprivation turns Julia into a person she never was before – forgetting to show up for an appointment with a business colleague or sick with a cold almost every weekend.

The days where Anna is in pain, crying, causes more stress on her family because they are trying to figure out how to best help her. Her cry causes a stress response in Julia's body. It's like a siren has sounded to take action. Julia constantly lives in the anticipation of the next crisis or mini-crisis Anna will need assistance with.

To try to obtain more medical data, a repeat EEG was conducted on Anna. The leads were glued all over Anna's head in a painstaking process which takes over an hour to complete. Complicating the test, Anna must be sedated because she cannot respond to commands or actions requested of her and needs to stay completely still. Following the test, a neurologist interpreted the results. The net was there was no new information; just that her brain still was sending abnormal signals, causing seizures. Despite all the medications and examinations, Anna was still in the same state as she had been months earlier.

How Anna feels during a seizure is locked inside of her. It is an unknown to the rest of the people on Earth. Others who have experienced a seizure and are able to verbalize the feeling describe losing consciousness. They have no memory of what happened during the seizure. Anna seems to go through similar circumstances – she twitches and shakes for up to thirty seconds. Her muscles receive signals from her brain, causing them to tense up and harden. This muscle tenseness is commonly referred to as a 'charley horse'. During a seizure Anna experiences this sensation in many of the muscles in her body – her arms, her legs. Anna's seizures can be triggered by a sudden loud noise, light, or other times nothing specific. She experiences them often, throughout the day and night. Considering what is going inside Anna's brain, she does remarkably well. Most of the time during the day she is able to calm herself, allowing the seizure to pass to return to her baseline state. Only when she needs something does she vocalize/make a sound.

Nighttime is a completely different world for Anna. It seems like another force takes over, disturbing Anna in her sleep. Her nighttime seizures cause her to wake up crying in a visceral reaction of confusion and probably fear. Her cry pierces the night, jolting her mother out of bed to come assist her. The impact to her brain causes her to not sleep and function like others. She can be awake almost all night and stay awake through the following day. Her body is set to a clock that is not of Earth – she regulates herself on her own time. To make matters more frustrating, one neurologist had even told Julia that Anna couldn't be having seizures during the night (which is completely incorrect). This neurologist is no longer practicing medicine.

Julia is like me. She did everything she possibly could for her family. She rises each time Anna cries out – night or day. It must be the mother instinct, to do whatever it takes for your child when they cannot help themselves. I wish I could tell her how well she is doing, to offer some encouragement. Many of us mothers subvert our own physical needs for our children. After a night of Anna being awake much of the night, Julia tells herself to just get through this one day, that tomorrow would be better and easier. The catch up on sleep and rest is always a day away, not here and now.

Machines begin to be added as a part of Anna's daily life. She has a machine to help her receive nutrition at a constant steady state so she can absorb and process the food. It must be delivered in small amounts, so as not to overwhelm Anna's digestive system. Almost like feeding a baby bird with an eyedropper – Anna's system is so delicate that it can easily be pushed too far, causing her pain.

The suction machine came next into their lives. This is to assist with removing the fluids in Anna's mouth that she cannot handle on her own. Fluids accumulate in her mouth, causing her to gag or cough because she cannot effectively swallow. Each of Anna's coughs wrenches Julia's heart. It is a wrangling sound of Anna struggling to clear her airway. They start out with coughing, most often quickly escalating to a gag. The sound of Anna attempting to inhale air, making a loud gasping sound, makes her parents wonder each time if she will recover. Her face becomes flushed from both the coughing and the temporary lack of oxygen. There can't be many worse sounds in the whole world than hearing your child literally gasp for air. Anna experiences many of these episodes, gasping for air, daily.

While both of these machines are necessary for Anna's continued health, they add a greater level of complexity to Bill and Julia's life. Both the feeding pump and the suction machine must be by Anna's side every hour of the day. They must be cleaned, primed, and prepared to ensure they are effective to meet Anna's needs. The administration or use of the machines must be enacted at the moment Anna requires it, which is all unknown and unpredictable. And the machines require electricity, so they must be charged up to ensure they are ready to assist Anna.

Anna was now three years old. Despite all the suctioning her parents assist her with, she landed in the hospital with pneumonia. Fluids from her throat had seeped into her lungs and became infected. She had a high fever, breathing difficulties, and was refluxing/gagging/throwing up. In her hospital room, fluids seemed to be coming out of every aspect of her body – her mouth, her feeding tube, her backside.

She lost too much fluid and food. Her body just couldn't keep pace with the (liquid) food being pumped into her stomach. Anna cried out in pain as food was pumped into her stomach, being unable to sustain the demands of processing. To alleviate a probable cause of Anna's pain, her feeding pump was stopped. An IV remained in Anna's vein to infuse fluids and electrolytes into her system.

After a few days Anna cannot sustain herself and her body weight on fluids alone. A typical person can last for maybe a week, seven days, without food before the body begins its process of shutting down. Anna's IV site had failed twice in the previous three days. An IV failure is uncomfortable in and of itself; fluids go into the surrounding tissue, causing it to puff up and inflame. Each time, no matter of the hour of the day, an IV placement specialist is called to try to locate another vein to insert the IV in. Anna's hands, feet, arms and legs are all checked for a potential IV site. Sometimes her vein just won't support the IV, and the whole process must be restarted.

It is difficult for Anna, of course, with the pain of being poked by the IV needle and having her limb constricted. She sometimes tried to swat the offending item away with either her arm or foot. The medical team resorts to covering the IV site up with a 'dog cage' - a piece of plastic cut out to cover the site, then wrapped with medical tape. Another strategy was to put a hospital sock over the entire site on either her hand or foot.

Anna's parents were worried about her – she couldn't absorb nutrition. The days stretched into a week. Anna was crying, cranky and irritated also because she was hungry by this time. Anna's doctors made the decision that she required TPN (Total Parenteral Nutrition), because she could not absorb any food through her gastro-intestinal system for almost a week. TPN is difficult for veins to support, as typically humans process foods via the stomach, a path that enables filtering and sorting of the nutrients out to the blood stream. With TPN that is all bypassed to directly deposit them into the bloodstream. And it is very expensive (over $100 per day), as each person's exact nutritional needs must be calculated before their TPN mixture is prepared.

In July of 2000, it was one of few sunny months in Seattle. Most people in Seattle have summers where they get out and enjoy the outdoors, maybe attending barbeques, going camping, or going to outdoor concerts. None of that was a possibility for Bill, Julia, or Anna. Anna's parents were round the clock attending to Anna in her hospital room, almost sick with worry and fear that she wouldn't be able to absorb any form of nutrition. They would bring their youngest child, who was not yet walking, and put her in an empty crib in Anna's room. Their summer was filled with medicines, fever, reflux, medical equipment and worry.

Bill and Julia learned that summer that parents, friends and relatives that are visiting or caring for a child in the hospital are oftentimes in a daze of confusion, terror, dread, and concern. They try to continue functioning as usual – making small talk with others sometimes helps push their fears out a few minutes farther. And sometimes they simply cry seeing a child's toy – maybe thinking of the similar one their child has at home or maybe, as in Julia's case, thinking how Anna would never be able to use that toy. It is a fragile balance of emotions as a parent to keep it together when your child is in the hospital, to keep the wheels turning to move forward.

During the weeks Anna was hospitalized that summer was the first time Julia had a discussion with Anna's doctors about the possibility of Anna dying. The doctor indicated the seriousness of Anna's situation, along with her opinion that Anna "wasn't there yet" (i.e. at the end of her life). There were still other things that they could try to sustain Anna's life. After two more weeks in the hospital, Anna rallied and slowly began to be able to take food via her gastrostomy tube in her stomach. Slowly is an understatement – the feeding pump would be increased by 1 cc per hour over the course of a twenty four hour period. If Anna started to cry, which came out as a sharp, painful cry in her discomfort, the increase for the next hour would be postponed. It was a long process, taking almost a week to get back up to the 90 ccs per hour that were required for Anna's adequate nutrition.

One resident, a first year medical student, had ordered Anna's feeding pump to be set at 120 ccs per hour. He had consulted his medical books and found, for her height, age and current weight, this was the recommended number for her caloric intake. The order was enacted by the nursing staff during the night, when Bill and Julia had taken a respite away from the hospital.

The next morning as they walked into Anna's hospital room, Anna was crying in agony. No one seemed to know what to do or how to stop Anna's crying or pain. Additional pain medication wasn't really an option, as it has the effect of slowing down the bowel system, which in Anna was already too slow for her comfort. Bill looked at the feeding pump and saw the rate was set at 120cc's per hour. Right away he walked over to the pump and turned it off. Then he asked the nurse who had ordered the rate set to that level. Standing six foot three inches tall, Bill is somewhat of an imposing figure. The nurse scurried off to call the doctor who had ordered the feeding rate increase.

The young doctor, having worked all night on call, walked into Anna's room about a half an hour later. Bill asked him why he thought 120 ccs per hour would work for Anna. The young doctor replied "That's what my book said". Bill then proceeded to give the young doctor a lesson not contained in medical books. He told him that while the book may give guidance, each person is individual and the doctor needed to listen to either the patient or those responsible for the patient to advise on their care. Bill told him what pain the doctor's decision had caused Anna, and warned him not to make the mistake again with anyone else. Lastly, he told the doctor he would not be allowed on Anna's medical care team going forward.

Bill was protecting Anna and championing for her needs. Watching all this I marveled at how far fathers had come in participating in care for their child – particularly this father. It's wonderful for a child to have such champions in both of their parents. I couldn't imagine Charles advocating for anything for our children, with the possible exception of Herbert's schooling.

Decisions

Bill and Julia are cornered by the circumstances of Anna's life. They cannot avoid their situation or the decisions that must be made for Anna that affect the quality and the extent of her life. Do they authorize a different feeding tube inserted into Anna's intestine tract? When Anna has "feeding intolerances" – where her body cannot accept nutrition through the digestive track – do they force feed nutrients directly into Anna's blood stream? Do they provide supportive oxygen if she cannot intake enough oxygen on her own? They have to face this music, it is continually playing.

Given Anna's medical needs and condition, it had become clear that her life expectancy is shortened. During Anna's following hospital stays, of which there are many and almost innumerable, doctors each time must ask what decisions and actions Anna's parents want the medical team to enact if Anna were to go into distress – i.e. her heart stops beating or she is unable to breathe. Julia was choked up; it is a difficult topic to comprehend. Julia would rather not think of decisions and planning of the possibility of her child's death. On the other hand she wants to have thought through the scenarios and possibilities, so that if or when an event to Anna's livelihood occurs, guidance has been established. She knows she needs to answer the doctor's questions to best advocate for Anna. How much to intervene? A personal decision for any parent – or any individual on Earth. Lucky ones get to choose; some don't have the luxury of deciding whether they want treatment or to know of their diagnosis. Others choose not to know, proceeding along without the knowledge of the situation.

The doctors ask Bill and Julia to fill out the POLST (Physician Orders for Life Sustaining Treatment) form, which is written, medically authorized instructions of her parent's choices for Anna if distress occurs. It is similar to an advanced health care directive for an adult. Checking one box indicates one thing – checking another box means something different is intended for Anna's future. As a parent caring for a living child, it is difficult to even think about the choices on the form. All of the emotions of protectiveness and help for your child are laid out. No parent would wish to be facing these sorts of decisions. Julia decided it would be best to push through her own hurt, fear, concern, and love for Anna to make the decisions ahead of time. The situation is almost like a Greek mythology story where a parent has to choose what life their child will have, where none of the options are all that great.

Facing the possibility of death is hard – no one wants to talk about it, even though we all realize at some level that it is going to happen to all humans at some time. It is even more difficult when the person is a child, your child. As parents we gave our children life. The natural order is that we parents would pass away before our children. Facing the thoughts and likely reality of your child passing away before you as their parent, any sort of 'natural order' has been disrupted.

Others ask "How is Anna?" a question that would normally come up in conversation about how another person's child is doing. The answer chokes in Bill and Julia's throats – to answer it honestly and factually would take way too long and is not the happy answer most people are expecting or looking for. They can barely answer – sometimes Julia squeaks out "fine" and then changes the subject. It is just so painful to revisit every moment how Anna is not tracking to a typical child's development and her lifelong expectations for achievement. On a different level it is like a relative asking "When are you getting married?" if you are single.

Bill and Julia had discussed having a third child. Their dream came true with the birth of their third child, a healthy daughter. Three girls. Throughout Julia's pregnancy she was closely monitored, given the past history with Anna. This would be Julia's last pregnancy – carrying a child while trying to lift, move, and care for

Anna (who weighed over sixty pounds at this point) was very cumbersome and difficult.

Connecting in Sweden

Julia's life was filled with her work during the daytime, meeting Anna's demanding care needs, caring for her younger two daughters, and running her household. There was not much time for her and Bill to nourish their relationship, with all of the caretaking demands they had. There is no blame between Bill and Julia as to why Anna was so impacted. They both continue to try to care for Anna they best they can, given the knowledge they have of what she needs to survive.

The relationship between spouses is especially vulnerable to strain when caring for a child with disabilities, with the rate of divorce being over sixty percent. Parents of typical children often experience marriage difficulties relating to child rearing. The situation is amplified when there are so many and complex decisions and actions that must be made to care for a child who is medically fragile.

With Anna's medical complexity and all of the other tasks Julia was juggling, that left little time for what might be called a 'hobby'. Now that Anna's health had stabilized for a period of time, she began to think about spending some time on activities that were for her interest. One of those was in our family's history. She had lacked the time and energy to pursue information than anything more than casually asking about our lives. Her interest remained dormant from inaction for many years while she was submerged in her work and building her adult life. An impetus to visit Sweden, to find where I had emigrated from, surged toward the top of Julia's list of priorities. She was eager to find more details on our family regarding those of us that had long since passed away.

To start her journey she had bits of family information, compiled from various sources. One of the sources was Nilla's youngest daughter, Ethel, who had detailed out Nilla's family tree. Julia also had a copy of the first page of Charles family's bible that had been passed down to him from the first entry in 1750. This bible was given to one of my great-great granddaughters when our home was emptied after Edith's passing. Edith had also written down for Julia the name of the city I was from in Sweden as Skone. (You may recall from my earlier description, the region of Skane, which is what Edith was referring to, not a city name.) These scraps of information provided Julia clues on a trail that was dormant for over one hundred years.

Julia planned and booked a trip to Sweden, my homeland, to attempt to locate the place where I emigrated from and learn more about our family. Her mother, my granddaughter, and Julia's second daughter, my great-great granddaughter, would accompany Julia. I was so pleased to see that three generations of my descendants would travel to Sweden, to see the country and research our family history. While Julia, her mother and her daughter were on the trip to Sweden, Anna and her youngest sister would be cared for by their father, Bill. (A father caring for his children would have been outside of any expectation in my days on Earth. Julia had a much better balance of childcare than I could have ever dreamed of.)

The three arrived in Göteborg (this is the Swedish spelling, Gothenburg is the Anglicized spelling), on the west coast of Sweden, in May of 2004. The last visit from one of our American family members to Sweden was Nilla's son Ben, my nephew. He and his wife visited Sweden in the 1970's to see our sister Johanna's daughter, Anna. By this time Anna had lived in Stockholm for over forty years – long ago and far away from the farmhouse my sisters and I had grown up in. While Nilla and Johanna were alive they corresponded, keeping in touch at least every year. They had encouraged their children to correspond with each other, and the links between their families were sustained across the ocean that physically divided them.

From Göteborg my three descendants drove to Lund, where my husband Charles had a niece still living. Lund is also where the Landsarkivit is located for the region of Skane. My daughter Edith had given Julia the woman's name and address, who was my children's first cousin, as both Edith and Ruth had corresponded with her when they were all in their younger years. Julia made this town a stop on their trip to visit the relative who was ninety six at the time and to conduct research at the Landsarkivit. The relative didn't want to meet in person, however, they did talk on the phone. She spoke English very well, but was nervous about meeting in person, owing to her age of over ninety years and her language skills. The conversation didn't lead to any more details about Charles' family.

While Julia was at the Landsarkivit researching the archives, my granddaughter and great-great granddaughter passed the time together in the city of Lund. They went to the playground in the center of the city, where there were many children playing outside, who had just been released from their school day. Julia's daughter was six years old and spoke no Swedish. She tried to join into the games of the playground, without speaking the same language. Her efforts to participate in the play activities were somewhat successful – although she spent much of the time running to and fro in the grass trying to figure out what next step she should take via nonverbal communication with the Swedish children. It was interesting for me to watch the children, as young as four through about age eight, interact with each other. Spoken language wasn't a requirement for playing together at that age. They all just played together, without verbalizing. It was apparent to me, though, that my great-great granddaughter was trying to figure out the rules and expectations for the game being played on the playground in Lund.

Meanwhile, literally across town, Julia was successful at the Landsarkivit. She had found an English speaking docent who was able to help her find the rack of microfilm that applied to Verum, the area where I was born. Another challenge presented itself when

301

Julia had to make her way to the newer building of archives, located on the outskirts of town, to find the microfilm records from the parish I lived in. Between a taxi, a bus, and walking, Julia found her way to the other location of the archives which held the greater detail of the parish I was born in. Julia didn't speak Swedish, which hampered her efforts to find the correct bus to her destination. She did somehow make it there within not too long of a time.

It was at that location she found the exact entry of my family's history in the parish records kept by the country of Sweden, showing all my family members listed and our christening dates. She knew she'd found the correct entry and location for where I grew up; she learned and verified additional details about me and my immediate family, over a hundred years later. She was literally tingling with excitement of having found the records of where I grew up, after over one hundred years had passed.

The next day the three drove to the area where my family's farm had been. Being remote from a larger city, none of the local people living in the area spoke English. Julia had become confused as to which farm was probably ours in the area, and stopped at a farmer's home to ask where the Nilsson farm was located. She was asking, over a hundred years later, where my family's farm was. Somewhat improbable that anyone would even remember. However, this was a small farming community, and most everyone's family who lived there had been there for hundreds of years. Through some hand waving, pointing, looking at the names written down on paper, the farmer pointed to a direction down the road.

Coming up to the location of our farm, they stopped the car and got out to walk around. They found no buildings on the land; the farmhouse no longer existed. They walked through the clearing where the house I grew up in once stood. All that is left now is the outline of the house's frame. The trees gently swayed in the wind –

whispering their call of welcome. That was all that was physically there. I was there, in spirit, watching them, guiding them. It was a joy to see they had found the location of the home where I had grown up. On a different level, they had found me.

Filled with a sense of connection, my granddaughter, great-granddaughter (Julia), and great-great-granddaughter climbed back in their Swedish car. Their next stop was to find the church, the parish, where I was christened. They found that relatively easily, as the church is located in the small village which is the county seat, Verum. There didn't seem to be any businesses in the village, just the church and very few residences (recall that in Sweden most of the buildings farmers lived in were relocated to their farming plots back in the 1800's). They didn't see anyone walking around. It was as if they were visiting a village with no inhabitants.

They saw the spire on the building that was the church and drove towards it. They parked the car in the graveled lot near the church and approached the church building. Around the church, marked off with a waist high picket fence, was what looked to be the church's cemetery in the church yard. They walked past the grave markers to approach the steps of the church. Julia felt a reverence for the graves of people who had been buried there over hundreds of years, as signified by dates on the grave markers. She realized some of the grave markers could have been family members of hers who had long ago passed away. It seemed to her irreverent to walk past these graves of people who had left Earth so long ago. What were their stories? What were there lives like? So many details of people's lives that were now silenced.

Looking towards the church building refocused Julia's intent to go inside the church. For the time being, they passed the gravesites to ascend the few steps up to the vestibule, the small room that opens into the sanctuary. These were the same steps I walked up every Sunday as I grew up.

Julia was impressed with the ornateness of the church. It was apparent to her that the church was supported financially - it was well maintained. Finances were accrued through the government's collection of dues or fees to the church. The government then paid for the church buildings and upkeep, along with the pastor's salary and support. This was accurate up until 2000, when the church was removed from the country's governmental control and finances.

Looking around the sanctuary, the main room of the church, Julia saw the stained glass windows and the lectern set apart from where the congregation would be seated in their pews. These were fixtures of the building that were there when I attended this church. From her eyes she was seeing the same scene I had, with the expanse of over one hundred years between when each of us was physically present there on Earth. The format of the church service has changed so that the lectern is no longer used. Presently it is now the custom for the pastor or minister to be on the same physical level with the people of the congregation, not feet higher where they have to incline their necks to look at him or her.

Julia was struck with amazement to think she had found a physical building where I had been during my growing up years. Especially so given that prior to her visit to Sweden, the place I grew up was unknown to the rest of my descendants. After surveying the rest of the church, to which an addition in the 1950's provided extra floor space, they paused a moment in front of the altar. Julia thought about that this had been the exact place I had been christened in 1867. Close to one hundred and forty years separated our physical presence in this church. It was a moment of connection between us. Julia knew she'd found the places that had been important to the beginnings of my life on Earth. She whispered to me that she was there in the church of my christening. I whispered to her in response, which Julia received on a subconscious level. Her rational brain wasn't processing my message to her, but she did know in her heart of my presence.

Julia composed herself and readied to go outside to the church yard, to the cemetery and grave markers. My three descendants walked up and down the rows of grave markers, looking for a name they have on their family history list. The list detailed birth and death dates, which provided a means to ensure they had the correct "Elna Nilsson", as both Elna and Nilsson were typical names during that time period. There were quite a few men named Lars, Nels, or Anders. Last names didn't vary much, either – there are many Johnssons, Anderssons, Nilssons, and Larssons. "son" is the Swedish spelling of last names – Norwegian last names tend to end with "sen", and very few of these grave markers had names ending in "sen".

Some of the grave markers are made of stone, large and ornately engraved. In other sections of the yard are wood grave markers, set close together, their etchings sometimes weathered away by the snow, wind, and rain, unreadable. Julia located my sister Johanna's (Julia's great-great aunt) grave, verifying it must be hers, as the marker had the same name, dates of birth and death shown in the family history documents Julia has. This was a validation of my family's history, that it had been accurately recorded and successfully passed down through multiple generations across the world. It was a thrill for Julia to realize she had truly found where I had spent my youth and where my family, her family, was from. The pieces of the puzzle fit.

Johanna died August 22, 1918, three years before her husband Olaf passed away. My sister's headstone was etched in a flat marble slate, but not located anywhere near her husband's in the cemetery. Olaf would have been responsible for the choices about his wife's grave marker and the costs for her burial. The proximity of her grave is in the area of the cemetery with less affluent people, signified in their plainer grave markings and further distance from the church building. Julia wondered if the proximity of their graves indicated how Johanna's life was – separate and distanced from her husband Olaf? What did Johanna experience during her marriage and later years? What was her daily life like? Did Johanna somehow disgrace herself in Hagnarp's society to be buried so far away from her husband? Maybe they were not living together as a married couple any longer during their lifetimes? Given the timeframe of the late 1800's in Sweden, Johanna likely had to follow what her husband had decided. Julia's questions go unanswered – this piece of my family's history has long since been buried.

Olaf, Johanna's husband, is buried next to his parents. His grave marker is prominent in the cemetery, made of limestone rising three feet tall. This piece of extravagance displayed his success in his business endeavors, an indicator to all who passed by then and now that he was a monetarily successful person during his life. He must have had some standing in the community and wealth to be able to afford it.

It was an overwhelming day for Julia, to know she had found the location of where I grew up and the church I had attended as a child. The travelers went back to their hotel room and fell asleep within a short time from the exhaustion of the day.

Following their visit to the locations where I grew up, the three travelers went on to general sightseeing activities in Sweden and Norway, including the cities of Stockholm, Oslo, and Bergen. They saw the Orrefors crystal factory which has been in operation since 1898 in Smaland with its beautiful sculptures of glass. They sampled Swedish food, which is somewhat bland compared to all the tastes and spices available in the world today. Julia's daughter, who was six years old, ate a lot of ham, as that was the only food she was certain to like. It was served at breakfast, lunch, and dinner, although she did vary away from ham for Swedish meatballs.

In and around Stockholm they visited Drottningholm, the stunning palace outside of Stockholm. It was humorous to watch the three of them driving there – they were a bit lost trying to follow their guide book while Julia was driving the car. After a few, several really, wrong turns they finally arrived at the palace. It was worth the trip for them. I loved watching them explore the many rooms of the palace, and seeing all the finery that is there. Some of their history via my Father's money is in that palace, as he was a taxpayer for all of his adult life. Julia's daughter, then six years old, was feeling tired and cranky by this time in the day. To help her mood, Julia purchased her a gift from the gift store. My great-great granddaughter then toured the remainder of their visit at the palace with a tutu over her clothing. (This was not something that would have ever been done in my time on Earth. I tried not to frown on them...I guess sometimes parents have to let things go.)

Their trip was a success – Julia had 'found' me. It deepened our connection and satiated her interest in our family's history. Upon returning home to Seattle, Julia had written up the family history knowledge she had uncovered. The information was then filed away for reference at some other time – maybe when she had more time.

Accepting

Throughout Anna's life, Julia and Bill lived in a constant state of not knowing. Not knowing if they would get a frantic call from Anna's school, be taking Anna to the hospital for medical attention, or knowing why Anna's brain injury occurred. They had to learn to let go of the thought that a person's body can be controlled. It seems medicine is more of an art than a science – every person is different, each body adapts in its own way. Each body succumbs to differing circumstances in different ways. Every human will encounter something which causes their physical death. There is no way around that.

They also had to let go of the thought that there is a reason for everything that happens. They lived for many, many years not knowing why Anna's brain had been injured or why this happened specifically to Anna. They had to learn to push those thoughts out of their brains and move forward with the day that is here, the day that is now. The past cannot be undone. That point rings so true for Anna; the past injury to her brain is irreversible.

As a mother Julia would love to erase the part of history when Anna's brain was injured, to take away the impact and the subsequent complications of not being able to function as a typical person. But she cannot. She is powerless in that dimension. Once the impact to Anna's brain had occurred, there was no 'going back' or recovery. The task at hand was to manage the impacts that had occurred to Anna and continue with life. The other choices as Julia saw them were to be completely devastated by the loss of Anna's function, freezing in pain to inaction or to blame someone else, not taking responsibility for what happened.

During this time period Julia had to let go of her preconceived notion of what Anna would become and accept Anna for who she actually is. And choose to love her for who she is, now, today - not who she 'should' or 'might' have been. Julia realized Anna is, along with the rest of the human race, perfect as she is. She's here now; that's what's important. Julia isn't unique in that no one on Earth knows what the next hour or day or month or year will bring. She has to learn to accept that and adapt to the circumstances that Anna brings.

Anna's health can rapidly decline; one minute she is doing fine, the next hour she could be going into respiratory distress. Anna lives close to the edge of the precipice of health and circumstance. The line is razor sharp in between health and distress for Anna. All humans live close to the line; some will not cross it until very late in their lives. A typical person could be driving down a highway and meet another car and driver who have crossed the centerline of the road. Their lives will change in an instant, as Anna's life was changed by the instant(s) that occurred before she was born on Earth.

The "well meaning" people, those curious and/or acquaintances who are not that familiar with Anna's circumstances, want to "do something". They ask Bill and Julia "what can be done?" Again this is a difficult question for Bill and Julia to answer, as they have already been through the scenarios, racking their brain for what else can be done and acted on. The answer is : nothing. There is nothing else to be done. This is not what the well-meaning people want to hear. It sounds so defeated – like the game is over – there's nothing else. That's not how Bill and Julia feel or act. They are not giving up on Anna. They are doing all that they can to ensure Anna's life is made as comfortable as possible; that *is* the answer to the question "What can be done to help Anna?"

Often there truly are medical miracles where a child or adult's life is drastically improved by medicine and doctors. That is fabulous there are so many talented people who are making others' lives better. But this is not the answer Bill and Julia can give to the "well meaning" people. In Anna's situation there is no 'cure'. Medicine can only manage the effects of her brain injury. Medicine and healing cannot make her brain grow; there is no way to insert brain function into Anna's earthly body.

Many of the "well meaning" people tire of the subject of Anna – once they realize she isn't going to 'get better' they shut down their interest. She is left behind, much like the excitement of a crowd before a sporting event. All the people are clamoring to get to their seats, anxious for the game to begin. In the shuffle and the hustle of reaching their goal, they forget about those that are behind them, who maybe cannot walk as fast or know where exactly to walk. Anna is one of that group – she must rely on another person for every aspect of her daily life – from eating and toiletry to physical therapy to keep her muscles as limber as possible. Unless continual attention is made for Anna, she couldn't survive even another day. After the number of times Anna had been admitted to the hospital with pneumonia, feeding intolerances, or a common cold, Anna's lungs have been taxed by the infections they've undergone.

Yet she does survive. She has blown away all predictions and estimates for her life span, as inspecific as they are. There is no timetable, no course of predictability for how Anna's life will unfold. The milestones that humans typically achieve, sometimes on their own and sometimes with others' assistance, are not going to be met. Her journey is not typical, to be sure, but just as unique to her as an individual. She is mapping her own destiny – fighting for each breath and bodily efforts.

Anna does all that while attempting to communicate to others what she needs. Her only mechanism is to vocalize sounds – either crying or making sounds. She is a great signaler as to when she needs assistance. She also knows how to endear herself to her caretakers, who care for her with concern and attentiveness. It is a win-win relationship. Anna fights on through each hospital stay and recovery time period. She is tough, a formidable competitor to any marathon runner for endurance and tenacity.

During the time periods where Anna is maintaining her status, Julia plans some diversions for her other two children. In Seattle her family visited the Swedish American museum located in the Ballard neighborhood of Seattle. Ballard, having a port and the locks between Lake Washington and Puget Sound, has an active marina where many Scandinavians settled to be near their sea-going professions of fishing or transportation. They walked to Larsen's bakery, a long time Danish bakery in Seattle that makes some of the best Kringle (almond paste filled pastry). Their shelves are lined with Scandinavian food and groceries – canned fish, Limpa bread, cheeses, canned goods from Sweden, Denmark and Finland. For many years residents from Finland, Norway, and Sweden lived in this neighborhood and never learned to speak English. They simply patronized the businesses associated with their homeland, and conversed in their first language.

As time progressed, the caretaking needs for Anna grew in demands and enormity. Anna required constant attention – whether for feeding, changing her diaper, suctioning her mouth secretions or comforting her crying. That level of attention made it difficult to even have moments to complete other tasks – such as housecleaning, laundry, or reviewing the household's bills. The bank of energy was depleted from Bill and Julia's reserves.

Julia came to the realization that she needed help, physical help, with all the activities that had become necessary to keep their household running. They needed to hire a helper for Anna, to attend to her needs. It was difficult to find individuals who would want to help with Anna's care. It is the most personal of levels of care for another human being: toileting, bathing, dressing.

It's also challenging for Anna's family members, with the caregiver's presence inside their home, which is their personal refuge from the outside world. With this additional person there is now a listener to family conversations, another person to negotiate space in the home around, and another opinion about how care should be delivered to Anna. Anna's family has to adapt so that they can receive a respite from the constant demands of Anna's care. It's not easy for the caregiver, either, having to come into the predeveloped structure of the family and adapt to how Anna's parents want them to perform their work in caring for Anna. (This is the role I can relate to, as when I was a domestic for the Peterssons I had to learn to only observe; it was not my role to discipline the children or tell Mrs. Petersson how to run her household.)

Breakthrough

One of the people who have made a significant impact on the lives of Bill and Julia's family was introduced to them when Anna was eleven years old. Up until that timeframe, Bill and Julia had made a sort of peace with the unknown of why Anna's brain injury had occurred. They accepted it as a resident of their memories and experience. Still it was frustrating, as scientific based people, to not have knowledge of the origin for Anna's circumstances. As parents, and secondarily as engineers, they want to find a scientific reason as to why this had occurred to Anna, so that steps could be taken to remediate. The problem with that logic was, with Anna, they cannot even start such a process – the secret or key to start was locked up inside Anna.

Over the years of Anna's life the question of why this impact had happened to Anna was a nagging force in Julia's mind. It was a concern that had to be fought off many times. Each time Julia had asked the doctors had no explanation. They'd stated that sometimes it 'just happens' and there would likely be no actual determination as to what and why Anna's brain injury happened. Julia was frustrated into keeping her questions dormant. Her parents were also just trying to keep Anna going, keep her alive and surviving through the hospitalizations. They had little energy left over to go on a knowledge quest.

The field of practicing pediatric neurologists in Washington State in 1997, when Anna was born, was limited to five. The field was further narrowed as to which of the neurologists was accepting new patients. Anna was a complex case whose prognosis wasn't good; there wouldn't likely be any dramatic improvements in her brain function. Her issues were not the subject of any new research, the damage to her brain being irreversible. Thus as a neurology patient, she wasn't of much interest to neurologists seeking new research findings and / or improvements.

Luckily for Anna the number of pediatric neurologists had expanded in ensuing years in Washington to over thirty. This presented a greater choice in which neurologist to see, who could really focus on Anna and what her individual needs were. The time that had passed had seen great advances in medical technology and research. There was new information available that might be brought to bear on Anna's situation.

Anna was referred by another of her doctors to a pediatric neurologist based at Seattle Children's Hospital in 2008. This neurologist, Doctor Scott, was refreshing to work with. She listened to Anna's history (as described by Julia) and formed some possibilities of how to best help Anna. She adjusted Anna's medications to manage Anna's seizures. Anna was scheduled for follow up appointment to check on her status every three months.

During one of the visits, Julia mentioned her ongoing concern as to the reason or source for Anna's injury. The neurologist carefully considered possibilities for investigating. Much had changed in medical technology in the past eleven years – in only eleven years the medical knowledge had made leaps and bounds forward! The CAT scan that had been taken after Anna's birth, the technology available in 1997, was not precise enough to show the details of the impact to Anna's brain. The only conclusion that could be drawn from that CAT scan was that an impact had occurred, affecting both hemispheres of her brain, the left more than the right. Anna's subsequent developmental progress indicated her brain's development had been almost arrested near the time of her birth.

The benefits of newer medical technology are great. One factor in their administration is cost - many technologically complex medical procedures are prohibitively expensive – thousands of dollars for one MRI (magnetic resonance imaging). Thus it was a large investment of money which might yield no new information about Anna. The neurologist decided to go ahead and order an MRI performed, to yield a clearer picture of Anna's brain and anticipate discovering clues it might display. The MRI would require Anna be sedated, as the patient cannot move during the scan, and Anna is unable to control her movements (as before in the EEG test).

A few weeks later Julia brought Anna to the appointment for the scan. The logistics of having a person such as Anna undergo an MRI are also a significant factor. It takes hours of preparation to bring Anna to the hospital. Her supplies for the entire day must be brought with her – feeding pump, feeding bag, extra liquid food, toiletry items, medicines, applicators, medication documentation, insurance cards – the list is long.

Before Anna received anesthesia, the anesthesiologist went over the risks of administering it, which include greater chances of death due to stopping breathing, since Anna was already impaired in her breathing abilities. A sobering consideration. Julia signed the consent form, and the procedure began. Anna was put on a gurney/stretcher and wheeled into the MRI room. Julia waited outside the room in the long, seemingly endless hospital hallway. The huge machine took successive slices of pictures of Anna's brain. The results would be pieced together into pictures, where after a doctor would examine them and determine the results. Anna went to the recovery room, where she was slowly brought back up to consciousness. Julia was then able to take Anna back home in the van.

A few weeks went by when the results of the MRI were compiled, interpreted, and summarized. Julia and Anna returned to the neurologist's office, when the results of the MRI were explained. It was a day of anticipation to hear if there would be additional information regarding Anna's injury. The neurologist began by stating that an injury had occurred to Anna's brain due to a loss of oxygen. It occurred across her entire brain, so that indicated the oxygen source that had been reduced or cut off was probably the passageway into her brain, though the subclavian artery. Because of the injury, most of Anna's brain function comes from the brain stem, located at the base of the brain, which provides the basic functions of regulation of a person's breathing, heart, and central nervous system. Her upper frontal lobes of her brain simply couldn't develop much further, which impacts all the higher level functioning such as speech, motion, and (what is commonly thought of as) intelligence. Now Anna's parents knew what had happened; still no answer for the question of why.

Luck and fortune smiled upon Anna when her neurologist, Doctor Scott, came onto her care team. After delivering the news of the MRI results, she was willing to push forward to see if they could find an explanation for Anna's brain injury. The doctor had kept current on the latest research, and decided to order some specialized blood tests, to check a variety of factors in Anna's blood.

The blood testing is also expensive. Some would say it's not worth the money when the results would not change anything for Anna's capabilities. The effort is great, also, where highly trained doctors analyze the results to provide their analysis to Anna' family. Dr. Scott didn't give up. She felt it was important enough for Anna and her family to investigate.

Julia wheeled Anna across the clinic to the blood draw clinic. The phlebotomists know Anna from previous visits - both her hospital stays and clinic visits where blood draws were necessary to monitor the blood levels of her medications. Because of the number of blood draws and IV's Anna has had in her veins over the years, it was particularly difficult to get enough blood from Anna to be able to conduct the blood tests ordered by the doctor. Anna cried during the attempts – she was helpless to resist or stop the needle's insertion. Finally the phlebotomist had to prick Anna's fingertip and squeeze it to get blood from there – one drop at a time. Julia held Anna's arm, wishing it would be over soon. She felt helpless to be able to help Anna with the pain of the tests. She was praying the information the blood tests might yield would benefit Anna by providing increased information regarding Anna's condition.

The phlebotomist had asked to be the one to help Anna that day. His level of skill was one of the best in the whole hospital – he was often called in when other staff were having difficulties completing the necessary actions. He is patient and calm, speaking in low tones. This type of communication soothes Anna, and helps her not get too upset. She listened for auditory cues as to what would happen next. He told her what his next steps would be in trying to find a spot on her body to draw blood from. Anna listened to him, but couldn't help crying in pain as her finger was squeezed to extract blood, drop by drop.

The phlebotomist is an example of someone who doesn't get paid enough money in the world for the consideration he shows to so many people here on Earth. He is a kind, gentle, persistent provider to assist in the health care of so many children that are in need of it. His ethnicity is from a completely different place in the world than our family's. Thankfully the world is a smaller place with all the new technologies (like airplanes for transportation) and needed resources can be brought to their locations across the world.

The vials of blood were sent to a laboratory for technicians to complete the tests. This part of the process was unknown to Julia and her family. All they could do was wait for the results. They didn't know when that might be that they would receive either a report summary on paper in the mail or a phone call stating the results were ready. It was a timeframe of not knowing, of anticipation of what they might learn.

Another two months went by before Anna and Julia were scheduled to return for a follow-up visit. In the meantime a nurse had left a message on their home telephone answering machine stating something about the blood test results and laced with several acronyms Julia had never heard of. Julia was absorbed in her day to day life of working, getting the kids off to school, and shuffled the message off to a corner of her brain to ask at the next visit.

Continued Discovery

Julia was anticipating the next visit to the neurologist, to obtain more details as to what Anna's blood tests indicated. At their next in person visit with Doctor Scott, she explained what the testing results had shown to Julia and Anna. The information provided a life changing moment for Julia, Bill, and their daughters. Finally the key had been found to unlock the mystery of Anna's brain injury and medical condition.

Julia listened as the doctor explained that Anna's blood tests had indicated she has a genetic factor in her blood which elevates her risk of experiencing a stroke. In fact, this is what had caused Anna's loss of oxygen to her brain; she had a stroke before she was born. The factor, recently identified by medical science, is identified as MTHFR (methylenetetrahydrofolate reductase). MTHFR is an enzyme that is produced from instructions contained within the MTHFR gene. It is needed for the remethylation of homocysteine in the blood to produce methionine. If the enzyme is inactivated by a lack of MTHFR, an increase in plasma homocysteine occurs, increasing a person's risk for heart disease or stroke. Medicine tells us that 10% of total risk for coronary heart disease may be attributable to elevated plasma homocysteine. Differences in the MTHFR gene have also been studied as possible risk factors for many other conditions, including heart disease, high blood pressure (hypertension), high blood pressure during pregnancy (preeclampsia), glaucoma, psychiatric disorders, and some types of cancer.

This discovery of the link between the MTHFR enzyme, the gene makeup, and associated risks was monumental for Anna's family. They, along with 30 to 40 percent of the Caucasian population, carry this mutation of the gene in one of the two copies each person possesses. If a person has one copy in their MTHFR gene, this is called "heterozygous". The risks of clotting and heart issues are lower with this status. However, 12-15 percent of European populations, with the exception of the Dutch and Finnish which see 5 percent, are "homozygous", meaning both genetic pieces of the gene are affected. This is the case with Anna. She inherited a copy from each of her parents, putting her in the higher risk category for heart disease and stroke.

The doctor explained to Julia that a blood clot in the pathway delivering blood to Anna's brain had caused Anna to experience a stroke. I was literally singing from my viewpoint; I knew my son, Herbert, had died from a stroke at age 42; I myself died of the same cause close to the same age. Anna was unlucky in our family to inherit this genetic combination that caused her stroke to occur. The clot caused a loss of oxygen, for a significant enough amount of time, to impact and impair her brain's function and development. It was as if it had arrested her brain at that exact moment in time when the clot appeared. Dr. Scott continued to explain that strokes most often occur with either infants less than one month old (including the months in utereo) or people over the age of 60. They can, however, occur at any age.

Another piece of huge significance for Anna and her family is that this status is *genetic* – meaning it wasn't an external factor that caused Anna's injury. The cause of the clotting tendency travels through her veins every second – it is contained within her blood. It is part of Anna. In a terrible win of the lottery when the clotting factor and other circumstances collided, a blood clot blocked oxygen from travelling to Anna's brain. That event forever changed that path of Anna's life and that of her family's.

Dr. Scott explained that one of the primary methods to treat this blood condition was to take folic acid, also known as B9 vitamin. It is readily available in many foods and as a supplement vitamin. If consumed above 1MG per day, it has been shown to decrease homocysteine levels in human blood. The amount of folate contained in foods of a typical calorie diet is not enough to meet the need of a person with the MTHFR factor. A person would have to eat about twenty cups of broccoli per day to satisfy the level of folate needed. Supplements are the means to ensure the higher level of folate is present in the body. With each 5microsmol/L increase in total homocysteine levels, the risk of coronary artery disease increases by 60% for men and 80% for women. Reducing these levels is of significant impact to a person's overall coronary health, if they have the MTHFR factor.

Medical recommendations in the late 1990's recommended pregnant mothers take folic acid supplements of 400mg. This amount, which Julia took daily during her pregnancy with Anna, wouldn't have been enough to alleviate the homocysteine risk. It took Julia awhile to realize, and eventually come to accept, that given the information available at the time of her pregnancy with Anna, she had done the very best she could.

For individuals with MTHFR factor, taking any substances known to increase the risk for stroke push their risk for stroke even higher. Some that fit into this category are commonly known including birth control pills and estrogen. This finding was significant to Julia's family, as it would affect future medical decisions.

The handwriting of Anna's predisposition for risk of stroke is etched in her genetic makeup; it was undecipherable until Doctor Scott provided the key. The medical knowledge of the MTHFR deficiency was not available during Anna's formative stages. The mystery of why Anna's brain had been impacted was finally unlocked, after being trapped inside for eleven years. The information freed the thoughts that had swirled in Julia's head for those years. The information discovered by Dr. Scott allowed her to understand that the impacts to Anna were from a genetic source.

Julia's own brain was swimming in absorbing this news and what it meant for their family. It took her several days to read the additional materials Dr. Scott had given her. She also searched medical journals for additional information. What powerful knowledge Dr. Scott had given them to help improve her family's overall health – the knowledge was a gift which would benefit them immensely. It was up to them to act upon the information, and remain consistent in taking the vitamin supplements.

This information was vitally important as it indicated the rest of the family could have an increased risk for stroke. I wanted to cheer aloud that Julia and her family were now aware of the source of Anna's brain injury and the associated medical risks for individuals with the MTHFR factor. The other members of the family, besides Anna, could also now find out more about what their genetic makeup is. I also wanted to congratulate Julia for continuing to ask the questions that would help Anna and the rest of her family's health.

With this knowledge Julia had a feeling of success. She had kept at the quest for information to help Anna. Even though, for years, the doctors had stated there was no identifiable origin for Anna's brain impact, Julia hadn't given up hope an answer might be found. Julia had made peace with the thought there was no answer to the "why" of Anna's situation. Yet she didn't give up the thought that someday there might be more information made available. Much like caring for a skin wound, you have to keep up the pressure until the flow has abated. You can't stop before you've solved the issue, before you've solved the puzzle. Partway doesn't yield the benefits that are sought.

I would like to think this is part of Julia's Swedish heritage imparting the lessons of working hard and consistently keeping at a task. This approach to situations, especially the difficult ones, certainly worked for my son, Walter, Julia's grandfather. She saw that, learned from that, and used it in her own life.

All of this is not to say that Julia didn't have her doubts and fears along the way – of course she did. As a mother she wants to make it all right for her children. There is just no way to 'fix' Anna's situation. All that can be done is to care and love Anna for who she is, right now, today.

Looking at the World Sideways

Following the landmark discovery of information about how Anna's brain injury had occurred, one of the resultant conditions Anna experienced was that her back had grown into a scoliosis of a ninety degree angle. This was because her brain wasn't able to send the signals to the rest of her body for typical growth patterns which would allow for her muscles and bones to develop to support walking and sitting up. Imagine looking at the world sideways throughout a day – that was the view Anna had.

The pain she felt was excruciating – every turn of her back hurt the nerves and her muscles. She cried out, sharply, indicating the pain she was experiencing. When she was put in her wheelchair, for transport to school or physical therapy, the pain was even worse. The wheelchair's back was flat, and held her, via side supports in an upright, linear position. It hurt to have her back be put into a linear, unyielding support system. Anna could only tolerate being in her wheelchair with this back pressure for about half an hour before the pain became overwhelming. She cried to be set free from the restraint of the chair. It was hard for others to care for her when she was in so much pain; she needed constant attention to move her and adjust her position. For caregivers it is stressful to hear someone in pain, crying, and be unable to correct or assist the person.

The challenge was that if she was to go to school, she had to sit in her chair during the bus ride, which was at least forty five minutes each way. It became, understandably, more and more difficult for her to be able to endure the bus ride. Strong pain medication was not really an option, as the side effect of slowing down one's gastrointestinal tract would impact Anna even further.

Finally all the symptoms and hurt Anna was feeling invoked being scheduled for a spinal fusion surgery. The plan was to fuse the entire length of her spine, from the base of her neck to her tailbone, together via the insertion of two metal rods. The waiting list for the surgery was six months, due to the resources of the skilled surgeon and the hospital facilities. Anna's pain was on a waiting list, along with all of the other patients who desperately needed care at the Seattle hospital.

Anna's surgery timeframe was settled on as November of 2008, the next available time for the eight hour surgery. She would have to live with the pain level through the next six months. After her school year had come to an end, the summer time offered Anna a respite from the pain of riding in her wheelchair to school and back each day. She spent the summer at home in a reclining position. The chair was an evil device in her mind that hurt just thinking of the next time she was going to be put (forced) in it.

Julia received a phone call in late August. A surgery spot had suddenly become open, months earlier than had been planned. Another patient had to give up their scheduled spot – maybe they had become too ill to undergo the surgery. Julia hesitated for a moment, thinking of the other family's difficulty of not being able to proceed with their scheduled surgery. Then she accepted the schedule. Bill and Julia scrambled to rearrange their work and life schedules around the surgery date that was the following week. It would be completed just before Labor Day, the start of the school year.

On the appointed day, Julia, Bill and Anna met the surgeon in the pre-surgery clinic room. The surgeon was enveloped in surgical scrubs, a mask, a head cap, and goggles. His friendly face they'd seen in the clinic visits was hidden behind the medical garb. He reiterated the risks to Anna of the surgery and the steps he would take during the surgery. As Bill and Julia had heard from earlier surgeries, Anna, as a medically fragile person, was at increased risk for complications during surgery, including from anesthesia and from the difficulty of her body going through this extensive surgery. Her spine would be flexed back into a straightened position, by the surgeon literally pulling against her muscles and nerves. Once Anna's spine was in a straightened positioned, he would insert two parallel metal rods, the entire length of her spine long, and then fuse each of her vertebrae to the metal rod. Anna heard the surgeon's calm voice from her medically induced groggy state. She heard her mother and father's voices soothing her, telling her everything would be alright.

The surgeon informed Bill and Julia that the medical team would now take Anna into the operating room, and that they could wait in any location within the hospital. He would let them know about half way through the surgery, four hours from now, how it was progressing. Bill and Julia said their wishes and farewells to Anna before the surgery, and then watched as the medical team wheeled her gurney towards the operating room.

Bill and Julia left the surgery prep room and were in a foggy state themselves, wondering what to do next. What do you do when your medically fragile child, who has difficulty breathing on a typical day, is going into a non-conscious state for about eight hours? It was difficult for them to concentrate on anything – reading the newspaper, a conversation, eating lunch – anything. They both were worried about Anna making it through the surgery. Luckily her heart and breathing had always been strong; that was a good sign. At the halfway point the surgeon paged them for a few minutes of update / consultation. Bill and Julia happened to be in the cafeteria, trying to swallow the food which seemed to stick in their throats due to their concerns for Anna. They tossed their remaining food away and walked quickly to the surgery waiting room.

The surgeon explained things were going well with Anna's surgery, and that she had not lost a great amount of blood. They were able to reuse much of the blood Anna lost during the surgery, using a special machine that centrifuged the blood. He stated he would contact them again once the surgery was completed.

Anna came through the eight hour surgery very well. For only the second time in her life, she was in Intensive Care for 2 days and nights, with a nurse watching her twenty four hours a day. All of her vital functions were mapped, tracked, and measured. Bill and Julia appreciated the heightened level of attention for Anna's medical status, and in a selfish way they wished she could always have this level of care while in the hospital. However this level is too costly to maintain for any longer than absolutely necessary.

Anna was released to a general surgery ward of the hospital after the 2 days in ICU. She continued to do well, remarkably so. She was able to resume her feeding schedule within a few days after surgery. For her this was a truly rapid recovery – during other hospitalizations it had taken her *weeks* to be able to tolerate feeds that could sustain her health. However, she just couldn't seem to regenerate the blood she'd lost during the surgery. Anna remained overly tired and irritable, with her blood cell counts too low. When it was apparent to the doctors Anna just couldn't regenerate her blood cells to the necessary level, a blood transfusion was ordered. A match for her blood type was found, and she received the gift of blood from an anonymous donor. Someone gave blood to allow another person to have a better life. The transfusion was a gift of new life for Anna. The next day she had much more energy and color had come back to her skin.

Eight days after the surgery, Anna had recovered sufficiently to go home. This was record time for her to not require an IV for medicine and or feedings. She was still in need of twenty four hour care at home. She did remain in an extraordinary amount of pain from the impact of the surgery to her spine and nervous system. Anna's cry was not a 'please come help me' kind of cry – it was a jarring, sharp, tense cry that signaled the severity of the pain she was experiencing. Julia rushed to her, day or night, to help assist her by repositioning, soothing, or administering medicine.

Julia called the doctor to attempt to explain the level of pain Anna was in. Over the phone the severity just doesn't seem to be clear enough, despite Julia's attempts to provide a detailed description of what Anna was experiencing. The dosage of typical pain medicines had to be limited and managed, due to the side effect of slowing down digestion. Anna's digestion ability would now always be restricted even further because she had no mobility in her lower back due to the spinal fusion. It was almost a circular argument of what could even be done to help Anna's pain from both her spinal surgery and her digestion motility.

One doctor who, at the time followed Anna for her developmental milestones, suggested Julia give Anna a warm bath and ibuprofen to help her pain. His advice was like a verbal slap to Julia. He was suggesting a remedy that might be offered for a typical person with typical circumstances; he didn't seem to understand the level of pain Anna was in. Several types of prescription pain medications weren't even able to help Anna. Julia felt that to be basically told that Anna should "take 2 aspirin and call me in the morning" by the doctor was ludicrous. After this immediate crisis had been worked through, Julia removed this doctor from Anna's care team.

Deprivation, Continued

In the time and space after Anna's back surgery, only Anna and Julia had a detailed understanding of the extreme level of pain Anna was still in two, three, four, six, nine weeks after Anna's surgery. Anna, as the person experiencing the pain, woke up crying out several times every night. Julia was then alerted to Anna's pain. She stumbled out of bed, groggy from whatever level of sleep she was in at the time. For some of the cries all Julia could do to help Anna was to try to make Anna's bed and position more comfortable for her. Medication could only be administered at specified time intervals. Too much medication would have an adverse effect on Anna. Anna and Julia were alone, in the dark hours of the night, in their knowledge of the detail of Anna's pain.

Julia became almost hysterical from lack of sleep. For the occasional night that Anna slept relatively well, the one night of sleep wasn't enough for Julia to recharge. Her 'battery' of rest had been worn down to close to "no charge". She needed many more nights of good, consistent night's sleep to restore her body's need for rest. It just wasn't possible to care for Anna during the months following her spinal fusion and get a good night's sleep. Julia's attempts to describe her sleep deprivation level to medical professionals were met with sympathy, but not a practical, real time approach as to how to alleviate the lack of sleep both she and Anna were enduring. Julia was going to have to figure out how to get additional support on her own.

The deprivation of sleep, restful sleep, is one of the most dangerous ways to get to a person's psyche. People can't think rationally and respond calmly when their brain has been unable to rest itself with deep sleep. Lack of sleep has been proven to be an effective means to crack a person's willpower and mental health. Prisoners are subjected to it in attempts to disrupt their thought patterns or obtain information. Common side effects are crankiness, confusion, general tiredness. Most new parents experience this for some number of months, where the responsibility often falls on the mother to get up in the night (and day) to feed, change, and position an infant. Typically as a baby matures they begin to sleep through the night – it is a milestone parents relate to and await the arrival of continuous sleep through the night.

Julia's daily life had consisted of an erratic sleep schedule for twelve years now. She felt it like a marathon of sleep deprivation to see if she would crack under the pressure. Was caring for Anna in these circumstances somehow a test of her resolve? How could this be a situation anyone could successfully survive? Like a gambler at a blackjack table, Julia had hit her limit. The cards were being called in as a result of her exhaustion. She was cracking due to the pressure.

Finally, after a long night caring for Anna, with her repeated outbursts of crying which couldn't be abated by anything – medicine, comforting words, music, *anything* – Julia had a moment where she hit the bottom – the absolute lowest she could go. After the months (and previous twelve years) of sleep deprivation, Julia was so exhausted she just couldn't continue meeting all of Anna's care needs – her body just didn't have enough energy to keep going. The situation had become truly overwhelming. The state that Julia had arrived at wasn't somewhere she was proud of. She felt terrible for not having the physical energy to care for Anna, who was experiencing extremely high levels of pain and medical issues.

Julia struggled with the depth of her emotion, pondering her next step. Her issue with asking for help was blocking progress for Anna and herself. In our Swedish family we encourage independence and reliance on one's self to achieve. It was difficult to even admit, even to herself, that at the present time she couldn't meet all of Anna's care needs on her own. Could she ask for help? Who would she ask for help? How would she ask for help?

Sitting on her bathroom floor, sobbing, Julia decided that she was going to have to get help with Anna's care or she was going to have to drive her to the hospital and not bring her back home. She had to either 'give in' or 'cave in'. She realized she simply couldn't keep providing most of the care for Anna on her own resources and power. She had to ask for, and accept, help. This crisis had forced her to make a choice for sustaining both Anna and herself. She made phone calls to the doctor and the state social worker, letting them know she would be bringing Anna in to the hospital, so that Anna's pain could be evaluated at the hospital.

Julia then packed up Anna to transport her to the Emergency Room (ER). Julia was driving to the hospital and wasn't going to be turned away from getting doctors to assist with Anna's pain. She wasn't going to accept being put off, not reaching the attention of the specialized medical attention for Anna's care needs. Enroute to the hospital was another grief, anxiety filled trip in the van, with Julia sobbing in frustration, sadness and reaction to her feelings of defeat. She felt she was losing the War, as if she was not doing enough. Anna cried also, in her continued pain, and listened to Julia, her mother, apologizing to her that she had to ask for help. Watching them travelling in the minivan, they were quite a pair – the distraught mother driving her distraught daughter to the hospital.

Julia and Anna arrived at the Emergency Room entrance, the well-known, established route for Anna to check-in to the hospital. Some staff who were working that day knew Julia and Anna. They greeted them and smiled their welcome. It was comforting to see some friendly, familiar faces. They knew as they looked at Julia and Anna meeting again in these circumstances couldn't have been for a positive reason. Something must be pretty impacting to Anna's health for her mother to bring her in unannounced to the ER.

Once inside the room where Anna would be checked over, the game began again – the game being the dance of the steps of

331

diagnosis for Anna's current situation or symptoms. First the nurse came in to perform the first level checks – blood pressure, temperature, oxygen saturation. All these were normal – there was "nothing" immediately "wrong" with Anna. Next came the intern (1st year medical student), who asked general medical history questions and the preliminary reasons behind the visit. Then came the medication reconciliation person to ensure the hospital had the most current information of the medicines Anna was taking. Yes, they were all the same. No, there had been no changes or side effects. Julia tried to be patient in her responses to their questions about Anna; she had answered them all many times before. But she was anxious for Anna to get the detailed medical attention to figure out why Anna was so uncomfortable.

Julia sat in the hard chair next to Anna's gurney, where she was laid out with her head inclined to reduce the reflux and gagging. Anna's care needs were ongoing during these hours spent in the ER – Julia was at Anna's bedside to provide suctioning and personal care. She jumped up from her chair to respond to Anna. They waited for the next step in the game. Anna continued her protestations, vocalizing her pain. After some number of minutes, the resident came in. She asked several additional clarifying questions, all of which Julia reported from Anna's recent experiences. Outwardly there didn't seem to be a crisis in Anna's overall health. The resident could see, however, how distraught Julia was, that she was tired to the point of exhaustion. Because of Anna's medical status, her care needs were overwhelming.

This visit to the Emergency Room was different than some of Anna's other experiences. The medical team had received the message. None of the doctors suggested Julia give Anna an extra dose of some medication and go home. After reviewing the complexity of Anna's symptoms, medicines she was currently taking, and observing Anna for a while, they explained that it would likely take at least a few days to sort out what the cause(s) of Anna's pain were. Anna was admitted to the hospital with severe pain. This effectively took over Anna's care to sort out the pain issues Anna was experiencing. Julia was relieved that they weren't shuffled off to go home and 'keep trying' or try some insignificant effort that wouldn't resolve Anna's issues. Julia accompanied Anna to her assigned hospital room (which happened to be one Anna had stayed in on previous visits – it was quite familiar to them) and, along with the nurse who had previously cared for Anna, got Anna settled in her room. It was 1 am by this time; Julia was exhausted. Another night of interrupted, patchwork pieces of sleep and rest. She lay down on the fold out couch and tried to sleep.

As is typical in the hospital, nurses come in at least every two hours to check on Anna. At other intervals Anna's vital signs must be taken, which also generate noise and movement in the hospital room. Sleep for Julia came in fits and starts, in small slices of time. Eventually the sky outside began to lighten with dawn. The busy daytime hours at the hospital were dawning. Julia decided to abandon attempting to sleep further; she would just continue on with this new day as if she had slept a reasonable number of hours. She didn't see many other choices – she had to keep going to advocate for Anna.

Julia stayed by Anna's beside until the team of doctors would care for Anna during this hospital stay came by for 'rounds'. Rounds are when the medical team reviews a patient's status and symptoms, then discusses their plan for treatment of the patient. Parents at the Children's Hospital are invited to be a part of this discussion, often times presenting part of the history and uniqueness of their child. Julia or Bill want to be there to express Anna's needs, to be her voice where she cannot vocalize it herself. It is a key piece to unlock the knowledge the medical team has to bring it to bear on Anna's wellbeing. They stay by Anna's beside to be sure to be present when the medical team arrives at Anna's room.

Over the many hospital stays for Anna, rounds becomes like watching a student take an oral exam. The residents, who seem to be younger and younger (the reality being Bill and Julia are getting older and older), present their 'homework' – Anna's history, diagnosis, planned next steps. After the plan was discussed, Julia took a short break from attending to Anna to go purchase a cup of coffee. Even stepping away from Anna's bedside is hard for her parents to do – what if someone isn't right there to suction Anna when she coughs? They are in the constant struggle with themselves to let go some aspects of Anna's care; it is not a comfortable decision for them.

Julia remained with Anna for the rest of the day until Bill could make it to the hospital after his work shift had completed. Their other two girls were at school – Julia's mother (my granddaughter) had gone over to their house to help them get off to school in the morning. Julia was coordinating the family's activities from Anna's hospital room to make sure the family's schedule was meeting their previous commitments for the day.

"Schedule" becomes a ghost, unseeable, unpredictable, unknown, when Anna is in the hospital. For Julia that is frustrating, because she is a person who likes to set commitments for the day and keep them. Anna's health is also like that ghost; if she needs to stay in the hospital for care it is often uncertain in the early days how critical her care will need to be. To best support Anna, Julia and Bill have to shove the rest of their lives out of the picture to clear their calendars.

Other peoples' schedules are impacted by this, as either Bill or Julia needs to be present at the hospital to advocate for Anna. Thus carpools to dance lessons, writing out checks for the school field trip, or preparing dinner all get pressed down the priority list. Other people outside their family are also impacted – confused or irritated by the interruption of scheduled tasks. They call to ask what is going on, why Anna isn't going to school, etc. Julia is put in the situation of having to both deal with her daughter's current medical needs and explain and coordinate with many other external parties.

Strangely, some lean on Julia for their emotional support during these times. That adds extra pressure on her, given that Anna is her main focus at that time. Julia is focused on processing and dealing with her own emotions seeing Anna struggle.

The medical team at the hospital performs a vital service for so many children; most are not in pediatrics unless they really want to work with children. Most of the team are also generally not prepared to work with children who do not track to their age, who do not have all the functions that most typical children do. The somewhat ironic part is the whole reason a child is in the hospital is because something typical is not happening at that time in a child's life.

Julia went home the next night, after staying with Anna at the hospital for twenty hours straight, and slept in her own comfortable bed. She was exhausted from the physical toll of attending to Anna for many hours and the emotional toll of seeing her child in pain, knowing Anna needed to be hospitalized to have her needs addressed. This reminded me of when the doctor had told me of my heart condition. Something simply had to change or else there would be dramatic health consequences. It wouldn't help anyone if Julia became ill – Anna needed her, the rest of Julia's family needed her. And she needs herself to be rested to effectively function.

Anna remained in the hospital for a total of three weeks while her pain issues were sorted out. The sheer length of Anna's stay indicated how complex Anna's issues were to source. The number of doctors, nurses, therapists and technicians that helped her was staggering. She needed a huge net of specialists to help her get through the life affecting issues she was experiencing.

This hospitalization had shown that Anna had a collision of medical crises. Her back pain was indescribably painful, even six months after the surgery. Since the surgery had immobilized Anna's entire torso, the lack of mobility had caused Anna's digestion to slow, causing another source of great pain. The pain a person experiences from the stretching of the intestines is infinitely worse than if they had been sliced through. In addition Anna was experiencing muscle spasms and cramping in her legs and arms; like having a "Charley Horse" almost every minute of the day. Anna battled through it all.

Julia realized she had to take time away from activities she had planned for herself to be present at the hospital to advocate for Anna. She was the only person on the Earth that could be selected for these tasks. Julia heard the call to help Anna by being near and an advocate during these times. Clearly her priority was helping Anna through this rough patch.

She put her work life on hold – literally only responding to requests that could not wait, such as one of her employees or paying taxes (since it was April). It frustrated her that she wasn't able to get much done with her work – she just didn't have the concentration, dedicated time, and mental acuity. Due to being tired, she would misread sentences – her brain skipping over or adding words. She transposed numbers when looking at her business' financial information. When speaking, Julia would sometimes say words aloud she hadn't meant to – as if she wasn't able to form sentences. Her brain had been dulled by the lack of sleep.

Additionally Anna was having difficulty breathing, and Julia and Bill wanted to be at the side of her bed every hour each day. Logistically this is albeit impossible, after some number of days work commitments expect you to show up for work. To keep their jobs and funding for Anna's health care, they had to go to work. It was terrifying to think if they left Anna's bedside and she was no longer able to breathe they wouldn't be there, that they would lose Anna while they were away from her bedside. It is a wrenching choice to have to "pay the bills" or be by your child's bedside. Fortunately for Bill and Julia, and of course Anna, one of them was able to stay with Anna at her bedside.

Caring for a loved one requires you to let go of some notions of what you think you must do – at some point you also must shower, pay bills, grocery shop. You cannot give your entire life over to the care of another person *all* of the time; you'll have forgotten about yourself and your own care. Julia was within range of that happening – but Anna's hospital stay abated the situation. And Anna was getting the medical attention she so desperately needed to help her out of the constant level of pain she was in.

Fighting

Anna made the choice during this hospitalization to fight – yet another time. She did not want to be in pain, and had to express what was happening inside her somehow. The only way she had to do that was to cry. A high level of stress is invoked in a person hearing a baby's cry. A person's system releases cortisol in the bloodstream to provide a rush of energy for your body's response to the stress. The sound becomes damaging to your ears after 90 minutes (at 90 decibels). Anna made her point through her cries and received the right level of attention to help her. She is a fighter, a tough Swede I'd like to think. Despite this taxing situation she had found herself in, she continued to fight for her place in the world, as a living human being.

The medical team assigned to Anna that first week was concerned, made up of mostly medical students and first or second year doctors. They were reading their textbooks coming up with suggestions for Anna's care. The attending physician (the doctor in charge of the medical team assisting Anna) had been with the hospital for almost forty years. When he started in medicine there were no children like Anna that survived to be twelve years old. His team was made up of a resident (a first or second year doctor) and four interns (doctors in training, currently in the last year of medical school). As a team they seemed to be going by the book, reading the recommended medications and dosages.

Anna was writhing in pain in her hospital bed. The team of doctors came in to say they were going to try more of a particular medication, although it hadn't yet been determined if this medicine was causing some of Anna's pain. Julia asked why they thought that would work, given that Anna was still in pain. The resident cited that the book stated Anna should be able to tolerate more of the medication. Given Julia and Bill's history with Anna and medical professionals quoting their textbooks for Anna's care, alarm bells were sounding in Julia's brain. This just didn't sound right – Anna's entire life had not followed what had been previously documented in a textbook.

As had happened during other hospital stays for Anna, a resident (or even more rarely an attending doctor) made an assumption that since they read a plan of treatment in a medical book or journal, that will explicitly apply to Anna. This is an error in judgment that couldn't be more off the mark – Anna doesn't follow the typical, already described cases noted in books or medical literature. Wouldn't part of their medical training include the fact that each person's body is different in how it will react to medicines and care plans? Somehow that can be forgotten, when a doctor attempts to apply a specified path, especially when the individual has already started with an atypical path. Anna tries to explain, through her nonverbal sounds and actions, what she needs and is going through. The words are trapped inside her, yet she is trying so hard to communicate. The barrier of no spoken language to communicate through makes caring for her all that much tougher – it's a combination of an anticipator, observer, responder, and problem solver that is needed to help Anna.

The resident's response setoff firestorm in Julia's head: Early in Anna's life it was apparent that there is no 'book' for Anna. No child comes with a book that explains their differences, likes, dislikes – which every parent would likely benefit from if there was such a thing. In Anna's case it is tricky because she cannot verbalize what she needs or is feeling. Her caregivers need to try to read her mind, to know what her vocalization means or what she might need done for her next. The documentation that does exist covering Anna's medical condition and related symptoms are not specific enough as to what she needs as an individual. They are a starting point, to be sure, but are not the authority on Anna. Anna is.

Another thing Julia and Bill learned from Anna is that each person reacts to medications differently; what works for one person doesn't work for another. For this medication in question at this point, she had been on it for a few years with no side effects. Anna has taught us that she simply doesn't 'go by the book' — she writes her own script for her life. Anna was still crying a sharp, painful cry when the attending doctor walked in the room to join the resident to complete his rounds of his patients.

Julia asked that the medical team step into the hallway, so as not to have a potentially heated conversation near Anna. She knew it would upset Anna to hear her mother's voice rise and strain. Anna would likely react by crying herself, adding her voice to her mother's. Anna wants to protect her mother. If her mother was upset, Anna would become upset.

Julia felt a surge of energy (more accurately, a surge of stress hormones — cortisone and endocrine - released in her blood) to discuss Anna's medical treatment with the team of doctors. She wasn't going to give up on Anna, to let them proceed down a path that was causing Anna pain. For some reason the analogy of a battlefield had popped into Julia's head. She has no personal experience of what military personnel go through in battle. It just occurred to her that Anna's current situation was similar to her lying on a battlefield, with many other wounded that needed medical attention. Given the circumstances of the battle, it may be that the medical team must triage (identify) which people they can save with the supplies and resources they have. Some can be aided and possibly transported to a safer location. Some are left to die on the battlefield; their injuries are too great.

Julia's voice, shaking with anger and fear, rose in volume. She told the medical team: "If you are telling me this situation is like a battlefield, where you can only save some, and you have to make the decision to leave Anna behind, because she cannot be saved, then tell me now. And you better give Anna the best pain medicine you've got, because I'm not leaving her here to be in this level of pain." Julia couldn't leave Anna to endure that level of pain as acceptable for the rest of her life. She asked if there was another medical team that could give a second opinion.

Towards the start of Julia's tirade, doors to the other rooms in the hallway began to close, like when cards are shuffled. Ffff, ffff, ffff, the other doors closed in succession, so that other patients and their families wouldn't hear Julia's words. Julia noticed in her peripheral vision. It made her aware that others on the floor understood the level of concern she was expressing.

Watching this scene unfold, I was proud of Julia for standing up for her daughter Anna. Although I must say I was a bit taken aback. In my day talking to a doctor in that manner was not even thought of; we would not question their authority and stature in the professional field. And because Charles & I had nine children to tend to, neither of us had the amount of time and energy to dedicate to just one of our children. Of course children with the medical complexities of Anna wouldn't have survived when I lived on Earth. There wasn't the medical knowledge and interventions to sustain their lives.

It's been said that each person has about ten pivotal moments in their life, where the choice made forever affects the future of their, and others', life. I know this was one of the pivotal moments of Julia's life. She went outside her typical zone of calm and rational thoughts to yelling at the team of doctors. A wave of courage, anger, and fear had washed over Julia. Her instincts as a mother protecting her child had taken over. She stood up to a team of doctors who were telling her that they were doing all that they could for Anna and indicating that Anna's life was likely to include the high level of pain Anna was experiencing. Julia was speaking on behalf of Anna, for her quality of life, as Anna lay in the hospital bed, hurting from the pain inside of her body.

The attending doctor retreated, non-committal. From that point forward, the hospital staff changed. A different team of doctors, the Medically Complex Care (MCC) team was assigned to Anna, where they brought their knowledge and experiences with medically fragile, complex children to shape a plan for Anna's future. It took *weeks* of trying alternatives to figure out the combination of factors that would make Anna's daily life more comfortable, so that she wasn't in a constant, high level of pain.

During this hospital stay, Anna's breathing was labored; her chest went up and down in rolls of effort – like a wave of wind rolling through a field of grain. Julia wasn't sure if Anna was going to make it through this episode of difficulty or not. She functioned through the three weeks that Anna would stay in the hospital on auto-pilot. She didn't know what to expect in the next five minutes, hour, or day. Julia was really worried for Anna's life; she just didn't know how Anna would come through this experience. She just had to trust that Anna was receiving the best care possible and that Anna would pull through.

After a few weeks of being constantly by Anna's hospital bedside, Julia took a one night respite. She slept, not a deep, restful, restorative sleep, but still more continuous sleep than she'd had for weeks. The next morning while Julia was showering, Anna sent Julia a message. The message was clear in Julia's mind; it said : Momma, Let me Go. Anna was voicing her discomfort and pain, saying "I've had enough of all these medicines, needles, tubes, and hospital stays." It startled Julia to think that Anna was so directly communicating with her. Julia received the message as a symbol from Anna that if it was Anna's time to leave Earth, Julia should stop fighting that thought. It was a scary, but somehow comforting message, that Anna was ready to go if this was her time.

After returning to the hospital, Julia walked into Anna's room. They were there, alone. They had a talk. Julia reminded Anna how much she loved her, that she was proud of her, that she was so strong. And then Julia explained to Anna that she had received her message. Julia told Anna that whatever Anna needed or decided to do Julia would be ready for. Julia let Anna know it was alright if this was Anna's time to leave Earth. Julia emailed friends and relatives Anna's medical status, which had not improved in several days.

After reading Julia's email, like two Florence Nightingales in a much later time period, two of my granddaughters, Walter's daughters, went to Anna's hospital bedside. They rearranged their schedules to fly out to Seattle to be with Anna, as each had their own grandchildren and families. They made Anna their priority for those five days they came to Seattle. One had just been through a grueling round of chemotherapy; the other had survived a stroke of her own and the subsequent therapy and effects. They arrived at the hospital to offer support and encouragement to both Anna and Julia. Julia was grateful for their support and concern for Anna. What a wonderful gift they gave to Julia and her family. They just did it, and did so with a free heart.

Anna's breathing and pain level gradually improved. The hospitalization had been a success. With her new team of doctors and medicines, Anna's daily life was much more manageable for both her and Julia, her mother and caregiver. The additional doctors added to Anna's care team were a more appropriate Neuro-Developmental specialist and a team from Pain Management. Thankfully they were there to offer their expertise and concern for Anna, to provide solutions and options for helping Anna's daily life improve. Because they looked at the 'big picture' for Anna and her medical needs, they solved the crises of this hospitalization.

The Pain Management team was a relatively new team for a Children's hospital. In years previous to the early 2000's the predominant medical theory was children should be given little pain medicine, in part because of the side effects and part because it was thought that children didn't experience pain like adults do. How unfortunate that for years children had been experiencing pain that had gone either under- or un- treated. Adults (including medical professionals) had not found ways to communicate with children to understand what levels of pain they were experiencing. So the pain continued.

Granted children are likely less able to relate or verbalize exactly what level and type of pain they are feeling. However that does not diminish the severity of their feeling and hurt. The adults were not understanding what was actually occurring in many children's lives, whether they were patients in a hospital or dealing with a medical situation at home. The responsibility of understanding how a child experiences pain is put to adults, primarily those who are trained in medicine and psychology. Finally the medical field began to understand that children do indeed experience pain, at levels in accordance with adults. Some examples of scales that are now used to understand a child's pain levels are pictorial (such as the Beyer or Wong and Baker faces scales) and the Oucher scale, where a number indicating severity is assigned. Just because adults couldn't receive the message does not make pain children experience any less hurtful or real.

Anna went through that - where she was in pain, yet no one seemed to understand how much and how awful it was for her. Finally a team of doctors were finding solutions for the high level of pain Anna was in, day after day, hour after hour. At the end of the hospital stay, Anna was much more comfortable and could actually make it through a few hours without crying out in pain.

Upon Anna's leaving the hospital, Julia had a new awareness of what Anna's care needs had now become. Julia realized she needed to take steps to obtain nighttime help for Anna, so that she could get more sleep during the night times. Anna's hospital stay was a crisis that needed to happen to get Anna the medical attention needed to move Anna into a more comfortable phase of her life. It also had caused Julia to experience a crisis in planning for Anna's care; it could no longer be done by her as the primary caregiver.

The entire family's lives had been put back on track, with Anna's health improved to a stable condition. They all could now sleep better and go to their activities. They went about their schedule of work, school, and activities, trying to keep up with the constant demands on their time.

Balancing

Years are measured by the number of hospitalizations Anna has for Bill and Julia. It was a good year if Anna was in the hospital less than a week. Some years Anna topped out at six weeks; those weren't such good years. Some years they just got by – did what they had to do, covered the bases with their family. That was success for them. They weren't achieving greatness by an external scale – developing new companies, marketing new ideas, making zillions of dollars in the week's latest IPO. They were surviving – going to work after being up much of the night with Anna, contributing to their savings account when they could, and caring for their other two children.

It is a delicate balance that Bill and Julia strive for to balance the efforts and time they provide to Anna Christina with their other two children's needs. Like children playing on a see saw, the balance cannot be all in Anna's favor all of the time. Sometimes Anna must lean towards her siblings' attention needs, when her parents hire a caregiver to be with her so that they can attend their other children's activities. The caveat is Anna has to be alright – no medical crisis or high pain level – for the balance to tip away from her.

Anna's siblings, also my great-great granddaughters, are attentive to her. They accept her for who she is. They talk to her as if she could answer them back verbally. Anna does answer in her own language of vocalizations. It's just the message she is sending isn't always clear to the receiver. I love seeing them interact; the three girls support each other as siblings. I think they are special people (as my descendants I am especially proud of them) to not judge Anna for her lack of abilities, rather they embrace her and the abilities she does have.

On New Year's Eve of 2009, just before 2010, Anna was again hospitalized for respiratory issues with breathing. She was in isolation, as tests were still being conducted to find the source of her illness being either bacterial or viral. Until that was determined, the hospital had to enforce precautions so that Anna wouldn't transfer an infection to others. Thus they were in Isolation within the hospital, to be separated from other patients and staff members so any viral infection wouldn't be transmitted. Julia and Anna spent the evening hours of New Year's Eve together, just the two of them.

The business of the hospital around them had quieted down; the halls were mostly silent. Any patient who could have been released from the hospital had left, as it is generally easier for both the patient and the medical team during holidays. Thus the feeling of being alone was both physical and psychological for Julia. It seemed as if everyone who had been invited to a party had already left, and those left behind could either not leave their child's beside or were not in that sort of social group.

With Anna asleep and her condition stabilized, Julia left the hospital to drive to a New Year's Eve party given by friends. It felt funny to try to attend a 'typical' activity when Anna's status was definitely not typical at that time. On the other hand Julia wanted to connect with a community of people, to not be isolated in the world of illness and hospitalizations. It is a dichotomy. When your child is in the hospital, you cannot go on like everything is fine, yet you also cannot completely shut down everything else that is going on in your life. Going to the New Year's Eve party with their younger two daughters was a brief moment of 'typical' experience.

Before the clock struck twelve, as is typical, people were talking about the year that had just passed and what they might expect for the next year. Julia thought some different thoughts than she had in previous years. How could her life get any worse in 2010 than it had been the past year? How could she set goals and resolutions for a year which could be so derailed by Anna's health needs? She was thinking there must be a way to go up, after hitting what felt to her like a bottom in her life during Anna's health crises the previous spring.

It is difficult to rebound from stressful events in one's life – a major health crisis of a close family member, the loss of a job or home. It is not easy for anyone to go through these sorts of experiences. As someone who sees these events occur and the variety of ways individuals respond to them, I can tell you that everyone goes through difficult experiences, some more than others and with greater impact to their lives. Yet everyone is going to have some sort of event that will not be what they wanted for their lives. That, also, is just how life on Earth is. The differentiating factor between people's lives is how each person handles the events and their actions following them. Their responses to the stressful events shape their future. Any one of these types events could be devastating to a person; they could go into a deep depression and not be able to get out of bed. The reality is that response won't help anyone, most of all the person going through the situation and those that depend on them (such as children).

Every person deals with stress, worry, and concern differently. Anna's parents are no exception. That night Bill needed to be by himself, thinking about Anna and how she was doing. He went to their backyard, built a campfire, and stared up at the moon shining brightly that night. The same questions came back to Bill's mind: Why Anna? Why did her injury have to be so impacting? What will her future hold? Would this current illness be the one that caused her to leave Earth? The questions floated out into the night sky. No answers returned to these questions. The questions remain, hovering over their daily lives.

To face Anna's life experience Bill and Julia have to make some sort of peace with the unknown. It is unsettling and an uncomfortable place to be to not know, not have an answer. Even knowing about the factor in Anna's blood that puts her at higher risk for stroke doesn't explain the other questions her parents have.

There will never be a definitive response. To continually revisit these types of questions doesn't help the situation or anyone. Her parents have to leave a portion of their lives reserved for what is unknown and will never be. They can't keep searching for something that cannot be found; it is not within their reach. The answers to those questions are somewhere in the Universe, very far away from their lives on Earth.

Others (the "well meaning" people) still continue to try to make sense of Anna's injury. Frequently they ask the same questions of Bill and Julia they have themselves. It is difficult for anyone to accept that there is no answer to the question "Why Anna?" There isn't a reason. The answer is outside of any person's realm of impact on Earth. This thought is confusing, annoying to a person who wants to rationalize.

One such rationalization that the "well-meaning people" present is that "God doesn't give us any more than we can handle". While people likely do mean well when saying this to Anna's parents, what they are not aware of is that God doesn't dole out difficult events to see how much each person can handle. Anna's injury didn't occur because God decided to see how far Bill and Julia could be pushed or to punish them in some way. God is a force of Good. There also exists a corresponding force of Evil that impacts the lives of people on Earth. That force has always been there, resulting in many terrible, horrific events and actions. Given that 'bad' things do happen, people on Earth must figure out for themselves how they are going to respond and behave.

Signals

Breathing. Something most all of us take for granted. Hardly anyone in the world thinks about it. Other things top on people's lists in present day America might be what will be made for dinner, who might be invited into their home, or why they didn't get something that they'd wanted for themselves. Yet one very important factor I see people forgetting is that none of those activities are possible if you aren't breathing.

Anna increasingly began to struggle with this most basic task. She would cry out in confusion, pain, concern. Her cry asks for someone to help her, to tell another person she was uncomfortable, scared, or not getting enough oxygen. Sometimes someone else (such as her mother, Julia, or a hired caregiver) was right next to her, telling her it would be alright, comforting her, rubbing her arm. Other times it was the lonely middle of the night – her mother upstairs in her bed – no one else around. Julia would come running, half stumbling down the stairs to Anna's bedroom; even this short delay in attention would cause Anna to require more attention to calm her enough to rest, to quiet, to eventually go back to sleep. It was scary for Anna to be awakened, the lights out, her room dark. She was trying to get in enough oxygen, and when her lungs didn't feel full she would cry out. Her cries were signaling distress; this was the only means she had to signal what was going on.

After months of Anna's crying out in the night, Julia finally decided she had to get some assistance to have someone attend to Anna during more of the nights of the week. Anna was quieted just knowing someone was nearby, that they would attend to her if she needed it. Another machine was also added to her daily life; her doctor decided to have Anna placed on a pump that would provide a consistent level of oxygen. This meant additional upkeep and tasks for her parents to make sure the machine was working correctly. The effort was worth it for Anna, as it enabled her to obtain a higher saturation of oxygen while she was sleeping, improving her ability to sleep more consistently. If Anna's sleep was improved, there is a direct correlation to her parents' sleep improvements.

My son Walter (who had passed in 1997) and I scored a communication victory in late January of 2010. We saw our opportunity and acted on it. It happened to occur during the 2010 Super Bowl, where 106 million people all over the Earth were watching this football game. Julia is not typically one of them; she is most often preoccupied with some other activity on that Sunday in late January when the game is played.

This year their family happened to be at home, with no other prospects to occupy their time. They turned on the game and watched as the opening coin was tossed to determine which team, either the New Orleans Saints or the Indianapolis Colts, would kick off and which would receive. Just prior to the opening kickoff, the television cameras focused on the head referee for the game and displayed his name on the screen, a young man about 35 years old; Walter Anderson. Julia was folding laundry while this occurred and happened to have looked up at the screen. When seeing her grandfather's name on the television screen, she realized it was a message that he is looking out for her, even when he is not on Earth.

Rarely if ever is Anna not with her family. Anna's needs for care, primarily from her parents, caused the rest of the family to take vacations in segments – two or three of their family would go on vacation, with one of Anna's parents staying with her. It was a brand new experience for their family, when Anna was twelve years old, that the rest of the family boarded an airplane to experience the sights and sounds of New York City.

Julia had arranged for Anna to be cared for at home for five consecutive days. The plan for Anna's care during their first vacation with only their youngest two daughters generated concern in her parents' minds over the possibility of something falling through. What if a failure occurring in meeting Anna's care needs. What if one of the caregivers became ill themselves? What if they simply forgot or couldn't come to care for Anna – who would stay? There were many more "What if…" questions. They took a chance on the patchwork quilt of caregivers to attend to Anna, with Julia's Mom (my granddaughter) as the fallback plan. They so wanted a brief respite from Anna's care requirements, having never been away from her for more than one night of her life, other than her hospital stays.

One of their destinations was the MoMA – Museum of Modern Art on West 53rd street in Manhattan. Bill became particularly fascinated with a painting that hangs in a somewhat obscure location in the museum on the fifth floor. It is by an American painter, Andrew Wyeth, of a young woman who is on the ground, appearing to try to reach a house far in the distance. She seems to be having to crawl her way toward a goal, the house, way off in the distance. The painting reminds Bill of Anna, who is also unable to walk, reaching towards a goal that is far off in the distance.

The name of the painting is "Christina's World". Julia and Bill were struck by the coincidence the name of the woman in the painting being the same as mine and their daughter's middle name. Mr. Wyeth had painted a woman, who was his neighbor on the Maine coastline. She was unable to walk as a result of being disabled by polio. The woman in the painting and Anna Christina face similar challenges: reaching for a goal via painstaking efforts, their physical body unable to transport them to where their mind wants to go. A print of the painting now hangs in Bill and Julia's living room as testament to Anna Christina and her daily struggles to reach her goals.

Just a few weeks after her family's trip to New York City, Anna was rushed to the Emergency Room with high fever and breathing difficulties. One minute Anna seemed to be doing fine. About an hour later she was struggling to breathe, her chest heaving up and down, rolling with each breath. Her temperature had spiked to one hundred four degrees Fahrenheit. On a Saturday, when many others were watching an NBA basketball game or baseball's spring training, Julia and Anna were in the all too familiar Emergency Room – even the chairs and walls were the same. They were escorted to room ten of the ER; the same room where they had spent many hours during several other ER visits. Anna's fever was able to be controlled with antibiotics and fever reducing medicines. She went home instead of staying in the hospital. It was easier on her family to care for her at home instead of having to shuttle themselves to the hospital.

The following week Julia and Bill tried to once again return to the routine of their lives. Work meetings, kids' activities, preparing meals. Even after all of the hospital stays Anna has had, each time still shakes her parents' confidence about life. Each visit to the hospital for Anna brings up the question "Will this time be hers to move to another world?" It feels to Julia as if Anna has a ticket booked for her passage, yet it is not known for what day and what time. Everyone will have a passage – Anna's will be sooner than most others'. Her parents let out a breath of relief, knowing she is still here.

Anna did recover from this bout of illness at home, and routines were settled back into for almost the next year. Glorious days of routine and regularity – specific events occurred at the time they were 'supposed' to, activities were attended, meals were served, and rest was obtained while Anna was cared for by a nighttime caregiver. All was well with routine.

Resurging

In February of 2011, after a long day of work and school, Bill and Julia and their daughters were home for the day. They were tired from the daily stresses of their lives – commuting and the demands of their work and school. The afternoon entered its typical pattern of homework for the girls, Anna's digestion tasks, and preparations for dinner. Anna's caregiver was in her room with her, ready to assist Anna when she needed toiletry help or suctioning. Julia walked in Anna's room to check on her; she thought Anna seemed a bit warm, so she put a thermometer under Anna's arm. Beep, beep, beep – beeeeepppp it was finished reading Anna's temperature. 39 degrees Celsius – hmmm. Julia, still, after all these readings of Anna's temperatures, thinks in Fahrenheit temperatures. She had to look up on a conversion chart what the Celsius number converted to in Fahrenheit. She knew 38 degrees Celsius was considered a 'fever' by the hospital, which equated to 101 degrees Fahrenheit. She found the conversion chart, which was torn and tattered from when she'd printed it out off of the Internet some number of years earlier. Julia scanned down to 39 in the Celsius column and looked to the corresponding number in Fahrenheit. 103. That got her attention – not a good number.

Anna had spiked a fever – within the space of an hour. The War had kicked into another phase, another formidable opponent having surfaced, and another battle to be fought and won. As many parents have seen with their children, fevers can occur rapidly in children. For Anna a fever makes it even more difficult for her to breathe, her chest rolling in effort to get air in. Anna's nostrils started to flare with each intake of breath; her breastbone/chest 'pulled' where her esophagus travelled down to take air into her lungs. All of these are signs of increased work to get oxygen in to one's body.

Julia's mind and body snapped into a state of high alert. The enemy had returned, after having been kept at bay for almost a year. Germs were on the offensive in Anna's body. Julia was thinking through the possibilities of what could be happening inside Anna's body, what responses might be needed, and what effect all of this would have on the family's schedules for work and school for the next few days. Her brain flashed through tasks that needed to be completed in the next few days; everything but helping Anna would be put on hold. Julia alerted the on-call physician from Children's Hospital, the doctor who would answer patient needs outside of typical business hours. This was an emergency for Anna.

This situation of their daily lives completely upended had happened almost countless times and days before this, where Julia's plans for how the rest of her day or week or month would be shoved into an "unknown" status. Their family would focus their efforts on Anna's health, forgoing any sort of previous plans. The focus on Anna would overtake other aspects of their lives. What if Anna needed Julia's attention in the middle of an important meeting? What if Julia happened to be in a spot where she was somewhat unreachable (such as a movie theater – which rarely occurred anyway) and Anna became severely ill? The ongoing stress of always having to be available in case Anna needed her was a constant presence in Julia's thoughts and life.

Luckily the on call physician that night happened to be Anna's regular doctor, the person who saw her in clinic every three to six months. He was very familiar with the details of Anna's health history. He advised putting Anna's oxygen on to help Anna with oxygen saturation and seeing if the Tylenol would help Anna's fever go down. The nighttime caregiver came at the usual time; she administered Anna's nighttime preparations and everyone attempted to go to sleep, hoping the situation would get better. At midnight the caregiver noticed Anna's temperature was at 104 degrees Fahrenheit; it had crept higher. She went upstairs to wake Julia. Julia came downstairs, saw Anna's chest going up and down, working even harder to breathe. Julia made the decision to take

Anna to the hospital. Anna's respiratory status had reached a level where she needed help from the medical team at the hospital. Julia called the doctor, who alerted the emergency room to let them know Anna was on her way.

Julia drove Anna in the minivan through the dark night. It was about one o'clock in the morning. The freeway that would take them over the bridge to the hospital displayed signs with flashing yellow lights. Julia was surprised by the messages and hoped somehow they were incorrect – that the bridge wasn't closed for repairs during the nighttime hours. She drove on, her brain hoping that the road and bridge might be open so she could save precious time by taking the most direct route to the hospital.

Despite Julia's hopes, the signs weren't incorrect. The path over the bridge was indeed closed. She had to exit the freeway via the off-ramp and take another route. There was no way for her to change these events to make Anna's trip to the hospital more expedient – she had to adjust her path. Julia worried about the extra time it would take to arrive at the Emergency Room, if Anna would be alright until then. As had occurred with other medical crises in Anna's life, there was nothing else to be done at that point than the effort already underway.

The entire route to the hospital Julia was primarily focused on listening to Anna's breathing; secondarily she was attending to driving. The thought passed through Julia's head that she needed to pay close attention to driving, as it was both the middle of the night and the typical traffic pattern had been changed. She thought of the statistics for increased risk to be in a car crash with both of these factors. She still had a hard time concentrating on driving with concern for Anna's breathing being forefront in her mind.

As Julia and Anna arrived at the hospital emergency room door, the now familiar process of admittance would begin. Julia approached the sign in desk, where Anna's doctor had already informed the ER staff that she was on her way. This saved Julia the incessant round of questions as to Anna's history and why she was being seen.

A nurse emerged through the double doors to the waiting room and ushered Anna and Julia into a room. That was the fastest time to a room that Julia could remember. Julia pushed Anna, who was crying in her wheelchair, through the halls, surveying the staff for who was working that night, scanning for familiar faces. Several staff people waved or said "hi" - they had helped Anna on previous visits. It was welcoming, warming to know and have been helped by so many staff people. On the other side of the coin, it was tinged with sadness that they knew so many people working in the emergency room, resulting from the numerous previous visits over the past fourteen years.

Staff were waiting for Anna as she entered the room where she would be cared for. There were easily six to seven hospital staff to help with getting Anna onto the hospital bed and start figuring out what steps were needed to stabilize Anna's breathing and temperature. Julia was apprehensive as more and more people came into the room, performing various tasks to help Anna. The attending physician came in and introduced herself to Julia. Julia looked at all of this activity with both appreciation and wariness. She was grateful for the high level of attention and care Anna was receiving. She was also wary because she knew that meant that Anna warranted that many medical staff persons' attention at that time. Anna continued to labor in her breathing. Her chest rolled with the up and down motion of breathing, much like a rollercoaster. Julia was at her bedside holding her hand.

The (now typical) tests were conducted that had been many times before; blood tests, X-ray scan of Anna's chest, oxygen saturation, heart rate. The phlebotomists obtaining Anna's blood draw looked at her somewhat apprehensively. There weren't many sites that looked even promising. Over Anna's fourteen years she had needles for IV's or tests in practically every possible location. The sites that were available were tricky to get the needle inserted and not have the site fail. Her beautiful pale white skin is scarred where there have been multiple IV's inserted over time. Anna endured the needle pokes to obtain blood and begin an Intravenous drip to provide her more fluids.

Anna was admitted to the hospital to learn of what was causing her temperature and current illness. Cultures were taken, blood tests were run. After a few days, Anna's temperature responded to the steady stream of Tylenol and/or Ibuprofen. The tests came back that Anna had "the common cold". She had needed the care level offered at the hospital to bring her through just a slight infection, the common cold. It illustrated to Julia how on the edge of health Anna is – one small flinch off of the center and she is in respiratory distress.

Anna's Purpose

Through all of Anna's almost fifteen years, she has been an instructor of some great life lessons. One of the primary lessons has been the significant, intentional purpose for Anna's life on Earth which is to teach people about the dimensions of life that are not based on function or ability. By her presence she teaches others about unconditional love, caring for another person who cannot perform functions for themselves, and the joy of health. Days without physical pain are a gift. When she is in public settings in her wheel chair, she is teaching others by vocalizing sounds that, besides a few people on Earth who know her well, are incomprehensible. Yet she has a language. She is communicating with other human beings.

Her physical presence offers the instruction that she is a participant in society, given that her level of capability and participation is different than most. She has a place on Earth, just as millions and now billions of other humans do. Anna's physical presence also shows the devotion that is required to ensure her ongoing physical health and wellbeing. I, along with the others that are with me now, call out to those on Earth to help those in need. Special needs are truly that – special. They take more time, effort, and emotional investment. The care efforts of feeding, bathing, administering medications, and providing enjoyable activities require extra effort. This time is an investment in the person being cared for. There is no monetary payment or worldly gain for doing so.

She brings to light for many other people that one's health is a key component of life. If you are healthy you have most of what is necessary to make a good life for yourself. You have the foundation – it's each person's responsibility to build on that. If a person doesn't have the fortune of good health, they have a more difficult path. There are many shining examples of this including

Para Olympic Athletes, cancer survivors, and developmentally delayed individuals.

Anna illustrates the difficulties of a human body fighting through pain, where the physical body just cannot perform optimally. She has endured excruciating levels of pain that she cannot verbalize; no one else on Earth truly knows what her experience has been. Yet through me she is transmitting her message. She does have a message; she is aware of what is happening around her. Anna calls out for others to assist her, to value her enough to help her along her journey through life on Earth.

The pure light from where I am shines through Anna's physical body. The beauty, seen in the sparks of light in Anna Christina's eyes, shows others on Earth that she is a messenger – she is well known to many. The spirit within Anna is transmitted to others who choose to be around her, the messages flowing nonverbally.

Within Anna's body, it demands her to handle all of the functions she needs to keep her going – breathing, processing food, sleep – along with all of the external stimuli which can so easily overwhelm her. Her brain has limited capabilities to adjust and recalibrate her body's response to temperature swings, noise, and crowds of people.

Anna is a unique person, just as every other person living on Earth is. She knows what is happening around her, she sees through the clarity of another world. She is enveloped within an Earthly body that cannot perform functions that others can. Even so she makes the best of her situation. She hears people, she knows what they are saying, she understands. All this without being able to respond verbally.

She has to rely on others for daily care. She is grateful for the assistance; she like everyone else doesn't want to be in pain or unhappy. Anna smiles when others try to cheer her up or say something funny to her; her smile indicates when she is feeling good and appreciation to another person. She knows when to laugh at a typically speaking person's joke; she gets it.

While Anna does not have the capabilities that most other people do – to walk or talk – she does have the capabilities of interacting with others, listening, laughing, and experiencing calm or peace. She maximizes the use of what she has been given. Her brain does it's absolute best given that it has the power of an infant's brain, but is now asked to drive a fifteen year old's body.

Anna is a fighter; she has to fight every single day to keep breathing, keep her organs functioning to sustain her life. She has fought through twenty or more hospitalizations, accepting food, medicines and treatment to restore her to health. Anna has defied the odds in her body's growth. She grew to be much taller than anyone would have predicted. At five feet five inches tall, she is the tallest person the hospital team has seen for a person with the extent of her brain injury.

On the surface of Anna's human body it may seem that she is, what the out-of-date medical terminology labeled an 'idiot'. This word is assigned by some measurement scale made up by humans in the nineteen hundreds. Although Anna cannot speak in verbalized words in a language other humans understand or purposefully complete self-care tasks such as eating or walking, she is mentally aware, more so than most people on Earth realize.

Yet her body and brain do have many functions that are observable to others. She makes her own decisions. Socially she knows who she likes and trusts or when she is uncomfortable. She vocalizes in her language. While not spoken words, her sounds she makes indicate different things – boredom, restlessness, sleepiness, happiness. It is up to others on Earth to interpret what Anna is saying and then take action. Sometimes she needs to be moved to a quiet place because there is just too much activity going on for her. The signals in her brain already are causing multiple actions and firings of her synapses – adding extra noise and churn and it becomes too much.

Anna is able to calm herself despite the mental storm that she lives through each moment. Her brain is firing off electrical impulses constantly, sending messages that aren't able to traverse the intended destination. She is constantly thinking a mixture of thoughts. Through all of this Anna is able to put those signals at rest. Her brain, even given that it is of the size of a newborn infant, is able to calm itself and allow Anna moments of clarity.

In the current times of the 2010's people have a barrage of items asking for their attention – people at work, drivers in traffic, emails, tweets, and texts. This barrage is similar to what Anna deals with inside her brain, except that it's Anna's brain creating the firestorm of activity. She has no control to stop the barrage as others do, where they can turn off the external factors of work, traffic, and electronic communication.

She knows she is loved. She knows there are people on Earth that value and cherish her. She knows to keep trying, to hang in there because there is someone always around that wants her to 'do well' – feel alright, not be in pain. She isn't giving up. The love she feels has sustained her through many difficult and perilous medical challenges.

Anna and I are in constant communication, since any communication with me is on a nonverbal level. She listens to what I have to say better than most anyone else on Earth. She lets me know how she is doing and if she has any concerns. We have lots of time to converse. When we're not in communication, Anna knows I am watching out for her. She is my namesake - I have special place of love and concern for Anna Christina. I watch over her, just as I do the other of Walter's twenty five great-great grandchildren (who are my great-great-great grandchildren).

I would like to be able to say my husband Charles loves Anna. Unfortunately I cannot with a clear conscience. He remains very intolerant of any sort of 'short coming' or disability. There are many others that feel as he does, who will never understand, or care to understand, Anna's (and others like her) purpose. He went about his life not acknowledging that people have different needs to be met – whether it's extra help with their math homework, a special diet, or medical attention. He blocked out the possibility that disabilities of the mind and body exist. He told himself it would never happen to him or any of our children, believing he as one person could make it so. Charles felt that a person with special needs takes too much time and effort, that the money and resources to keep their life sustained should be used elsewhere. He put minimal value on a person that wasn't physically capable.

Charles chose not to realize is that he, like everyone else, was just one step away from having special needs. Had he had an accident while working in those hazardous conditions, laying stone while twelve feet in the air on a ladder, that could have been part of his life. I think he was too scared, in a layer way underneath his external body, to even think of the possibility of becoming disabled. He chose to not to try to understand or acknowledge disability of any form. The thought presented an annoyance and disturbance in his mind.

Gratitude

From my viewpoint I have the benefit of being able to see situations all around the world. I see Anna being cared for by her family – part of my family – and many others. I see across America where laws have been passed and funding made available for the standards and care of people with Earthly disabilities. That makes me proud to be an American, that the lives of disabled people are valued.

Across the Earth, the approach to caring for the disabled varies widely. I see many places on Earth where people who are disabled are valued much lower than typical people, sometimes not at all. There are places where disabled people are literally left by the side of a road or in the wilderness to die. Other cultures and societies house the disabled in their populations in a human warehouse, where they eke out an existence with minimal food, human interaction, and environmental comforts such as heat or cooling. There are other places where if a baby is believed to have a congenital defect, the country's doctors advise (or force) the mother to terminate the pregnancy.

People on Earth have a choice as to how to approach people that are different from themselves. It may be they are different in appearance, religious views, level of cognitive ability, or social grace. As we know from learning more about how the human brain works, people try to push away subjects or situations that are unknown and unfamiliar to them. Thus when encountering someone who is different from what a person thinks of as 'typical', the person may subconsciously or consciously try to avoid the other person.

It is wonderful to see when someone on Earth steps out of their own life, cares, and concerns to help another. On Earth now things are so busy – schedules, automation, activities. People rush around with multiple things to do and attend to almost every hour of the day. Many people make an extra effort to think of the needs of another person. It is especially wonderful to see when a person who isn't involved in another's day to day life or has something to gain steps out of their own comfort zone to show another compassion, assistance, and caring. Their positive actions are recognized, although it may not be a tangible sign seen on Earth.

There are many who choose professions through which they help others. Some examples are the woman who, day after day, week after week, delivers clean bedding to the units of beds in the hospital, the nurses who want to work with the Medically Fragile community, and the phlebotomist who approaches the challenge of Anna's blood draw with calm and persistence. For Anna she has had the benefit of many doctors who do truly care, who want to make others' lives the best they can be. Julia and her family are grateful for all of the people who offer assistance, whether it is through providing services or simply taking a moment to try to understand a difficulty they are going through.

It takes time, energy, and thought to assist someone else. People risk a part of themselves and some of their resources when they choose to spend time with others who could use some assistance. These people might be in the checkout line at the grocery store, a volunteer in a hospital, or a motorist on a freeway. Anyone has the opportunity to do this. The question is if they have the capacity, as part of the way they live their lives, to give something of themselves to someone else.

There are payments of gratitude that will be realized by caregivers. Sometimes the caregivers on Earth see a glimpse of their payment – the reward of a smile, giggle, or blink of a person's eyes. They may receive messages from those of us not on Earth in their sleep, through their subconscious of appreciation for their efforts. Other times the caregiver is so consumed with the effort they are closed off to the messages trying to be sent, like a postal mail letter being returned as "undeliverable". We'll keep trying to get the messages through.

Granted there are times in peoples' lives that they just cannot give to others as much. They may be going through a particularly challenging time – the death of a close family member or friend, a surge of effort required at their work which sustains their family life, or moving households. These time demands create an ebb and flow pattern, much like the way the tide rises and falls in the oceans, in the time and energy people have available.

People who assist others must reprioritize their own lives, something not everyone is willing to do. The assistance may be a lawyer arguing for a just decision, a teacher taking a few extra minutes to answer an individual student's questions, or a caregiver attending to the personal care tasks of another required in daily life. There are times when a person who is assisting someone else gives up a portion of their needs to care for another. Their reward is most often not in monetary currency. The reward is in the smile of someone who cannot speak, the laughter of a child overcoming an abusive situation, or the continued health of a medically fragile person. These situations do not go unnoticed – those of us not on Earth see, we notice, we understand. And sometimes others on Earth give recognition and support to caregivers, which is a wonderful gift to let them know how much they are appreciated.

Living with What's Next

The age old question of what will happen next is ever present in everyone's lives. No one on Earth knows what the next day, next hour, next year will bring. That is also true for Anna and her parents who are constantly watching her, as Anna is constantly struggling to keep her airway clear and consistently breathe. Her cough, originating in her chest, could visit any time of the day or night, propelling her parents into action to respond. The ever present possibility of being called on for assistance leaves her parents on a high alert almost every hour of the day. The sound of her cough, then gasping for air, then sucking air in is wrenching – it causes escalation of stress in her parents' bodies every time it occurs. The feeling of desperation, helplessness, and fear mixed together is omnipresent, ready to surge back into their consciousness each time Anna coughs. They wish they could somehow cough for Anna – somehow get inside her body and clear out or stabilize her airway. When Anna literally gasps for air, in those moments she seems to teeter on a precipice – will she recover? Will she continue to breathe? Or will she go into respiratory distress? Her parents let out an inaudible sigh of relief each time Anna is able to recover and continue breathing.

Like deciphering a baby's cry, Julia and Bill learned to gauge Anna's coughs – does this one need attention (i.e. suctioning) or did Anna recover from that one on her own? Their home is a zone in the War for Anna, where they are constantly standing by, listening for a sound from Anna that requires them to spring into action. It's hard for them to relax because the possibility of action being required is always present, similar to the response required from a military person in a War zone.

Someday Anna's body will fail her, as will be the case with every human on this planet. She is like an extreme athlete, pushing her body to the limits of what it can do. Her body has been optimized – every ounce of function that could be available has been

367

investigated and utilized. Anna's body simply doesn't have the capacity that most other human bodies do. Her potential was cut short all too early with the loss of oxygen to her brain via her stroke that occurred in utereo.

As I have mentioned, all nine of my children outlived me. I was thankful for that. As Julia's great grandmother, I don't have some undiscovered depth of wisdom to impart to her about facing Anna's life when it ends on Earth. How does one counsel a mother on the topic of the death of their child? It's almost inconceivable notion, that a parent would have to watch their child lose function and be in pain for years. The natural order of things is out of sync – that the older, more frail pass away and the younger, more vibrant live on.

Starting from when Anna was conceived, her life, and therefore Julia and Bill's, hasn't gone 'as expected'. The thought of a typical child leading a typical childhood was evaporated – vaporized into the atmosphere – gone. Anna's life is similar to many others', though, in that their lives don't go 'as expected' either. Life on Earth sends twists and turns people never imagined would happen. Maybe a person didn't get an opportunity for work they were hoping for, or maybe a parent is disappointed by a child not being able to attend the preschool of their choice. Anna has chosen to make the best of what she has, limited by physical challenges most others do not face.

Anna's needs are the same as all humans – nutrition, shelter, ability to breathe, love. The path to meeting her needs is windier than for others. Yet she bravely claims her place every single day, traveling through her life unable to visually identify, to complete her own bodily functions without several forms of assistance. She forges on for her position, her bunker, in the War every minute of every day. Her comrades are those who help her with her tasks of daily living – getting nutrition, eliminating, breathing, sleeping. These are people with many more physical abilities than Anna has, people who value her as a person and invest their time to help her. They are not abandoning her as wounded and unable to save. Included in this group are the vast array of healthcare workers, her doctors, her nurses, her personal care assistants, her parents, her family.

There might be some on Earth who think that a person like Anna is a nuisance, not worth the effort to provide for her care and life. To them I say – someone cared for you. Every person starts out Earthly life unable to care for themselves. There is a time period where every human needs the care of either their parents or some other human who can feed them, shelter them, clothe them. When I was on Earth, I cared for my nine children as a mother does; feeding, bathing, clothing, cleaning, loving. In the best of situations there is someone (multiple people!) to love and educate children. And many times as a human grows up and enters adulthood there are special times of need for care, such as emergency appendectomies, birth / delivery care, or dental extractions of decayed teeth. Everyone needs some sort of intervention by others at some point in their lives.

As for the future, of course those on Earth are unaware as to what plans have been made for them. I do know that someday every human will leave Earth, each with their own specific reason and timing. Because of Anna's medical impacts, her life will be shorter than others'. Each day she perseveres is a gift. Each day of less discomfort, each day her bodily functions work to meet her needs is a successful day. No one on Earth knows what the next day will bring. It's a funny thing watching people think they do – where they'll be, who they'll be talking to, what they'll be eating. It's an illusion – in reality there is no way to know exactly how life will occur every day.

The day I call Anna to me – the day her heart and body fail her as mine did – will be too early for those on Earth. Her family, her parents, her sisters, are aware that most likely Anna will depart Earth before they do. They don't want to think about that situation, but it is something they must face, and then come to terms with. They have learned to focus on loving her each day on Earth for the person she is.

Few people on earth are comfortable about talking about death. Seems kind of odd, because everything – including all humans - will die at some time – the question is when and how. Julia and Bill have had to stare death in the face, looking at its terrible claw of emotion and feeling. They have almost befriended it; they know it is waiting, lurking, and going to snatch their beautiful daughter Anna before it really should be her time. They have come to a place of acceptance of it. It will, they know, eventually win the War for Anna's life. They cannot make the hurt and pain go away for Anna - they can't minimize the risk to a small micro percentile. Anna will make the determination when it is time for her to leave Earth.

Anna has changed the lives of many around her to an immeasurable extent. Her parent's and family's lives are reordered constantly by the demands that must be met to care for Anna appropriately. It is my hope that the stories of my family give a voice to people who have a physical or emotional circumstance which alters their life course from that which is considered 'typical'. Maybe our story will spur people will spend time to help others, to care for their fellow inhabitants of Earth.

I encourage everyone on Earth to focus on what's right with today. Tomorrow (or even a few hours from now) may bring completely different circumstances or conditions. Live today to the fullest.

Anna is a shining example that you can be happy despite the state of your physical body on Earth. Thankfully Anna has the gifts of the ability to laugh, giggle, and smile – she can show her happiness. That is pure happiness that can be seen through her eyes. That is a gift from somewhere other than Earth.

Epilogue

As my great-granddaughter Julia was writing this book, she uncovered pieces of information previously unknown to my descendants. During Julia's visit years earlier to Sweden, she had obtained a photocopy of the parish records of my family. The paper had been filed away in a manila file folder in a drawer. She hadn't looked at it since a few months after her trip to Sweden in 2004. While researching the writing of this book, she opened up the file folder and reviewed the contents. Typical items were in the folder, including restaurant receipts, bus tickets, and a copy of their air travel. Then she came upon the photocopy of the parish record of our family. The entries made by the clergyman on the ledger show my parents' names and their children. The entries show "son" and "dr" (meaning son and daughter) by Lars and Nilla's entries, respectively. The names next on the list are Anna, Johanna, Elna, and mine. My sister Johanna is listed in the registry as "(adopt)" meaning adopted into the house.

Julia suddenly had realized only Lars and Nilla were the biological children of Lars & Pernilla. The parish records do not show a "dr" (meaning biological daughter) in front of any of the names of Anna, Johanna, Elna or mine. During the 1800's the Swedish parish records listed all who lived in the household, not only those who were biologically related. The registry listed Anna's christening date as only nine months after Nilla's – quite unlikely that one mother could bear two children within nine months. Elna came to our household when our mother was forty four years old, which again is quite unlikely for a woman to bear a child at that age. Then when I arrived, my mother was forty seven; even more unlikely that I would be her biological child.

During the time period I was born in Sweden, in the mid-eighteen hundreds, an "orphanage", homes built for children to live when they had no caretakers (either parents or relatives), did not exist. If direct relatives couldn't take a child, other families in a parish were asked to take a child in. A family did so to help the child and also to have additional help on their farm or household as the child grew up. That is how I came to live with the Nilsson's, and how I would grow up with them as my parents. I was born in the middle of a widespread crop failure and subsequent famine. Many families were literally starving. My biological parents were probably unlikely to be able to feed me and gave me over to a family that would take me in. Or my mother may not have had the means or socially acceptable arrangement to raise me. During the years of intense famine in Sweden, adding another mouth to feed to a home would have to be seriously considered. It could have meant less food for others living in the home, where resources were diverted amongst more people.

I am grateful to both my biological parents and the Nilssons. Their decisions and choices allowed me to survive with food to eat and a warm place to sleep. If my parents, the Nilssons, had not chosen to take me in, I may have not even survived to adulthood – or ever had descendants that continue to thrive on Earth. As I grew up in the Nilsson's household, I was literally training for what would become my profession when I went to America - a domestic. The Nilssons provided me what they could, until I was twenty one, and then sent me out into the world to support myself.

My family – my children and my husband Charles - didn't know of this fact. I didn't share it with them, and neither did Nilla. We just never mentioned that we were not biological sisters. We both felt it best to leave that information in the past, part of our lives back in Sweden. My children and grandchildren always did wonder why they weren't treated quite as equals to Nilla's family. One rationale was that Nilla's husband Charles was a business owner who was financially more successful than my husband Charles, which put them in a different social standing. My husband was a laborer, and I was a domestic. We were 'working class' people, where Nilla and her husband had moved into higher layers of society via their economic prosperity.

I don't have any anger or regret over not being a blood relative to the Nilsson family. It was to my fortune that I was brought into the Nilsson household, to grow up with food, housing, and schooling. Their decision to take me in to their household allowed me to grow up and survive. They were kind to me, and that was the best I could hope for.

Now my descendants have another puzzle that will likely go unsolved – who were my biological parents? What were their life circumstances? What were they like? What was their genetic makeup? Where exactly were they from? In many ways those questions are no longer important. The fact is I survived and thrived with my parents, who fulfilled the Earthly responsibility of raising me in their home. This became the most vital role for my existence: sustaining my new life, helping me, a child, grow up. In the world of today the goals for raising children are different than they were when I had my children, and even more different than when I myself was a child. For my children my goals were to keep them fed, clothed, and out of harm's way. When I was a child in the mid 1800's, my parents' goals were to have children survive to be able to assist in sustaining the entire family, by tending crops and completing chores.

As I said, I cannot thank my parents enough for choosing to take me in and providing me an opportunity to grow up. The effect of their decision to take me in reverberates through hundreds of years and will be shown in my descendants who now live in many states across the United States. I even have great-great-great grandchildren now!

Julia also realized, after rereading the page of family history from Charles' family bible, more details of his family's ethnic origin. The bible's entries date back to the 1700's and lists a city where his family lived that is on the coastline of what is now the country of Norway. Charles' profession that he was Swedish was accurate for the time period he lived in, as from 1814 through 1905 the land area covering present day Sweden and Norway was united under the Swedish King. He and his family did not claim Norwegian as their cultural heritage. They felt they were 100% Swedish. In 1905, almost thirty years after Charles had left Sweden, Norway became an independent country of its own and no longer governed by Sweden.

As for the effects of Scandinavians on present day America, currently around 3.9% of the population is said to have Scandinavian ancestry. Much of the Scandinavian culture in America has been absorbed into the general population. Immigration from the Scandinavian countries to America slowed to a trickle after 1920. Thus it has been almost one hundred years for those that had immigrated to be absorbed into the American culture. A few American universities offer degrees in Scandinavian history or language, including Augustana College (now in Rock Island, Illinois, originally it was founded in 1860 in Chicago) and the University of Washington (Seattle, Washington).

The lasting effects of the Swedes in America have reverberated through my family. People that have gone before us have paved the way and made our lives that much easier, for which we have gratitude and thanks.

For the future, it is bright with the children of today. They should be inquisitive, continuing to reach for that next rung on the ladder.

This is my story, which has now found its path. I thank my great-granddaughter for giving it new life.

Appendix – Family Photos

Photo 1: Charles & Christina: Wedding Photo

Photo 2: Construction of our home on William Street

Photo 3: Ruth, Walter and Alice on our home's front porch on William Street

Photo 4: My Family in 1913

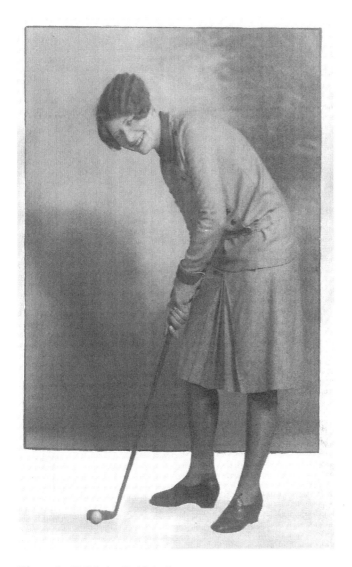

Photo 5: Edith in Golf Attire

Photo 6: My Family in 1936 in our living room

Photo 7: Anna at age 3

Made in the USA
Charleston, SC
17 May 2012